Deskilling Migrant Women in the Global Care Industry

Deskilling Migrant Women in the Global Care Industry

Sondra Cuban
University of Lancaster, UK

© Sondra Cuban 2013

All rights reserved. No reproduction, copy or transmission of this publication may be made without written permission.

No portion of this publication may be reproduced, copied or transmitted save with written permission or in accordance with the provisions of the Copyright, Designs and Patents Act 1988, or under the terms of any licence permitting limited copying issued by the Copyright Licensing Agency, Saffron House, 6–10 Kirby Street, London EC1N 8TS.

Any person who does any unauthorized act in relation to this publication may be liable to criminal prosecution and civil claims for damages.

The author has asserted her right to be identified as the author of this work in accordance with the Copyright, Designs and Patents Act 1988.

First published 2013 by
PALGRAVE MACMILLAN

Palgrave Macmillan in the UK is an imprint of Macmillan Publishers Limited, registered in England, company number 785998, of Houndmills, Basingstoke, Hampshire RG21 6XS.

Palgrave Macmillan in the US is a division of St Martin's Press LLC, 175 Fifth Avenue, New York, NY 10010.

Palgrave Macmillan is the global academic imprint of the above companies and has companies and representatives throughout the world.

Palgrave® and Macmillan® are registered trademarks in the United States, the United Kingdom, Europe and other countries.

ISBN 978–0–230–34233–0

This book is printed on paper suitable for recycling and made from fully managed and sustained forest sources. Logging, pulping and manufacturing processes are expected to conform to the environmental regulations of the country of origin.

A catalogue record for this book is available from the British Library.

Library of Congress Cataloging-in-Publication Data
Cuban, Sondra.
   Deskilling migrant women in the global care industry / Sondra Cuban, University of Lancaster, UK.
    pages   cm
  ISBN 978–0–230–34233–0
  1. Nursing homes—Employees. 2. Women professional employees. 3. Women immigrants. 4. Globalization. I. Title.
  RA997.C83 2013
  362.2'30683—dc23   2012045625

Transferred to Digital Printing in 2013

To my parents, Barbara and Larry, with love

Contents

List of Figures viii

Acknowledgements ix

1 Professional Women Migrants Becoming Care Assistants 1
2 A Homework Methodology for Researching Migrant Women's Lives 26
3 Care Industry Needs Skilled Migrant Labour 51
4 A Place of Settlement and Upheaval 88
5 The Disappointing Journey to Being 'Just a Carer' 123
6 Caring in Transnational Networks 159
7 Conclusion: Counting Migrant Women's Education and Expertise 194

Notes 218
References 221
Index 241

Figures

2.1	Sondra waiting at the airport	26
2.2	Mapping the nursing home	44
3.1	Duplicate log	74
4.1	Alice in her car	101
4.2	Miniature bear figurines	104
4.3	Rota	107
6.1	Alice's map (for meanings of abbreviations see text)	180

Acknowledgements

First and most importantly, I thank the incredibly perceptive women participants (whose names remain anonymous) and informants who are at the centre of this book. They put up with all my questions and kept giving me advice and comments. Their perspectives were so important and I hope that I have done justice to their stories and that they make a difference to women in similar situations. I also want to thank all the consultant experts whose candid thoughts brought me to the next level of analysis and whose names also remain anonymous. Thanks to Andrew James for shepherding this manuscript through to the end and Philippa Grand at Palgrave Macmillan for believing in me from the beginning. Cherline Daniel and her team at Integra (through Palgrave MacMillan) in Pondicherry did a fantastic job with the copyediting and a big thanks to these editors too. The visual team too were brilliant. And of course, a huge thanks to Abel Barroso, whose work I saw when I was in Cuba in 2012, for allowing me to use his provocative image for the front cover. I thank Wendy Hoag too, for designing the email with Barroso's artwork in it. Family, friends, and colleagues who supported the project, read drafts and gave feedback, or just plain supported me and engaged me in questions and conversations about women, migration, care, and labour during this five year period are: Larry Cuban, Barbara Cuban, Janice Cuban, Caryn Cheyfitz, Viv Cuthill, Gemma Wibberley, Betty Hayes, Nelly Stromquist, Angela Giacomini, Katharina Heyer, Anne-Marie Fortier, Alan Fraser, Susan Cueva, Hediana Utarti, Mark Minard, Corinne Fowler, Krisnah Poinasamy, Aviva Samet, Jamima Fagta, Gwen Sanderson, Linda Secker, Kimberly Coleman, Steve Reder, Clare Strawn, Rosie Cox, John Urry, and Christine Milligan. A big thanks to the special advisory board members of the Economic and Social Research Council (ESRC) project who kept me on track: Sylvia Walby, Anne-Marie Fortier, Margaret Bremner, Lesley Gill, Llaja Sterland, Benette Palanqui, Michele Cornes, Corinne May-Chahal, Pauline Rossi, Michael Duque, Carolyn Jackson, and Jo McVicker, who was the administrator of the project. Carolyn Jackson was my Head of Department and gave helpful comments on my proposal to the ESRC, in addition to giving me the time and support to finish the book. I can't thank Ozias Goodwin enough for driving me at all hours of day and night to the train station and back and forth from Cumbria and London to collect the data. And a huge thank you to my daughter Barbaraciela (Ciela) for her patience when her mother ran back to the computer because she forgot to say something else in her manuscript. Above all, I want to thank some special researchers who spent time and energy on this project: Georgia Spiliopoulos, Monika Glaz, and Kathy Pitt. Georgia (Joy) was the research assistant on this project and an especially good researcher. Without funding first from Lancaster University and then from the ESRC I couldn't have embarked on this journey, so, of course, I appreciate this financial support. I wrote this book in South Seattle during 2011–12 and it would never have been completed had Ciela not had the excellent care given to her by her babysitter, Tamiko Nietering, and her teachers at the Seattle Hebrew Academy, so I thank these special friends. As I run around the beautiful Seward Park for the last time before packing my bags to return to England, I am reminded of the musical inspiration of Jimi Hendrix, whose hometown is Seattle, and marching with Laura Love singing, 'We Shall Not Be Moved' during an OccupySeattle protest.

1
Professional Women Migrants Becoming Care Assistants

> If you trap the moment before it's ripe
> The tears of repentance you'll certainly wipe
> But if you let the ripe moment go
> You can never wipe off the tears of woe.
> (Blake, 1791, in Blake, Erdman, Bloom, and Golding, 1997, p. 470)

Introduction

This book is about the insidious role of the global care industry in professional migratory flows of women. This case study depicts what happens in England when professional women migrate to take jobs that they initially believe will lift their status but which fail to do so because of their location within the labour market and society. What I will show is that these women didn't move much from where they began. With this, I challenge notions of transnationals and their upward mobility and the highly skilled as privileged. Mei-Li's story illustrates this situation.

In just over a year, Mei-Li went from being a care assistant in a nursing home to being a cashier at McDonald's, where the pay was the same and there was less heartache. She took English and maths courses there because that's what she had done since her arrival on a student visa from China in 2008. She said: 'I have to think: how I will develop myself? So that's the reason why I don't want to work in a nursing home anymore.' Her manager (at her last nursing home) didn't acknowledge her development so she said: 'I just want to try myself.' Worse still, this manager didn't help Mei-Li when she was accused by a British-born colleague of assaulting a client. This colleague claimed Mei-Li was ignorant of the law and couldn't speak English well—an accusation that propelled her into court, becoming a major obstacle towards pursuing a care career in England—the reason she came in the first place. Mei-Li realized that working in nursing homes was threatening her livelihood.

After the trial, at which she defended herself well and was acquitted, she could not erase the verdict on her criminal record despite having gone to numerous agencies to remove it. She decided to extend her visa for a large sum of money and enrolled in a further education college, attached to a major university, that promised to advance her into the nursing profession. Still, her record raised employers' suspicions and she felt like, 'A total victim and framed. It is a real disgrace and a terrible thing that happened in my life.' Mei-Li added:

> I need my human rights back. I am ambitious, well educated and conscientious. I am hoping that I will fulfil my travelled nurse dream... but I never realized that the case will put me in the end of my future.

Mei-Li and other migrant women's skills benefited England's social care system and its public by bettering the quality of care for older persons. But where did it leave the migrant women? I was left with the question as to why so many women professionals like Mei-Li became care assistants and persisted in that role despite so many intractable barriers.

Context for the book

This was one of several questions I asked myself in researching migrant women like Mei-Li, for in trapping the moment, as Blake wrote, it had also trapped her. These questions came to be at the heart of this project: Why do professional women migrate for jobs for which they are overqualified? What strategies do they use to deal with their decisions and disappointments? Two years after meeting Mei-Li, I had responses to the struggles of Mei-Li and 59 other care assistants I listened to across England.

Lasting from 2007 to 2010, this project draws on an Economic and Social Research Council (ESRC) study[1] of a select group of professional women in diverse fields and regions of the world who migrated to England taking jobs in the elder care sector as part of a strategy to improve their capabilities and livelihoods. The study examined the reasons behind their gamble of migrating into an industry and country they believed would improve the quality of their lives. It also examines the effects of their work on the industry itself, especially the quality of care for clients. The scope of this book focuses on macro, meso and micro levels of analysis.

Concentrating too much on the macro level would give the study an overwhelming structural emphasis that would lose unique dimensions of migrant women's experiences. Macro levels are therefore integrated into the analysis to focus on the roles that the law, institutions, and policies, in both sending and destination countries, play that account for migrant women's status in this gendered employment niche. This part of the analysis was derived from a synthesis of theories and research studies, including interviews with over 60 experts in the fields of labour, care, migration, and English to Speakers of Other Languages (ESOL) as well as a literature review of other countries' care systems. A meso level of analysis focuses on migrants' networks and their transnational status in straddling different worlds. This level of data utilizes observations of the participants not only in their communities but also in their workplaces, and includes the perspectives of clients and other workers. Finally, a micro-analysis that focuses too heavily on individual experiences without attention to social context would not explain behaviour, attitudes, and practices of a group of migrant women struggling with similar issues. So drawing from interviews with 60 migrant women care assistants and their narratives of mobility in England, including their strategies, identities, aspirations, and actions, makes possible integrating the micro-analysis with the meso and macro levels.

My reasons for writing this book are threefold: (1) to sort out a muddled debate about exactly who the migrants who become care assistants are and what they do, (2) to correct a gender gap in the research on professional migrants, and (3) to advocate for migrant women working in this industry. Most literature on this subject only touches on these issues. First, real differences in 'care work' are under-theorized in the literature. Migrant nurses, domestics, and care assistants as well as nannies and au pairs, for example, are all classed as 'care workers' along a skills spectrum (Brush and Vasupuram, 2006; Huang, Yeoh, and Toyota, 2012) while other related occupations, such as teaching, are excluded. Second, the literature assumes a male migration model of professional migrants with high-tech and finance sectors highlighted, in which women feature as spouses to the global elite and are homogenized as passive followers. Factoring in both gender and care work into the picture warrants the existence of women pioneer migrants who are breadwinners and highly skilled, even if they are not viewed as such. Third, academic perspectives tend to rely on structural explanations of these migrant women's circumstances, overlooking the diversity of their voices and experiences, while mainstream media accounts highlight individual testimonies without reference to global migration and the labour market, conveying the impression that all care employees have the same issues and that interventions would be in their hands alone. This study emphasizes the roles these women play in the care industry but also their diverse strategies for settling into, adjusting to, as well as leaving it.

The participants in this study came from a variety of professions, many of which were in health care fields, like Mei-Li. Their reasons for migrating were diverse, and after migrating they went through a range of experiences in their care assistant posts. All of them, however, perceived themselves as being deskilled in one way or another. The book will focus attention on the ways they coped with this 'race to the bottom'; some felt duped, others felt unlucky and some re-evaluated the bargain they had made. Their reactions ranged from wanting to escape from their situations to desiring retribution, to feeling paralysed to act. Some attempted to use these jobs as a 'foot in the door' to advance to other sectors and positions. Still others embraced care work, toiling away as near-saints, deepening their relations with clients, and reframing their aspirations. Some even became whistle-blowers on companies and advocates for their clients. In clinging to their former identities and in using their skills and dispositions, they were able to survive in a new place of settlement and eke out new roles as well as consider different destinations for the future. This book, then, offers a dynamic profile of women migrants with myriad motivations and experiences. This diversity is important in understanding the growing trend of the 'feminization of migration' under globalization pressures and the resiliency of migrant women in adapting to, and even transforming their workplaces. In writing the book, I attempt to open up new conversations about gender and care work in terms of who does it and its meaning in society. While it is common knowledge that migrant women become downwardly mobile—Arlie Hochschild's landmark 'global care chains' (2000) begins with a story about a college-educated former schoolteacher turned nanny and housekeeper—the mechanisms for how this happens and the relationships between migration and skills, as well as the outcomes of deskilling for migrant women, are little known.

This chapter focuses on the post-welfare society and its dependence on gendered skilled migrant care. First, I introduce the issues of these migrant women care assistants who were once professionals. Then, I address concepts used in the literature and common occupational definitions focused on care for older persons. Next, I map the reach of the global care industry with its recruitment and retention of women from emerging nations to major advanced economies like England. I present the issues of staffing the industry, including supply and demand of the workforce with ageing populations and welfare reform to be discussed in Chapter 3. I follow this with a description of the participants' issues surrounding their opportunities, qualifications, and education, which are covered in depth in chapters 5 and 7. The ways they negotiate these transnational identities and networks inside and outside of the workplace are introduced and then explored in depth in chapters 4 and 6.

In this chapter I set forth the main argument about the high-stakes wager these women made to migrate for care work. Theories that address engendering transnationalism frame the argument. Then I return to issues that capture the discrimination with which participants like Mei-Li struggled. The last part of this chapter consists of a socio-demographic profile of the sample that will reveal the themes in the book.

Terminology

This book focuses on care for older persons. Known as 'women's work,' this type of care is part of 'intimate labour,' requiring touch, personal attention, and closeness in face-to-face encounters (Boris and Parrenas, 2010, p. 11). This book focuses on this type of care as part of a global *industry* that reflects its marketization and the risks for its migrant workers (Yeates, 2009, p. 33). Elder care employers and recruiters, operating in tandem with states, produce a 'migration industrial complex' (Yeates, 2009, p. 86) that is composed 'of institutionalized networks with complex profit and loss accounts including a set of institutions, agents, and individuals each of which stands to make a commercial gain' (Salt and Stein, 1997, p. 468). Intermediaries or brokers (like recruiting agencies), in selecting the workforce, turn care work into something that 'migrant women do' (Kofman, Phizacklea, Raghuram, and Sales, 2000, p. 25). This industry expands faster than other sectors by lowering prices to compete. It attracts low-paid and skilled migrant labour by crossing international borders, much like manufacturing. Saskia Sassen (1998) discusses the economic links that are established by companies and states in the organized export of a low-wage female workforce. As chapters 5 and 7 show, 'development' increases opportunities for women to receive a higher education in emerging countries and raises their information levels, at the same time that it reduces their opportunities due to weak labour markets. The Philippines, for example, is a middle-income 'developing country' where wage differentials compared to those in England are significant (Portes, 2009). The book also focuses specifically on labour migration and its feminization, where distinctions between the two are not often clear. While international figures show that women make up about half of all international migrants, what is less clear is how many of them migrate specifically for work (Parrenas, 2008). With this, the term 'migrants' is used throughout the book to connect to 'migrant workers' and their labour, an important point for those engaging in paid care which is often not considered 'work' (Ackers, 2004). These migrant workers often lived 'betwixt and between' two or more worlds at once (Grillo, 2007, p. 199). Although they travelled along care trade routes, they are not referred to here as 'transmigrants' because 'nothing is gained by calling immigrants "transmigrants," when the earlier and more familiar term is perfectly adequate' (Portes, Guarnizo, and Landolt, 1999, p. 219). While definitions of migrants vary, basically they are viewed as foreign born, having just moved to a country for a year or more, and are 'recent arrivals' (Anderson and Blinder, 2011, p. 2). Yet even these terms are unsatisfactory.

'Migrant worker' also connects to 'care worker,' a common term used in the literature along with 'migrant care worker' or 'international,' 'foreign,' or 'overseas social care workers' or 'assistants' (Cangiano, Shutes, Spencer, and Leeson, 2009; Hussein, Stevens, and Manthorpe, 2010; Spencer, Martin, Bourgeault, and O'Shea, 2010). A 'care assistant' for older persons signifies a *paid* care employee as opposed to an unpaid 'carer' who does similar work and may receive a stipend but is not bound to a 'legal' employment-based contract. Yet this distinction also undervalues the 'work' that unpaid carers do as a 'labour of love' and which is, in the public imagination, often considered to be of a high level due to its divorce from pay (Anttonen and Zechner, 2011). Although 'worker' is a progressive title that valorizes women's labour (e.g. 'sex worker' or 'domestic worker') it did not fit with the participants' identities as they referred to themselves as 'carers.' To be precise, this book calls them 'care assistants' to fit with the industrial vocabulary, job titles, and advertisements, as well as the work itself, which focuses on supporting and assisting older persons through agencies in private homes, and residential and nursing homes, as well as assisted-living or sheltered homes and day care centres for older people. The definition of this work, provided by the International Labour Organization (ILO) (ILO, 2008, ISCO 08 Code 5322),[2] entails provision of 'bathing, dressing, or grooming, to elderly, convalescent, or disabled persons.' According to the ILO classification, care assistants also maintain records of clients, help them move, provide them with emotional support, clean, read aloud, plan and serve meals, and ensure that clients take their medicine.

Prior to being care assistants the participants were 'former professionals,' a topic that is explored in chapters 3 and 5 and which is important in view of the neglect of these women's status in immigration and employment policies. To clarify, the term 'professional' suggests a person whose occupation is founded upon specialized educational training and standards that are regulated through professional associations and governments. In England the care industry is referred to as a 'sector,' with Chapter 3 describing its composition, including the different types of care homes and services that this system provides. These care assistants worked in nursing and residential homes, private homes (through agencies), day care centres, and sheltered homes or assisted-living homes. It is *social care* that is highlighted in this book, which focuses on long-term care for older persons, including institutional and private home-based settings. This differs from *health care*, which refers to hospital settings run by licensed professionals (Spencer et al., 2010, p. 17).

This book highlights the participants' qualifications, and I call them 'skilled,' as a proxy for education levels but also because they skilfully managed clients. The category 'highly skilled' usually refers to having both tertiary education and a specialized occupation. This leads to deskilling—a topic nearly always mentioned in the care migration literature, but rarely highlighted. Lastly, this book focuses on gender, which sees it structuring and constraining women's opportunities. A 'gender contract' is the logic whereby women commonly engage in care activities (paid and unpaid)—ones that are sanctioned by family, state, and the market (Anderson, 2000). Women engage gender through their caring roles, responsibilities, and practices.

Mapping staffing issues: Surplus and demand in the care industry

Care, once thought of as out of the market is now squarely in the market (Held, 2002). It is part of the new service economy, which has grown over the last three decades (Harvey, 2005). Unlike other service industries, however, care work is place-based; in other words, care for children and older persons is immovable to the extent that it cannot be outsourced to other countries (Crozier, 2010).[3] The workers, however, move. The rise of the service economy, and the care industry in particular, matched the surge in labour migration during the 1990s as income levels in advanced economies for those who could afford care services peaked. Neo-liberal policies, with free market principles, created weak workplace regulations enabling employers to drive down wages (McDowell, 2004). By outsourcing (or sub-contracting), this industry generated more low-paid labour (Wills, Datta, Evans, Herbert, May and McIlwaine, 2010). This move separated the men from the women, with over 80 per cent of women working in the service sector, especially in care (McDowell, 2004, p. 146). Care as a top growth industry relies on a female workforce for their soft skills and high-productivity performance.

The care industry, already gendered, became immigrant-intensified as a quick fix for solving labour shortages due to the low wages. Migrant women have a 'dual frame of reference,' comparing wages from their home countries to where they want to go, and often have few choices other than to accept jobs that no one else wants (Wills et al., 2010, p. 7). This global supply of female migrant labour is viewed as unethical because in caring for at-risk clients, workers are defenceless in negotiating for better conditions and pay (Crozier, 2010). This also creates a type of servant class (Cox, 2006).

England as a case study

England is an example of a 'migrant in the market' care model with its extensive outsourcing of services and high demand for low-cost workers (van Hooren, 2012, p. 12). England has a liberal system of social care that is heavily privatized and organized through means-testing (for determining ability to pay for services) and direct cash payments, with independent contractors providing most care services (Froggatt, Davies and Meyer, 2009). The government has promoted migration as a means of counterbalancing its vast ageing population with welfare reform. Care employers want to 'attract talent' through overseas recruitment of a population believed to have higher than average qualifications over British-born workers (Skills for Care, 2007). They do this by lobbying the government to brand care as an occupation with 'skills shortages' that can only be met through migrants. In reality, these 'shortages' are relative to sudden spikes in demand, 'inflexible' supplies of workers, and the fact that the state disbars certain work from paying (Ruhs and Anderson, 2010, p. 4). Standard economic rules—shortages incurring better wages, producing more supply—don't apply in this industry because of the existence of immigration laws and other constraining gender-based and industry factors (Spencer et al., 2010).

As subsequent chapters will show, the participants were self-selecting. But they were also aggressively recruited both inside and outside

England. Care employers often turn to agencies to recruit migrant care assistants (Spencer et al., 2010). These employers cite British-born workers as unwilling to do shift work, lacking the right work experience, and having high turnover rates whereas migrants work all shifts, have a 'good work ethic,' are respectful and compassionate with clients, and learn new skills (Cangiano et al., 2009, pp. 94–95). Employers rely on these workers, who are easier to retain and accept lower wages than nationals. They will also work flexible or unsocial hours (Spencer et al., 2010).

This type of selection occurs because England has a migration system that sorts types of workers for particular jobs, favouring some countries over others. This selective 'managed migration' system, beginning in 2008 in the form of a points-based system, stems from the mid-twentieth century. Race and gender have influenced this system (McDowell, 2009); single women migrants, for example, were recruited as domestics in England in the post-war years. The new immigration policies focus on tiers of workers based on labour market scarcities, giving a more prominent role to employers, with 'what they think they can get' (Anderson and Ruhs, 2010, p. 8). The state, as Chapter 3 shows, has played a regulatory role with care employers for risk-selecting migrant workers. A comprehensive case study of care assistants in England (Cangiano et al., 2009) showed that migrants are estimated to be about a fifth of the care workforce for older persons, that is, 19 per cent—with the USA having slightly more than this figure (Spencer et al., 2010). Experts predict that the number of migrant workers will rise in Organisation for Economic Co-operation and Development (OECD) countries to meet the needs of burgeoning ageing populations (Yeates, 2009).

Global economic restructuring in a post-welfare era

Migrants tend to be employed in greater amounts in countries with radical welfare restructuring (Misra, Woodring, and Merz, 2006). These 'welfare regimes' or 'care regimes' reflect austerity measures in state, markets, and the family (Esping-Anderson, 1999 in, Rubin, Rendall, Rabinovich, Tsang, Oranje-Nassau, and Janta, 2008; Kofman et al., 2000; Lutz, 2011; Rostegard, Chiatti, and Lamura, 2011). When emerging countries privatize, state agencies cut subsidies on goods and liberalize import policies, which has the effect of reducing wage, health and safety regulations and programmes, and leading to inequalities, unemployment, debt repayments, thereby inducing many women to migrate (Sassen, 1998). Migration policies go hand-in-hand with economic liberalization. Bilateral (rather than multilateral) agreements, for example, regulate migration flows and create complex power relations that benefit employers (Fudge, 2010). Regional proximity and colonial histories often direct and 'manage' these flows too. Of these factors, proximity is critical for recruiting migrant care assistants, as with England and Poland (Spencer et al., 2010). But it is also based on employers' national preferences for certain workers based on assumptions about what these migrants offer (Cangiano et al., 2009; Datta, McIlwaine, Evans, Herbert, May and Wills, 2010)—a reason why England has found ingenious ways to recruit healthcare professionals from outside the European Economic Area (EEA), such as Filipinos for care assistant work.

Although a globalized business, each country has different care systems for older persons. In England, as previously mentioned, care is purchased in a competitive market with workers receiving poor pay and conditions. This model differs from that in social democratic countries, which offer free care and have higher pay and conditions for workers, and Southern European countries, which operate according to familial models of a 'migrant in the family' (van Hooren, 2012). Yet most European countries appear to be drifting towards market-based models of care.

From global care chains to global care industry

A wide-ranging study of migrant care workers (including nurses and nuns) by Nicola Yeates (2009; see also, Yeates, 2012) maps out the political economy of care and, in doing so, enriches the concept of global care chains first introduced by Hochschild (2000, p. 130). This chain, according to Hochschild, starts with migrant women from emerging countries emigrating to advanced economies to care and remitting to improve their families' livelihoods. Hochschild (2000, p. 131) describes these chains as a 'series of personal links between people across the globe based on the paid and unpaid work of caring.' Households are linked through a downward spiral of care work, which in the end, depends on unpaid and very low paid care (a migrant care assistant depends on a 'helper' and her mother for the care of her children). Nations are linked through the extraction of human resources for care, specifically, the 'emotional surplus value' of migrant women (Hochschild, 2000, p. 130). All of these women are linked together as if in a chain in order to fill a 'care deficit' in advanced economies. Working women (and even those who aren't in paid employment) in high-income countries (Cox, 2006) become dependent on migrant women for care, with the latter's children bearing the brunt of this relationship.

This chain concept has also been used to describe male migration as with 'chain migration' (families moving in stages with women following). For women, however, the chain suggests a burden as they are tied to precarious jobs and vulnerable people (Escriva, 2005). Their physical absence is viewed as creating a care crisis in emerging countries. Yeates (2009) shows that not only does this chain metaphor not fit all migrant women (as not all are mothers, like Mei-Li) but not all situations either. The metaphor can be misleading too as this theory of one country's economy (with a care surplus) being dependent upon another (with a care drain) confers a sense of collaboration between actors and disregards other internal and subjective factors, as if women are simply swept along with state policies (Escriva, 2005). Although Hochschild has since expanded the chain concept to anchor it to a 'socio-emotional commons,' with migrant communities giving and exchanging care (Isaksen, Devi, and Hochschild, 2008, p. 407), the literature still refers more to domestic labour and households rather than care in institutions (and agencies). Moreover, it does not consider migrants' professional expertise in the making of care. The value of the care chain argument, however, is that it makes women migrant care assistants visible as a group and is a starting point for focusing on global care migration as a private solution to a public problem (Fudge, 2010).

Another way to look at migrant women's incorporation into the global care market is through a 'diamond' that includes other facets (such as the community) rather than a linear 'chain' (Raghuram, 2012). This diamond image of many sides to the face of a stone is multidimensional. It challenges the 'transfer' of care from one country to the next, as if it is all the same type or in the same direction. Many other facets *transform* rather than simply *transfer* care from one environment to the next, examples of which are in chapters 3 and 6 (Yeates, 2009). A 'transnational political economy of care' (Williams, 2010, p. 391) is another facet of this diamond. This economy is connected to migrants' care commitments, the movement of care capital and remittances, as well as transnational care discourses. Regardless of whether transnational care work is conceived of in terms of chains, diamonds, economies, circuits, or, even, carousels or conveyer belts (Eckenwiler, 2010, p. 26), it involves investments and risks on the part of these migrant workers, most of whom are women.

Central argument of the book: High stakes migration for skilled women

High hopes, low odds

Women like Mei-Li intended to maximize their resources by migrating as care assistants but in doing so had also maximized their risk. While they planned to exchange their 'social chits' (obligations to care for something better in the future) they ended up with just obligations (Portes, 1998, p. 8). In her mid-twenties, Mei-Li, like a number of the participants in the study, had reached a point in China where she felt she could go no further in her career and wanted to take the next step of migrating to England for more opportunities, as part of a 'travelled nurse dream.' Therefore, she had the qualifications and education levels to realistically aspire to move from care assistant to nurse again in a new country and paid for this opportunity. Mei-Li paid her recruiter £8,000 with money lent to her by her aunt and mother with 'pressure' to pay them back over a three-year period. After arriving in England, however, she wasn't sure she could fulfil this agreement, earning only £5.52 an hour, which in early 2008 was the minimum wage.

Mei-Li was a pioneer migrant—the first of her generation to migrate from her family to a particular place for a particular type of job[4]; like most of the participants, she relied more on agencies to migrate than on her networks. These agencies started them on this difficult journey. While Mei-Li's situation was unusual because she was charged with a crime, a number of the women experienced major difficulties which early on disadvantaged them, moving them further from their original goal of obtaining 'greener pastures,' as one participant remarked. These women saw these jobs in terms of insurance for themselves and their families in very uncertain times and, like many other migrants, took risks to start at the bottom (Hochschild, 2000). Although the participants were from different countries, former professions, and family circumstances, they faced similar problems.

The feminization of labour migration

The international migration of women like Mei-Li over the last 20 years has swelled, and is known as 'the feminization of migration' (Castles and Miller, 2009, p. 9). As previously discussed, this is due to the growth of the feminized service industry, which selects out women from specific regions, nationalities, and social classes (Castles and Miller, 2009; Sullivan, 1984). The feminization of labour migration is often seen as a development strategy for sending countries to resolve their problems (Phillips, 2009). However, there is little consensus about whether or not labour migration is empowering for women (Piper, 2005). Many women—skilled and unskilled—and their opportunities are thwarted because even as they rescue failing welfare systems in high-income countries, the remittance of their low wages leaves them few resources for their own personal progress. The feminization of labour migration, then, connects to the feminization of poverty (Sassen, 1998). Migrant women's important work as care assistants contributes to the modernization of nations but comes at a great personal sacrifice. Women like Mei-Li often find themselves within a 'globalization trap' in the care industry (Lutz, 2011, p. 185).

Parvati Raghuram and Eleanor Kofman have contributed the most in-depth coverage of skilled female labour migration. They show that women have always been active participants in labour migration but focus specifically on their *skills*. Well-educated women are motivated by a number of complex factors, including the power relations in their families, communities, and labour market. These women move through migration regimes, with their economic and social policies, practices, and institutional and colonial histories (Kofman et al., 2000, p. 49). These regimes connect to migration management systems with their power to issue visas that determine women migrants' labour market value.

The outcomes of selective incorporation in the labour market

From the onset, the participants in this study lost their professional prestige and social status by entering the bottom rung of the occupational and social hierarchy (Sullivan, 1984). Recruited for care assistant work, they were retained through social policies that exacerbated their problems and trapped them. Social stratification, gender, and labour market theories help explain the major troubles participants faced in the receiving country's labour market. These theories expose assimilation as a myth of upward mobility (Bauder, 2001; Portes and Rumbaut, 2006) and focus instead on the divergent pathways that migrants follow in adapting to a new country. Simply put, the place that many low-income migrants first grasp in a new country is the place that they often stay—this stratum of society first absorbs and keeps them there and they become active participants in this process (Fitzgerald, 2006). While the participants were indeed incorporated into the labour market, it was into the working-class rather than the middle-class—which was not a place to which they aspired. To be sure, the participants were not 'opportunity hoarding' (intentionally closing off opportunities to outsiders) (Waldinger, Lim, and Cort, 2007, p. 6). In other words, they were not 'holding' on to their care positions as a measure of job attachment so much as being trapped through gender segmentation, immigration laws, and other factors (Peixoto, 2009). Policy makers rarely concern themselves with women migrants' labour market integration as they are viewed as less skilled and reproductive rather than as productive dependents (Kofman et al., 2000). These views translated into policies that led to the participants' deskilling.

The participants knew they would be deskilled but did not realize that this work would be the end game of their experience. Deskilling, which is defined as a way to make the skills of a worker (in this case professional migrant women's expertise) obsolete, has a set of negative outcomes associated with it. This was especially the case for former health care professionals like Mei-Li, but it was also so for women from other fields. The care work did not utilize their educational knowledge, their professional dispositions, and the levels of decision-making authority they previously had. They were required to follow a narrow and scripted care plan when caring for clients, which prevented them from practising their former professional skills. The traceable barriers to professional advancement that the participants faced (to be discussed in Chapter 5) included immigration policies, professional closure by national associations, employment conditions, and limited resources that restricted their entry into professional careers in England, all of which were underscored by less perceptible problems, like the subordinate role of care in English society. These theories, while valuable for understanding economic barriers, say little about how the women workers themselves played the cards they were dealt. These theories do not account for the ways the participants circumvented these assigned 'contracts.'

Enter transnationalism

Transnationalism is broadly defined as 'the nature and function of border-crossing social networks, families and households, ethnic communities and associations' (Vertovec, 2007, p. 150). Migrants are viewed as having dual-lives (or more) in speaking different languages, having homes and family in more than one country, and moving back and forth across nation-states. Transnationalism is also not a new phenomenon but is 'old as labour immigration itself' (Portes, Guarnizo, and Landolt, 1999, p. 218), although technological innovations have increased expansionist motives built into late capitalism. On a broader level, migrant transnationalism affects economic and social systems, creating new complex global patterning. Peggy Levitt and Nina Schiller (2007) see transnational social relations and practices occurring in multiple locations and affecting participants' actions. This 'social field' is, 'a set of multiple interlocking networks of social relationships through which ideas, practices and resources are unequally exchanged, organized and transformed' (p. 188). In this field, actors interact across national borders, maintaining social relations across the miles: 'they ebb and flow in response to particular incidents or crises' (p. 191). By migrating to a new country that has a stronger economy migrants may gain more power in relation to those at home or not depending on the level of 'personal losses and gains' (p. 193).

Vertovec (2007) suggests that the term 'transnationalism' hides the types of changes that migrants make and that 'transformation' is a more accurate term. Migrants have 'bifocality' (p. 153), that is, they may form allegiances or political bodies to lobby for their rights as 'social citizens' in both receiving and sending countries (Levitt and Schiller, 2007, p. 204). This concept captures what happened to participants (see, Chapter 3) who with their expertise capitalized on their skills and were viewed as valuable by clients. Yet the effects of migration for women are often 'contingent and contradictory' (Levitt and Lamba-Nieves, 2011, p. 5). Few participants in this study, for example, fit the ideal transformative portrait of entrepreneurs and most of the participants remitted their limited incomes for basic amenities and savings to immediate families, which, while helping greater productivity and 'economic transformation,' did not lead to their political participation (Vertovec, 2007, p. 164). No surprise, since the costs of their migration were so high and they were constantly working to make ends meet. Again, the participants did not rely so much on their networks as much as the agencies that, linked to state policies, were key gatekeepers for their migratory experiences that led to their spatial entrapment.

Engendering transnationalism with care

The project of 'engendering transnational migration' (Boyle, 2002) means specifying women migrants' experiences in the actual places where they live and work. This includes the markets they become embedded in—often to their detriment—and the communities in which they dwell. This politics of location (and dislocation) entails the intimate, gendered, and racial, situation-specific experiences and practices, as well as particular global forces, historical and current, that engage marginalized groups. These dwellings highlight 'gender [which] is a constitutive element in the formation of labour markets' (Brah, 1996, p. 128) and includes skills, the division of labour, family roles, available and worthwhile jobs, racism, and immigration rules.

The care industry is at the centre of these transnational women's stories of the spaces they occupied and, as Chapter 4 will show, the participants' workplace experiences permeated the fabric of their lives. The care industry had seized the moment to attract female skilled workers like Mei-Li who paid the price for migrating. This view unsettles the linear modernist classical story of labour migration as a 'race to the top' of a destination country's social hierarchy. More attention, then, needs to be paid to the concrete gendered practices surrounding women migrants' *immobilities*. Their workspaces reinforced global power structures in a new social order.

A feminist geographic approach further highlights the patterning of gender, labour markets, and immigration together as part of social locations (Mahler and Pessar, 2006, p. 46). Documentation makes clear that women are in demand in the global service economy with occupations that are magnets to migrants and are employer-stimulated (Mahler and Pessar, 2006, p. 47). At the same time migrants have aspirations to better their lives, which are shaped by gendered ideologies (for example, to care), and migrate for this reason too. Recruiters groom, shape, and police expectations about being 'a good care worker' but give women migrants little information about their labour rights. Mapping gender with migrancy and care evokes a type of immobility in that the communities that these women belong to are not by choice but by place. Yet they may incubate ideas for future action. A good example is Geraldine Pratt's discovery of Filipinas who moved from being a 'registered nurse to registered nanny' (2004, p. 38) because of Canada's live-in care policies. She connects the globalization of care with ghettoization and deskilling within a number of social locations and, as such, reveals discrimination but also the ways her participants countered it. Pratt's first point of reference is the place where her participants started (the Philippines). She connects this to her participants' Vancouver workplaces and next to the Philippine Women Centre, where they performed their lives on stage, confounding negative stereotypes of them.

Intersectional explanations for understanding discrimination of migrant care assistants

Stereotypes and discrimination

The positive stereotypes employers have of migrants as more caring and hardworking because they come from 'more caring societies' have been articulated by migrants too (Datta et al., 2010, p. 102). National character traits (and race too) have been a selecting device (Anderson, 2000). One recruiter in the study, for example, claimed: 'Indians are very caring by nature—I don't know why but they are.' This connection between nationality and caring abilities, rather than educational experiences and expertise, led to the participants being treated as *outsiders*. This 'ethnic penalty' (Bach, 2003, p. 19) impacted their treatment and ability to progress.

These care assistants followed a long history, from the 19th century onwards, of discrimination that beset migrant nurses, who were channelled into less popular and downgraded areas such as geriatric care in the National Health Service (NHS) (Batnitzky and McDowell, 2011, p. 198; Raghuram, Bornat, and Henri, 2011). The pre-existing internal stratifications in conjunction with weak occupational categories reinforced migrant nurses' subordination, a pattern also found across the world. This legacy continues. One migrant nurse in this study claimed that Filipinos were used to cover the night shifts and were blamed when residents had problems. They were also excluded from promotions, given difficult tasks as well as the hardest clients.

Discrimination has only recently been documented among migrant care assistants in England (Cangiano et al., 2009; Poinasamy, 2009; Timonen and Doyle, 2010; Wills et al., 2010). Like nurses, it often starts with recruitment. In this study, an employer who recruited from Poland wanted more control in the selection process, a desire that landed her in Gdansk to directly interview prospective recruits. She wanted to select from a younger generation of Polish women, not those from the Communist era, describing one who returned to Poland after asking for two days off a week, saying: 'I can't work this hard.' For those from outside of the EEA, the stakes were higher as it was harder to leave. One participant, for example, was told by her Philippines-based recruiter that she would receive appropriate training in order to adapt as a nurse in England. Instead, she was given a cleaning job and stayed in England to recover the $5,000 that she owed her recruiter.

An Oxfam report (Poinasamy, 2009, p. 2) found that workplace exploitation was 'rife' in England's care sector and that this was related to the lack of labour rights enforcement for its migrant workers. Many workers had zero hour contracts (on-call basis), were not fully paid for their work, and were expected to operate at breakneck speeds. In this study, British-born employees noticed this phenomenon. One care assistant, for example, said that her employer used 'the Romanians as scapegoats and treated them like donkeys, running them around everywhere.' In addition to this ethnic penalty, there was also a language penalty that the participants faced, despite the fact that all of them were fluent in English, most of them emigrating from English-speaking former colonies (Philippines and India).

A language penalty

Employers preferred migrants but believed that they had poor language abilities, which they confused with accents (Cangiano et al., 2009; Spencer et al., 2010). An expert who was interviewed for this study, for example, claimed that migrants' 'tone is different, the syllables are different, and the peers will say that they don't understand what they are saying.' Yet 'language problems of migrants' is often an overused rationale for why they can't professionally succeed in England's labour market; it becomes a 'linguistic penalty' levied by employers and professional bodies who operate as gatekeepers (Roberts, 2010, p. 5). Cecilia Roberts (2010) shows how examinations for the professions discriminate against migrants due to the discourses in the test designs. The professional examination needed to enter the health professions—the International English Language Test System (IELTS)—may not reflect actual workplace communicative interactions or be relevant (Winkelmann-Gleed, 2004). Only those migrants from designated countries outside of the EEA take the IELTS, irrespective of their English language training, use, and proficiency. Labour market tests like the IELTS, which have shifting cut-off scores, create pressured conditions for prospective recruits by pushing up costs in sending countries (Lowell, Findlay and Stewart, 2004).

Migrants often internalize perceptions of their poor expressive language abilities and under-report or under-estimate these to employers (Rubin et al., 2008). In short, language proficiencies are highly contextual and subjective, like one participant in the study who wanted her English fluency to be 'a hundred per cent.' When asked to clarify what exactly this meant, she replied, 'a hundred per cent means speaking English confidently!' Many migrant care assistants like her attended ESOL courses in hopes of becoming more confident and raising their test scores too. The problem was that the courses were neither specialized nor advanced enough and were experienced as a 'big disappointment,' as one participant exclaimed. The participants' language skills, therefore, were not barriers for their advancement. Little attention is paid to the actual, non-language structural barriers blocking migrants' advancement. This issue is critical for women migrants in particular who face multiple obstacles (Rubin et al., 2008).

Intersectionality to explain discrimination

Intersectionality is a theory of specificity, of examining intra-group differences and acknowledging how women are different from one another (Crenshaw, 2011). These intersections crosscut along different lines of inequalities whereby migrant women are advantaged along some lines and disadvantaged along others (Lutz, 2011). This is a starting point for *decoupling* the experiences and identities of migrant women as well as their identities—how they carry and deploy different social categories (e.g. woman and migrant) creating conflict and privilege and the ways these intersect with one another and change (McCall, 2005). The analysis also shows ways that these divisions are used in social stratification (Yuval-Davis, 2011). Intersectionality, therefore, puts 'inequalities at the centre rather than the margins of social theory' (Walby, 2007, p. 451). Importantly, these inequalities should be made visible, rather than be reduced to ever fine points, so as to be included in anti-discrimination legislation (Crenshaw, 2011; Walby, 2007). An intersectional framework allows for an analysis of the discrimination migrant care assistants face as outsiders. They are 'insiders' to the extent that they deal with intimate issues in older people's lives but they are socially marginalized. Intersectionality offers a window into understanding unequal gendered and raced relations, with, for example, the ways the feminization of labour migration is central to organizing the global industry of care.

Consider Mei-Li again. An intersectional approach illustrates her situation well. She worked in a highly feminized and segregated environment with migrants on the lower echelons of her nursing home. She was also a Chinese woman in a new place of settlement. She was accused by a Caucasian British-born colleague of violating an older Caucasian British-born female client, with the English language being used as a weapon against her. Mei-Li felt, from the beginning, she was targeted because of her nationality. During the trial her solicitor, although saying it was a farcical case, did not highlight ethnocentrism in his argument due to the fact that he felt he could not prove this to be true. Loic Wacquant (1997, p. 222; see also, Nash, 2008) discusses the 'logic of the trial' in terms of the historical practices and mechanisms of punishing and controlling marginalized groups through legal processes that make race and gender invisible.

Intersectional theory, as discussed in the next section, also points to differences *between* migrant women (e.g. EEA vs non-EEAs), which are important for examining the participants' experiences in this study.

About the participants

The profiles of the participants reveal both diversity and clear patterns of selectivity for the care industry. Table 1.1 shows that although the participants were professionals from a variety of backgrounds, most (56%) had nursing degrees from health-care exporting countries (the Philippines and India). The highest percentage of nationalities was from the Philippines (46%), followed by Poland and India, representing the top nationalities for migrant care assistants in England. These data suggest that the Philippines, in particular, was a care-assistant source

Table 1.1 Participant Nationality, Education, and Profession

Nationality (sample size of 60)	Degrees (last one earned)	Professions (primary)	Degree-profession-work divergence	Advancement to professions
Filipino-28	Nursing (18); midwifery (4); physiotherapy (3); occupational therapy (2); medical administration	Nurses including a nurse educator (15); nursing attendant (3); midwife (3); occupational therapist (2); physiotherapists including a physiotherapy educator (3); volunteer nurse (2)	Five nurses were nursing attendants and volunteers	NOTE: One started her adaptation process but did not receive a licence during study period
Polish-16	Medicine; tourism/recreation; master's in economics; social work; business; language and literature; teaching (2); engineering, human resources; nursing (2): master's in psychology; accounting; post-graduate in public administration; economics	Paramedic; tax officer; unemployed; social worker; business owner; teacher (3); insurance broker (2); recent human resources graduate; nurse (2); occupational psychologist; IT specialist; web designer	– Engineering to insurance broker – Social work to waitress – School of public administration to web designer – Accounting to IT specialist – Master's in economics to unemployed	Two became nurses in nursing homes

Indian-8	Nursing	Nurse (8) including a nurse educator	0	Two became nurses in private hospitals; NOTE: Another participant adapted but did not obtain a job
Romanian-4	Nursing	Nurse (4)	0	Three became nurses, all in nursing homes
Various migrant groups-4 (Chinese, Thai, Cuban, Zambian)	Nursing (2), business administration; philosophy and linguistics	Receptionist; nurse (2); university lecturer and translator	Business administration to receptionist	0

country not only for England but also for Canada and the USA, as well as other countries that demonstrate selective recruitments (Spencer et al., 2010). The prevalence of Filipinos in England reveals the predominance of bilateral agreements over colonial histories or proximity for labour migration. Several of these former professionals could not find work in their degree areas in the country where they graduated, and worked in other jobs, often below their levels (participants with nursing degrees were voluntary workers in hospitals or attendants) while others were unemployed. None had degrees from countries other than where they were born and only a few had master's or multiple degrees.

Here it is clear that the Polish participants had the most variation in degree specialities and the most divergence as well in their professions and work. Of the non-EEA participants (40), 19 of them were on student routes, most arriving in 2008, the beginning of the points-based system, and all of these were Filipinos.[5] While most of the Polish participants arrived prior to 2008, this year showed more Filipino arrivals (half of them migrating then). Being on student visas caused stress among these participants when trying to renew their short-term visas, convert to work permits and other tiers in England's points-based system. Mei-Li as well as other non-EEA participants, for example, had to pay thousands of pounds to enrol in courses they essentially did not need just to stay in England. They believed that the longer they stayed, the closer they would come to acquiring citizenship status. Eastern Europeans (except Romanians and Bulgarians) did not need visas but were expected to register with the now defunct Workers Registration Scheme.

Although the participants are referred to generally as 'pioneers' in this book, several (5) followed or came with family (most EEA members). These family members, however, did not protect the participants from exploitation in their workplaces or by recruiters and once they reached England were expected to fend for themselves. In one case, two participants were sisters, coming one after the other, and considered to be 'troublemakers' by their employer, who lessened their hours so they would leave. In another case, a participant, in following her cousin (also a participant), discovered she had overpaid and received false information from her recruiter.

Eighty-eight per cent of the participants (EEA and non-EEA) used agencies as their migration channel. The high number of agencies featured in the study suggests the strong role of intermediary actors in the care industry and the roles they play in giving and withholding information, securing visas, setting costs, and putting in place debt repayments as well as expectations for recruits in the workplace. A number of these agencies had an overseas base and a sister recruitment company in England. These were often linked not only to the employer's company, but also to training agencies, colleges, and universities. When one link broke, others would point fingers and took little responsibility for remediating participants' problems. Due to these close linkages, it was also confusing for the participants to pinpoint where the exploitation started and ended and who did the exploiting. Only one of the recruits contacted a British employment agency and nearly all of them first contacted recruiters in the countries from where they emigrated. Additionally, some participants (9) had worked in other countries, especially the Gulf region, prior to migrating to England. Only two participants worked in the USA prior to working in England but none had worked in Canada or Australia, which were further destinations that were mentioned by participants, and suggested that England was a stage for onward journeys.

Seven participants (almost all EEA members) who were former nurses advanced to professional positions in England. However, most of these new nurses worked in nursing homes after they adapted (or converted their degrees) and some of these participants still did care assistant work. Some participants who were former nurses (13) were senior care assistants, showing that former nursing posts were indeed taken into account in establishing their status. Yet this was a minority and it was an arbitrary practice on the part of the management of particular companies. Moreover, the pay wasn't much higher. A few participants were promoted (e.g. to scheme coordinator) but they did not achieve much of a pay increase, as a supervisor, an assistant manager or a manager would command. There was little job mobility; apart from those who advanced to nurses, eight participants switched employers during the study period, five of which were in the care home sector. Three additional participants temporarily returned to their countries and back to the care homes where they worked.

The average (mean) age of the participants was 34.[6] The participants, then, were of prime working age, with a number of them having family responsibilities, including children (62% of the participants), making the stakes higher for them in migrating. Of those with children, six participants sponsored (or brought) their families to England. Other participants were planning to sponsor families. As Chapter 6 shows, even the single participants, and those in their 20s, carried responsibilities for family members and partners. A little less than half of the participants, were married, although there were also some divorced, separated, and widowed participants, signalling the existence of former spouses and/or extended families as well as children (all of these participants had children), which meant they had strong support roles. Being professionals in their countries of origin, these participants were seeking professional growth opportunities missing in their home countries. Taking a care assistant post was viewed as a 'stepping stone' for launching their dream careers, as one former physiotherapist expressed, and better lives. Yet the participants' motivations to migrate could only be discerned broadly from the socio-demographic data analysis. The qualitative data established more specific motivations. Yet as Chapter 5 will show, the participants had multiple motives to: (1) maximize a career, (2) earn greater incomes to support self and family, and (3) become more self-determined. These motivations, however, often had a bottom line of economic survival; all of the participants wanted to improve their financial situations and that of their family.

Conclusion

This chapter showed the costs and risks of caregiving for professional women migrants that amounted to what Nancy Folbre (2001, p. 22) calls a 'care penalty.' This resulted from a gendered contract, and linguistic and ethnic penalties. But the chapter also shed light on the ways women like Mei-Li persisted in the global care industry not just to get ahead but also to be professionals and, as will be evident in other chapters (particularly chapters 3, 4 and 5), how they confronted these penalties (see also, Twigg, Wolkowitz, Cohen and Nettleton, 2011). In migrating, these women gambled with a type of prisoner's dilemma (Folbre, 2001), which meant they put in their 'time' to do low-level care work and assumed that there would be reciprocity from employers and the government in fulfilment of their obligations that they could leverage to advance their careers. Mei-Li believed her care work could someday be traded in the market of care. Her decision-making was by no means flawed. The recruiters would either promise or indirectly communicate that this work would launch their careers in a new country if they were committed and worked hard. Many participants counted on this societal trade (Folbre, 2001). In working in this industry, however, they became trapped by this implied bargain and suffered as a result (Husso and Hirvonen, 2012). As pioneer migrants they took considerable risks to migrate on precarious visas in care assistant work and expected that they could use these posts to fulfil their upwardly mobile dreams. Although these expectations may be viewed as naïve, they were not necessarily out of line with many migrants who start at the bottom but work hard to move up in a new country: this, of course, is the grand narrative of immigration. But their journeys went off track. So why would they persist? What I discovered is that even the most motivated of migrant women, due to their responsibilities, endure these jobs and the 'double negative effects' (Boyd, 1984, p. 1094) of nationality and gender. Downward trajectories are often the norm for migrant women in the labour market, including the care industry (Rubin et al., 2008). This story is what happens when dreams don't manifest in the ways that are expected.

Chapter 2 will describe the participants over and beyond the sociodemographic data, and the dilemmas I encountered in framing the research in terms of my own migrant identity, positioning, and work. The aim of this chapter was to produce a reflexive account of a migrant woman researcher in academia studying migrant women care assistants in the service sector. By incorporating the research team's experiences, the intention was to create a more comprehensive and critical understanding of the full spectrum of skilled migration.

Chapter 3 expands on Chapter 1 by discussing the historical issues in the making of the 'care assistant' in England and the mapping of the sector with its power and the ways a select group of former health care professionals subverted it in line with their own values and aspirations. The aim of this chapter was to unearth the 'hidden' curriculum of the care industry workplace, especially the exploitative conditions in which all care assistants work. A big picture of the issues sets the stage for the rest of the book. Chapter 4 then gives a close-up view of the issues of a select group of migrant domiciliary care assistants in a particular region of England. By placing these problems within a place and time the issues surrounding the participants' mobility and immobility become concrete.

Chapter 5 presents profiles of the participants and their motivations and career trajectories as well as the mechanisms by which they became deskilled in these care assistant jobs. Again, focusing in-depth on a subset of participants, Chapter 6 focuses on the transnational worlds of the participants and the various responsibilities and allegiances that shaped their experiences. These chapters aim to develop knowledge about how professional migrant women's home and community lives interconnect with their work lives. I investigated their social support networks and how these shaped their mobility, opportunities, and identities in transnational contexts.

Finally, Chapter 7 is the concluding chapter and focuses on the practice, policy, and research implications of the participants' situations and, like the other chapters, highlights the gendered forces that impact well-educated migrant women, who in, Blake's terms, often trap the moment before it's ripe.

2
A Homework Methodology for Researching Migrant Women's Lives

Introduction

Figure 2.1 Sondra waiting at the airport

Smiling awkwardly, I stood next to a care employer at Manchester airport on a cloudy day in August 2008, waiting for two care assistants that she had hired from the Philippines (see Figure 2.1). How I came to hold a sign for her bearing their names was unforeseen. It was then that I realized how caught up I was in the fates of these care assistants. I wrote in my diary that

I felt implicated by using people in my study who I felt were migrating on very precarious visas, which the employer managed to obtain through loopholes in the government. I wanted to position myself with the care assistants and their experiences but in this I was clearly positioning myself closer to the employer through access to them.

Then two tired but happy people walked through the entry with suitcases in hand, making a beeline for me holding the sign. They hugged me, thinking I was their employer. I stepped back and made the introductions. The employer was not smiling.

These two care assistants, Elma and Sallie, were the last participants needed to fulfil the quota for my study and their recruitment had not come easily. The implementation of the points-based immigration system, in 2008, caused erratic fluctuations in the numbers of migrant care assistants arriving in England then and in the previous year. I found it hard to locate new participants who I could shadow. So when Debbie (the employer) contacted me to say that two were on their way I was pleased—although not for them because I knew what a difficult journey it would be once they arrived. Their recruiter in London had avoided my phone calls for nearly a year. But upon moving to a new company, she was more comfortable in telling me about her methods for recruiting health care professionals on student visas, including the two that I picked up at the airport. She didn't like the term 'recruiting,' and, instead, referred to her system as 'training.' She confessed that the student immigration route was a 'disguise' to draw migrants with the bait of training. Disturbed that her view was the same as mine, I became aware of how both of us were drawn into the care industry; this recruiter was also a migrant worker from the Philippines.

These research candidates (I had not yet asked them to be a part of the study) had met others like themselves in airports along their route who warned them about backstabbing colleagues, but said little about the employers they would encounter. In the Philippines, they had each applied twice to their recruitment agency and were unsuccessful, the first time being in 2006, and on finally consenting to travel on student visas after these disappointments, they were processed through the system. They said they were happy that I was there to meet them and nine months into the research, they turned to me to dispute their supervisor who told them that she 'bought' them from the recruiter. I had suspected that they would be exploited to some extent, although I didn't get a sense of the depth of it until the study was well underway.

It began with their financial exploitation, first by recruiters based in the Philippines and then by a London agency. Sallie and Elma paid much money for multiple services, few of which they actually received and many which they did not understand. Then the training company, affiliated with the recruiter, accused them of not paying their fees, which set in motion letters threatening their deportation. Without any legal recourse to gain reimbursement and no means to appeal, they had to enrol with another trainer, this time, at a reputable university, which offered a mandated vocational course and charged them an additional £1,500. Having had to pay this exorbitant amount of money for something that was offered free to British nationals in their workplaces, they could not afford to obtain British drivers' licences and therefore couldn't drive. The company then applied pressure for them to work overtime to pay for their own travel expenses and they took taxis and walked to clients' houses, even in inclement weather.

I have learned that migrants are alike and different. Elma and Sallie's visas, for example, were the same as mine and their vetting was similar too. Their credentials and professional experiences were important in getting them through the recruiter's door (even if the employer ignored these in the workplace). Like them, I was on a 'skilled two' work visa that barred me from having access to public funds or from working for another employer without first consulting and obtaining government permission. Unlike the 60 study participants who were on short-term student visas and work permits, however, I was able to get promoted and receive pay raises above a living wage and had decent working conditions. I was from a top-tier OECD country where British academics spend time and my union, too, had paved the way for my good treatment.[1] I also sponsored my foreign-born husband without problems and gave birth to my daughter in an NHS hospital without being regarded as a 'suspect.' While academic migrants like myself were viewed as endowing their skills to the destination country's labour market, the participants in the study were simply viewed as, 'aspiring' migrants (Bryceson and Vuorela, 2002, p. 11). Based on our tertiary education, however, we would all be considered 'highly skilled.' This category, therefore, conceals the wide range of ranks within it.

My visa and renewal of it was expedited in time to start work. I had no entry problems. My university credits and paperwork passed cleanly through administrative hands as if I had graduated in England. I did not have to tally points about the universities where I graduated nor answer questions about my English language competence. In fact, when I asked my colleagues and friends what I was, none of them considered me a 'migrant' but instead an 'overseas academic.' Nonetheless, I decided to affiliate as a migrant worker—after all I migrated to England to work and that's what made me valuable there. I worked at the upper ends of the feminized service sector, in education, preparing the next generation of teachers and researchers in this field. Care work, in essence, was the background story of our migration, gender, and labour.

The first part of this chapter describes the research team of four female migrants and how our tracks both paralleled and differed from those of the participants in the study. This provides the basis for understanding how the team perceived the problems the participants faced. But it also mirrored a feminist politics between academics and participants who were in the field of care at opposite ends of the spectrum. I will outline the problematic issues of the team in having both an insider and outsider status and the types of practices we engaged in to build relations and credibility into the study, especially in interacting with participants.

The second part is a discussion about researcher/reader/participant positionality and theorizes about skilled female migrancy with examples from my research project and the literature. Here I discuss the issues that I faced as an academic-based writer and my representations of the participants in terms of assumptions, interpretations, and pressures to glean findings that fit into contemporary policy debates.

The last section is a straightforward account of the research. It includes a discussion of the study methodology (see Appendix 1 for details of the design and timeline). I highlight the extended case study method as a means for moving through micro, meso, and macro levels. Next, I discuss ethnographic methods and their use in this study. Finally, I discuss data analysis methods that focus on themes and narratives of the participants' experiences. This analysis deepened the picture of these skilled migrant care assistants within the global polity.

Homework on caring

> The eyes on a woman's back are also her own eyes. They are everything she has seen in her travels and in her return home.
> (Behar, 1995, p. 2)

Keeping our eyes on our backs, so to speak, was an important exercise for the research team in accounting for our assumptions and cultivating reflexivity. This sense of vulnerability, of 'watching backs' allowed relevant material to emerge precisely because we, as observers, were conscientious about our viewpoints and our relations with each other and the participants. We wanted to focus on the work of care within the research process, especially when dilemmas emerged such as how the research team was implicated in problems the participants faced. This was one aspect of our 'homework.'

The other aspect was to glean knowledge about the invisible work that these migrant care assistants did, because there was an 'insufficiency of language' to describe their experiences with a vocabulary that adequately captured it (Smith, 2005, p. 153). They worked so long and hard that their home and work lives blurred. The term, 'homework,' therefore, questions the boundaries of home and work in the participants' making of care across different sites. Chapter 3 describes institutionalized workspaces and how they operated as homes for the clients as well as for the participants who spent long hours there caring for clients with their hidden expertise. Chapter 4 examines how private homes became institutionalized workspaces and how the participants' fast-paced movements hid their work; their employers failed to give them due credit for their efficient methods. Chapter 5 then goes on to demonstrate that these migrants' helpful interventions did not result in viable returns for their careers. Chapter 6 shows that 'home' is an unsettled concept for migrants caring for family in numerous places. Work plays an important role in the dispersal of families throughout the globe in pursuit of better livelihoods, making home, and work often indistinguishable with regard to care.

Writing about the hidden worlds of home and work requires a 'vulnerable observer' approach that is sensitized to the invisible labour of migrant women and their versions of care work. This approach was like a fragile, tenuous exercise in 'bearing testimony and witnessing,' with roots in basic activities of 'talking, listening, transcribing, translating, and interpreting' (Behar, 1996, p. 163). This type of 'homework' involved a process of tracking, documenting, and writing field notes of the veiled and mundane aspects of care engaged in by marginalized women. This 'homework' was important for reflecting on power relations surrounding what participants were 'doing, asking and observing' (Naples, 2003, p. 47). Most importantly this homework would help to ensure that 'false parallels' (Kleinman, 2007, pp. 31–32) would not be made between the academics and the care assistants (simply because we were all women migrants). Furthermore, each research team member had a different social standing that needed to be taken into account.

'Homework,' like after-school work that is assigned to students, represents the hidden valuable work that the participants did in their jobs. It also represents the training that was expected of them by the government and which was big business in England's care sector; the participants attended myriad care training sessions but because the advice did not fit with the realities of their workplaces they amended it while on the job. Furthermore, they studied in their own time, after work, without pay, and in their homes. These migrant participants had learned to follow the unwritten rules of this hidden curriculum.

Insider/outsider

I had to learn the hidden rules and retain boundaries and ethical practices in the research, which was an important homework practice for myself as an outsider. For example, when participants volunteered to pick me up at the railway station before their shifts I would give them money for petrol. A less straightforward example was when the participants 'forgot' they were part of the research in view of being unaccustomed to researcher–participant relations (Buch and Staller, 2007). These hidden care issues were negotiated in ways that went beyond the framework for institutional research ethics and meant relying on a care ethic and an intersectional approach. The research team was composed of women with different entitlements, and this became a practice ground for interacting with the participants. One activity, for example, involved a taped dialogue on our different and similar experiences of migrating to and working in England. Reflecting back on this reminded us of our diversity and how our experiences differed from each other and the participants.

It is important to detail the differences within the research team. We had different social statuses. As the principal investigator, I led the study, and, as a faculty member, I had seniority at the University. However, unlike the other team members, I was a complete outsider in the work world of care. The research associate, who was also a doctoral student, and lower on the academic totem pole, had first-hand experience of being deskilled as a care assistant; her social work degree did not count and to earn a living after migrating to England, she worked in a care home while attending a master's programme. There were also two paid informants on the team. One was from Poland and a former teacher and a care assistant. The other was a former nurse from the Philippines and, in migrating on a nursing student visa, eventually became a nurse and later, a manager of a nursing home. She, in particular, was caught between a number of worlds and could be considered as both an insider and outsider. The insider vs outsider terminology, therefore, is not ideal because it tends to fix one demographic variable (e.g. gender), which works against a more complex (intersectional) view of subjectivity and roles. Also, these terms are not static and shift with regard to social locations and people's ever-changing everyday worlds (Naples, 2003).

Recognizing this variability enabled me, as a researcher and an outsider in the world of care work, to gain insider knowledge of the participants. As an outsider, I used 'member checking' (literally checking with the participants about the meanings of their words), which was done informally and with staggered interviews over time and repeated participant observations. These prolonged interactions offered me ways to confirm understanding with participants (other than asking them to read their own transcripts which seemed decontextualized and labour intensive for them). Having informants check interviews also made possible the negotiation of different interpretations of the participants' words.

As a researcher, I not only depended on the indigenous knowledge of these informants but called on my own sensitivities and emotions—hence holding a sign at the airport. I welcomed the opportunity to *not* shield myself from the conflict and pain of acknowledging how I was, in part, an accessory to serious injustices (Naples, 2003, p. 51). Such issues have been taken up in feminist research (Stacey, 1988). In our case, sensitizing ourselves to the participants' predicaments helped us to understand the exploitation that occurred and the 'subjugated knowledges' that developed among participants as a way to cope with it (Collins, 1991, p. 228). It was also important in making this academic-based study accountable to migrant women participants and the politics of methodology (and empowerment) more transparent (Naples, 2003). Yet even this was not enough.

As an outsider, I took steps to enter the worlds of the participants. As an adult educator-activist with a genuine interest in improving migrant women's capabilities, I used my own professional training and identity (as an educator) to frame the research relationships as well as manage the project. I integrated concepts of identity, the politics of relationships, material realities of the women, as well as geographic location and subjectivity into the study, to focus on the impact of unequal power relations on migrant women. Using this pedagogy seemed 'natural' to me—it was what I used in classrooms with students, in my work, and in my life too. At the same time, this tripartite role of practitioner–researcher–activist entails inevitable conflicts when it comes to producing interventions, especially within academia.

Self-presentation was managed in the field through verbal and non-verbal means, such as appearance (as researchers we 'dressed down' although not to the point of looking like we didn't care about the participants' perceptions), but in ways which still signified us as different from the care assistants who were always in uniforms. Because I did not pretend to know the field meant that I could legitimately ask more questions. I used the social distance, usually used to designate differences between social groups, to engage in 'backstage talk' about problems. I did not draw on my gender for rapport for although their work settings were female-dominated they were highly stratified and bullying was common. That both the research associate and myself were in helping professions (education and social work) helped build empathy immediately with the participants who saw as champions.

Boundaries were drawn with our hats on as social worker and educator; this was particularly important for what was unsaid. As a former teacher of adult literacy and ESOL women students as well as non-traditional graduate students, I tried to honour the silences as much as the talk within my interactions. The silences could be strategic on the part of the participants to hint at something they felt they could not voice or as a space of resistance or healing. Yet silence can also signify a lack of opportunity to self-define oneself or of 'being silenced' by others or even self-silencing (Fivush, 2010). Voice, then, was viewed as a positive step and some interactions took the form of 'solidarity talk.' Some women for example experienced the interviews as cathartic, especially when they discussed the deviations from their life script of being upwardly mobile professionals, who were currently stuck in low-level jobs. My academic status reminded the participants of their former professional status and associating with me came to be a part of their own aspirations and a symbol of what they felt had been missing from their lives—affiliating with me made them feel ever closer to this goal of upward mobility; the Polish informant, for example, said she enjoyed talking to me so that she could use more 'refined English' than with her colleagues at work.

Nationality was perhaps the most concrete reminder of who was inside and who was outside, and this was reinforced in the research. While participants developed a type of 'strategic essentialism' (Spivak, 1988) to explain their situations, even sometimes covering over ways they were privileged, so did I as a researcher. The participants, for example, sometimes drew on cultural claims, stating that because they were not from England, they were 'better carers.' But the research team did this as well; for example, we encouraged participants to feel free to discuss their problems with English people, knowing we did not represent this country. I used my status as an American, something that I did not advertise, to discuss Americanisms with Filipinos who were concerned about losing their Americanized English accents as well as their connection to the USA where family members lived and to where several wanted to move.

Drawing on a care ethic

It would seem odd to pronounce *this* study as more 'caring' than another. Most feminist researchers use methodologies that honour participants' lives and lived experiences, acknowledging problematic issues that surface in participant relations and interactions, particularly around power. They often integrate 'care ethics' into research. In conventional research, however, ethics are reserved for the back pages of studies. It seemed appropriate, then, to focus on care ethics considering my research topic and the fact that the participants were largely *uncared for* by their employers. Much of 'caring for the carers' revalues care in its different forms. From the beginning participants wanted 'tougher skin' as one put it, in order to

> Talk to people if they don't treat me right. I shouldn't just turn back. I should talk about it—I should have the courage and the wisdom just to, you know, speak up.

This research would aim to help these participants to 'speak up.' To us, advocating for participants was caring.

This advocacy-based approach can also be deemed a 'feminist transnational praxis,' (discussed in Chapter 7), especially in the building of solidarity networks among migrant women. This is different from a 'global sisterhood' approach, which focuses on one issue—gender oppression—and may breach ethics unintentionally in trying to be helpful to 'third world women' (Stacey, 1988). The study in many respects was a project in 'remembrance' of these participants' invisible assets and capabilities, which they had lost through a process of migration. Joan Tronto (2003, p. 132) says that remembrance is part of a 'task of recognizing the past, of understanding time's place...that requires political imagination, courage and action.'

The research associate and I were in traditional caring fields, social work and education, that were revalued in this study. Yet we didn't celebrate care work so much as integrate the conflicts inherent in this work (discussed in Chapter 3). After all, we experienced the penetration of market forces into our fields through accountability regimes and austerity measures that were punitive; in these fields assessing 'performance' against a bottom line standard is now commonplace (Tronto, 2010). Building on our traditions of care, we asked participants about their needs for support in the interviews and built in advocacy interventions into the study, especially in Strand 3 (see below for an account of the different strands of the study). Yet this intention may be considered a 'do-gooder' activity to disguise power and privilege amongst women in highly unequal situations—academics, in the *knowledge*-based service sector, and the care assistants, in the *body-based* service sector. Our care ethics, however, enabled us to acknowledge that 'inequality, exploitation, and even betrayal are endemic to ethnography' (Stacey, 1988, p. 23), and so we took precautionary steps and attempted to be accountable.

Care ethics is a feminist response to contractual justice notions, which use guiding principles of objectivity that focus on individuals as autonomous agents and downplay power differentials around gender, race, and class. A feminist care ethics defines caring as a response to the needs of the self and as it relates to the needs of the community (Gilligan, 1982). As Chapter 6 will show, the women's transnational support systems centralized their informal care as something that was integrated, (mostly) positive, and important. But it also included stress related to their paid care labour. A feminist care ethic therefore includes 'both labour and feelings' (Waerness, 1996, p. 234) and highlights the giver of care as well as the receiver (Tronto, 2006).

A feminist care ethic extends into the social and political realm, acknowledging the ways care is positioned as a scarce good and the importance of class, gender, race, and other social conditions. This ethic is considered to be a public value that counters commercial care and its inherent stratifications (Tronto, 2006). Tronto (2010) for example notes that most 'caring institutions' are imbued with power relations and have a historical precedence. Noting that the colonialism project was to promote welfare *for* the colonizers (e.g. through missionary efforts to instil a Protestant work ethic) and know one's 'proper place' in the social hierarchy meant that often caregivers were disqualified from full membership in society. Therefore, care is 'the deep and ignored background to citizenship' (Tronto, 2006, p. 4). This doesn't mean that everyone *should* care, but that it is an active process and organized democratically for all participants rather than according to market principles. With this in mind, we can ask how a feminist ethic of care can revalue migrant workers' labour and expand their rights.

The conventional logic of care, however, is just not to think about it—something which is encouraged in the market-based language of purchasing a 'service,' hiding both the labour and the people behind it (Tronto, 2006). Not to consider the logic of care in the context of this research, then, would make the same error. Therefore an 'ethic of caring' (Collins, 1991 p. 215) guided the methodology and helped to deepen an understanding of otherness in the field through this homework approach, which focused on being responsive and empathic and recognizing the multiple intersections of gender, race, class, language, and other factors (Collins, 1991, p. 215). These traits are helpful for interviewing and developing relations in the field, but also for the analysis and writing stages of the research. At the same time, I recognize the cross-cultural aspects of caring and its different interpretations (Madge, Raghuram, and Noxolo, 2009; Raghuram, 2012).

The research team reflected on our own levels and types of giving and receiving care during the study. In terms of interviewing and observing the participants and in interacting with informants, I engaged in what I hoped was other 'caring' work, including writing references, putting participants in contact with legal and advocacy groups and resources, being a legal witness and support, as well as babysitting from time to time when participants were in a pinch. It is not uncommon for researchers to support participants in non-research hours. I was careful, however, not to use these incidents of desperate need as part of the formal data collection and drew boundaries, even if the participants had not, of what was ethical to include in the write-up. What *was* included, however, were cross-cultural and historical notions of care that I observed and which were discussed in the interviews. I made sure to also focus on the contexts and discourses of the participants' comments surrounding care. Without these, their words would sound one-dimensional, for example, statements that they believed they were better caregivers due to their cultural traditions (of caring for their elderly parents) or because they were women (see Chapter 3).

Positionality and reflexivity in the politics of representation

Representing myself

I understand that I am strategic in representing myself as a type of female care worker in the field of education as well as a migrant academic for the purpose of relating to the participants and for making claims. My social locations as educationalist, woman, and migrant contributed to my marginalization, but not to the extent that I was able to link to other postcolonial academics in the African or Indian diasporas who have written eloquently about this issue. While I wanted to situate myself in the contemporary skilled migration stream and write about myself as a 'migrant academic,' I did not want to be seen as an omniscient expert. Since 1999, the UK has aggressively increased its recruitment of highly skilled migrants and migrant academics, such as myself, through international agencies and migration systems, as well as new management and governance systems, leading to increased diversification of its faculty (Kim, 2009). But it is also because academic mobility, stimulated by US university proprietors that set international benchmarks, is now considered to be desirable and borderless (Marginson, 2008).

The participant interviews became reminders of the ways that I was also an 'outsider' in the British academy and in English society. Early on in the project, for example, I wrote in my diary: 'How is my situation affected by being a migrant at work in academia with the ways the academy is being entrepreneurial like the care industry?' My migrant badge, however, did not disbar me from potentially exploiting participants nor from making claims to being an 'insider' and therefore having my pulse on the truth behind migrancy or lending the impression that I was closer than most other researchers to the participants through listing our similarities (Wasserfall, 1993). I became aware, in writing up this study, of seeking out a kind of moral high ground in my research that was simply unobtainable and I found that I couldn't escape all of my different allegiances to *not* be implicated in both migration and care industry failings (Stacey, 1988).

Representing the participants

Although these participants were at the margins of English society, a population that is often viewed as 'trendy' to study, these women were privileged over many other migrants (e.g. undocumented migrant care assistants). However highlighting the participants' expertise and their professionalism did not negate the fact that they were also considered to be migrants and women and were low-valued workers too. By studying their professionalism, I was countering the image of the uneducated third world woman—'the bare-breasted other' (Pillow, 2003, p. 191) at the same time that I was creating a division between them and other migrant women with less formal education, which is not necessarily a feminist objective (of equity). In fact, I often had to defend the 'study up' charges that I was focusing on a favoured niche group. I was aware that being in the field of education, I had privileged their education (over other aspects) and used this to leverage my case for advocacy and to relate to them too as part of the club of 'well-educated women.' Perhaps if I had met more women with less formal education I might have switched my focus, yet participant after participant who I met randomly during my observations had tertiary education. While many good studies exist on migrant women care assistants, few of them point to education as a mediating factor in their employment, and so I decided to highlight this issue.

As chapters 5 and 6 will illustrate these women were often from the middle and working classes and were not the poorest of the poor. In the politics of representation, however, it wasn't enough to point out their middle-class status in their countries of origin. These participants' families were on the verge of going under and they were much more vulnerable than any 'middle-class' person in advanced economies. Many participants, therefore, were primarily interested in improving their household and family socio-economic conditions. Therefore any act of 'border crossing' including giving them co-author status was not sufficient because they didn't have an interest in speaking to other academics so much as improving their own lives (Nagar, 2002). However, finding ways to connect with their struggles through a focus on education appeared to me to be the best way forward with this group. Like them, I was ambitious to improve my life in a new country, even to the point of using this data (and hence the women's lived experiences) as 'grist for the academic mill' (Huisman, 2008, p. 373). In short, I was aware that my research on education could progress my own career path.

Going back and forth between theory and experience in the field, otherwise known as 'theoretical reflexivity,' was familiar to me at the writing stage, as it is to many other researchers (Clarke and Sandlin, 2006). George Marcus (1998) proposed three other types of reflexivity including: 'confessional' which is discussing the socio-demographic status of the researcher as in 'I am a white middle class American.' Then there is 'intertextual reflexivity' which is experimenting with writing such as integrating poetry and diary material. Lastly, there is 'deconstructive reflexivity' which evokes emotions and images as well as ideas that count on the reader to interpret the material. While the first two (theoretical and confessional) may seem to create higher levels of validity through incorporating the researcher's positionality (i.e. sociodemographics and personal stories), these have been critiqued as narrow (theoretical) and superficial (confessional) while the last two (intertextual and deconstructive) have been critiqued as self-serving approaches. Confessional forms, in particular, can become emblems of researchers who want to prove their legitimacy like, 'tropes that sound like apologies' (Nagar, 2002, p. 180; see also Patai, 1994). This move to centre oneself in the text creates an authorial invincibility.

Perhaps 'the crisis of representation' is simply a self-absorbed stance to win academic credits. While inserting oneself into the text may make the research more transparent, it does not make it unproblematic (Pillow, 2003). Daphne Patai (1994, p. 64) says, academics 'are spending much too much time wading in the morass of our own positionings' at the sake of real world problems. She claims (p. 65) that 'babies still have to be cared for, shelter sought, meals prepared and eaten.' I therefore worried that my efforts to display 'acts of location' could slip into empty gestures that did not attend to issues of inequality and left little room for political engagement with women migrants' struggles (Nagar, 2002). I became aware, that in writing, a type of 'hyper-reflexivity' could take over when I used my direct experience, which could be interpreted as 'navel gazing.' In this scenario, the researcher, in centralizing herself marginalizes her participants. In addition, over-determined explanations based on limited perceptions and experience in the field—'I was there, I saw it' or 'I was there, I felt it' could be the slogan for an isolated academic field worker who is newly entranced with her surroundings. Joan Scott (1992, p. 26) criticizes this type of self-absorbed observation and discusses the need for critiques of the conditions of difference, the circumstances of seeing 'not individuals who have experience, but subjects who are constituted *through* experience.'

Although reflexivity refers to some aspect of subjectivity, it does seem to differ from reflection not only in terms of a process (such as consciousness-raising on gendered relations) but confers the presence of another human being that gives feedback (Fonow and Cook, 1991). Reflection requires only one person then, and is an effort to do the same thing better (Pillow, 2003). It is important, therefore, to detect to what extent reflexivity is core to the research and writing and where it is simply lip service. Wanda Pillow (2003) says it's about engaging in critically thinking through how it is we do the reflexive work of subjectivity and representation—which means laying the barebones of the research out for the reader. Pillow (2003, p. 188) has developed 'reflexivities of discomfort' which she defines as pushing towards the unfamiliar—not as clarity, honesty, or humility, but as practices of confounding disruptions—at times even a failure of our language and practices. It's like an admission of messiness, and not editing this out in the final product. Pillow (2003, p. 193) says that qualitative research could benefit from leaving uncomfortable realities at the doorstep of the reader without trying to resolve them.

So I decided to look at situations that were 'messy' to me (Rose, 1997). As I got to know the participants over time, we became close, and sometimes too close for comfort. In one case, for example, a participant and her family came to stay in our house for two weeks while we were away because we were next to a hospital, which allowed them to have easier access to the patient. It seemed like the right thing to do at the time—yet this initiated a new relationship. In her narrative, I didn't mention this but instead represented her as resilient in locating resources from her community, including myself, in order to survive. How researchers answer to these feelings in the research came to be important for me in practising reflexivity. Another issue I struggled with was what to do when participants, who I liked as people, made derogatory remarks about their own ethnic group, or others, or on social topics. I wondered how I would represent these issues in my writing, especially in trying to make a sympathetic policy case about their situations. In fact, this particular participant made a number of comments to me about how worried she was about her children being influenced by talk show hosts like Ellen (who was an out lesbian), featured on English television. Another participant opposed sex education in schools because she believed it encouraged promiscuity. A number of the women had typically 'conservative' political and moral views (Levitt and Schiller, 2007, p. 194) on these topics while on other issues, such as labour rights, they were more open.

Another uncomfortable reflexive issue in my research were pressures I felt from other academics to align to policy debates. Many of these policies were polarized in the sense that they positioned migrant care assistants either as victims by an external oppressor or, the opposite, reduced them to underdogs overcoming major hurdles as 'ideal migrants.' The participants, however, were idiosyncratic and often pragmatic in their decisions, neither hero nor victim, so I knew I needed to write about their issues with layers of complexity including the contexts of their actions so that they were not made one-dimensional. My aim then was to write persuasive stories about the participants' struggles although I knew I could not escape the 'identity trap' of representation (Nagar, 2002, p. 184). In the end, I decided to represent them as 'professional migrant women.'

Doing the research

Extended case study

I used the extended case method to draw out the feminization of skilled labour migration in the context of global inequalities and sociohistorical change. I asked why well-educated migrant women at the cusp of the 21st century ended up in low-grade work in the care industry and how they became hidden actors in this sector. This was the anomaly that I addressed in order to dispel myths about migrant women as 'fit' for care and to create a diverse portrayal of this highly skilled population. The extended case method added reflexivity into the picture of skilled migrants, of which I was a part. I brought together their views with mine as well as theories (on transnationalism, gender, labour, and care). This method 'guides the dialogue with participants' through a type of mapping of the social order which is the first step in the research process, thereby making interviews and observations a type of intervention (Burawoy, 1998, pp. 5, 14).

The extended case method highlights disturbances in the system (e.g. an obstructive immigration system) and links these to social processes: an example would be analysing the tacit knowledge that the participants developed about the ways the immigration system limited their horizons. The next step was to focus on the social forces (such as rising costs in their home countries) affecting their families' livelihoods and on an analysis of the ways they saw their migration as a means of leveraging economic inequalities. A model that alternated between international and organizational levels was developed to visualize the forces impacting participants. The international forces dealt with structural adjustment policies as well as effects of the global recession while national forces dealt with dual issues of immigration and care sector policies together with demographic changes, such as a growing ageing population across Europe. This latter relationship led me to understand the ways that immigration policies went hand-in-hand with care sector privatization that saddled older persons, who had limited incomes, with the responsibility of care. This relationship was also discussed among participants in Strand 3 of the study at a deskilling workshop I created.

The cross-current of national forces laid the foundation for a multi-sited research approach in both the north and south of England. Then, in comparing and contrasting these participants' experiences to other cases in various countries through a literature review and expert interviews, I was able to generalize further.[2] This wider scope increased external validity by adding greater breadth to my case. But the extended case method does not stop at current social forces; it connects to historical research as well. This is why, for example, it was important to understand the participants' deskilling in line with a history of deprofessionalization of feminized occupations and the making of the role of the 'care assistant' (to be discussed in Chapter 3).

The extended case method focuses principally on the clashes between participants' practices and normative views of them through ethnographies, which situate their experiences within both immediate and extra-local contexts (Burawoy et al., 2000; Smith, 2005). In this case, it would be the ways skilled female migrants engaged in care in an industry that spans continents and has captured their labour. The intention is to contribute to a societally significant analysis (rather than statistical significance) translated through the eyes of a sensitized researcher who reconstructs theory with these problems in mind (Burawoy, 2008). For example, the global care chain, discussed in Chapter 1, was reconstructed to focus on an international industry to explain anomalies in the system and participants' experiences (see also, Yeates, 2012). The global industry perspective highlights the massive privatization pervading elder care in liberal countries such as England and its marketization. This reconstruction led to a new view of transnationalism that is gendered and linked to migrant labour and feminist movements. Constructs like domination, silencing, objectification, and normalization were integrated into the research to account for the research team's presence and our (possibly idealistic) intention to reduce these with the idea that 'in the reflexive mode, social theory intervenes in the world it seeks to grasp' (Burawoy, 1998, p. 22).

Ethnographic methods in data collection

Ethnographic methods are not mere data collecting tools but part of a socially engaged methodology (Burawoy, 1998), the aim of which, like feminist research, is to 'turn private troubles into public issues' such as the for-profit care industry (Burawoy, 2005, p. 266). Not just the participants, but also the industry itself, had crossed borders (e.g. trans-border care recruiters tied to training agencies and universities) and mobile methods were needed to capture these international interchanges. This encompasses researchers being 'moved by, and to move with, their subjects' (Buscher and Urry, 2009, p. 103). These moves were for practical purposes of dealing with multi-sited engagements of participants (virtual and physical) and the industry itself. Ethnographic methods were used to highlight the participants by framing their highly skilled mobility in terms of identity and belonging as they moved with economic, social, and business forces.

The ethnographic methods figured in three strands of the study (see also Appendix 1). Strand 1 included face to face and phone interviews with over 60 experts about macro issues—that is to say political, cultural, organizational, technological and social—affecting the study sample and a pilot study of 29 migrant care assistants that specified and expanded on many of these issues.[3] Strand 2 entailed three in-depth interviews with 22 participants. It also included observations at different sites, field notes, mapping, documentary analysis of workplace papers, and photographing relevant subjects and settings. Field notes were first written and typed and then inserted into a chart to analyse the interactions and issues that arose, including questions, ethical dilemmas, and surprising incidents. This chart focused on contexts of the observation, a summary of the visit, times, activities, relationships noted, and discussions with participants. Below is one section of an annotated observation chart of a Zambian care assistant:

> It seems that she is being treated by some of these clients as a 'migrant,' and there does seem to be overt racism with one man [client] who would not shake her hand. I was embarrassed to bring it up to her. She is just surviving and it appears that the company depends on her private car. She also told me about her mobile phone and the fact that the company was 'happy for her to use her own' until she brought it up to them. Her family is living on the edge of society—when I asked Tina what she is planning to do for dinner, she said she doesn't know. When I went back to her house I noticed she had no food in her refrigerator, she spent all her money on the visa for her niece, which was the third time she had to pay something. She said yesterday she was crying all day and said she wanted to talk to a friend to 'ventilate.'

Maps of the participants' movements were also drawn to understand how many activities they did daily and weekly with how many clients. Mapping movements was a non-traditional method for capturing life in care homes, which still is largely hidden from public view. Figure 2.2

44 Deskilling Migrant Women in Global Care Industry

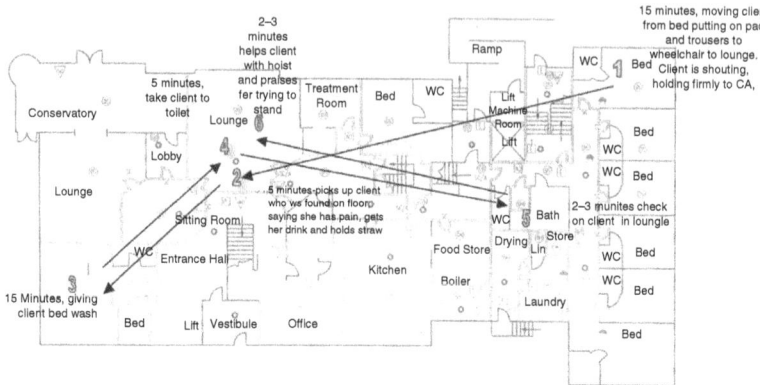

Figure 2.2 Mapping the nursing home

shows numerated series of movements of a participant with clients in her nursing home. These maps were accompanied by participants' activities with times (but for the sake of convenience, the content is summarized here).

Additionally two paid informants completed projects that with their insider perspectives illuminated their home lives, work worlds, and their transnational caring relationships. Their writing aligned more to migrant fictional accounts that contain rich imagery and turbulent emotional landscapes than to the sterile policy papers focused on abstract notions of targets, for 'social cohesion.'[4] Strand 3 consisted of study circles, video testimonials, interviews and assessments of participants' attitudes and beliefs about deskilling.[5]

Portraiture and Grounded Theory analyses

I used Grounded Theory (Strauss and Corbin, 1998) as an analytical tool to explore similarities across the participants and develop themes. For the narratives, I used a method, called Portraiture (Lawrence-Lightfoot, 1997) to enrich the contexts and unique dimensions of the participants. Portraiture captures the richly textured layers of participants' experiences while Grounded Theory encapsulates overarching themes as well as their strategies for handling problems. Examples of these are given in Chapter 4 and illustrate both common problems and particular strategies of migrant care assistants in a rural area. Both tools of analysis are the basis for the extended case method. They also compensate for one another. Grounded Theory tends to minimize context and reduce differences in order to compare cases and distil themes into commonalities (Burawoy, 1998) while portraiture focuses exclusively on unique actors and contexts. The themes produced through Grounded Theory were limited in producing knowledge about the issues in detail and therefore enabled the portraits to illuminate participants' individual struggles and their socio-historical contexts.

Grounded Theory

Due to the complexity and range of issues among a group of participants who had similar problems such as deskilling, I used Grounded Theory to analyse this phenomenon. The process consisted of creating codes and categories, gleaning themes and then creating hypotheses about the participants' experiences, along with the integration of experts' opinions on the issues and a literature review. Through an on-going process of comparing and contrasting data, connections were made between sets of relations.

I focused on the 'ground'—the data—to generate abstract concepts. To accomplish this, I needed to be 'flexible' and open to helpful criticism (Strauss and Corbin, 1998, pp. 12–14), while having sensitivity— which means tuning in to relevant issues of participants (p. 32). This style of research calls for creativity, closeness to the respondents and their views, immersion in the field and an ability to interpret situations and statements. The use of Grounded Theory allowed themes to be established across the participants' data, thus identifying crucial issues that have social justice implications (Charmaz, 2011, p. 361). Anselm Strauss and Juliet Corbin (1990) describes a procedure beginning with the use of analytical tools, such as finding key phrases or words in documents and experimenting with meanings at first by open coding which is a process of breaking down the data into distinct parts in order to label phenomena. Then, axial coding puts back the data together by making connections between conditions, contexts and actions. Next, selective coding is about creating a 'narrative about the central phenomenon of the study' (p. 116). Grounded Theory analysis requires re-evaluation of concepts/themes/categories at varying stages.

Initially, the research team, consulting with the informants, created 36 codes (open coding) in four broad areas. One example was called, 'Stuck in Stepping Stones.' We discovered that 'being stuck' was a repeated phrase among participants. A software program called AtlasTi helped make connections between codes in the transcripts that we analysed which then linked to larger issues; for example, the 'stuck' code connected to other codes such as 'educational desires.' We wanted to make sure, however, that the software itself didn't drive the process. For this reason, we used AtlasTi as a mechanical tool for confirming what we already learned from critically reflecting and discussing the data. Furthermore, demographic grids of the participants were used to supplement the thematic analysis. The constant reflexive comparisons/contrasts between our different data sets and analyses allowed for obvious and subtle factors to emerge that clarified the phenomena.

Portraiture

Portraiture is a qualitative method of inquiry developed by Sara Lawrence Lightfoot. It reveals stories in a rich way that provokes readers into identifying with and evaluating what is narrated. By bringing together art and science through 'empirical description *and* aesthetic expression' the aim is to develop 'a convincing and authentic narrative'(Lawrence-Lightfoot, 1997, p. 12). Portraitures disclose elements of narratives, which are often hidden, by highlighting the uniqueness of a person or situation. But they do more. Portraiture, as a research method, seeks to interpret and intervene, by appealing to readers by using accessible language, and to raise paradoxes. The latter allows the sketching of contradictions, which make the story come alive and gives it the fullness felt in real life. This doesn't portend the truth so much as picture it. Thus, through reflecting, interpreting, and narrating, the researcher engages the reader in a process of actively absorbing information about a person's experience of a particular problem and enlarges it to portray human struggle on a historical canvas. Similar to other methods of qualitative research, portraitures expose the narrator as well as the narrated; the researcher's self comes into play, while simultaneously emerging 'as an instrument of inquiry' (Lawrence-Lightfoot, 1997, p. 13). The 'art' in portraiture has been critiqued for the narrator holding the power of what the reader is accessing, thereby restricting inquiry. The portraitist does present extracts from interviews and observations, and in this respect, offers interpretations but also permits the reader's commentary.

The portraitures were first created by adapting and modifying the following analytic framework drawn from William Labov (in Riessman, 1993, pp. 18–19). Selected participants' interviews were assessed using a grid of six categories: (1) abstract (the summary of the narrative), (2) orientation (the set up of time, place, identities and situation), (3) complicating action (sequence of events that led to a crisis), (4) evaluation (how the participant interpreted their situation and their attitudes), (5) resolution (what finally happened), and (6) coda (a type of ending as the participant saw it and a return to the present). In filtering each participant's data through these categories, we could pinpoint specific elements in each of their stories. By selecting these elements, the story gains a structure that highlights the events affecting the person and the ways she dealt with her struggle. The particular interest in portraitures is in the metaphors that participants use to describe complicating events, feelings, and unresolved issues that both bear significant importance and raise questions. In this sense, the subjective experience of participants is revealed in emic (insider) statements against a background of social issues as well as the positionality of the researchers creating them (etic). Therefore, every portraiture not only included the participants' internal experiences of an event but also the contexts in which statements occurred and the researcher's inclusion of social history and their perspectives. Using portraiture as a method captured the participants' complicated journeys.

Conclusion

The messy and uncomfortable texts that come with the messy politics of power within research projects are often covered over in the final production (Nagar, 2002). I decided to incorporate these complex topics to make visible previously invisible issues. Doing this is not without problems. Marilyn Strathern (2000, p. 310) asks: 'What does visibility conceal?' After all, evidence is everything in research but like public displays, it may not be substantive enough because what is shown often consists of second-order descriptions. Calls for transparency are entrenched in accountability regimes that value more and more data: 'more information, less understanding, and in particular more information, less trust' (Strathern, 2000, p. 313). Making knowledge 'useful' often means deleting the grey and making issues black and white for policy-makers. But such 'clarity' also destroys the coordinate system that ethnographers build and use in the process of researching a phenomenon (Strathern, 2006). Connecting and reflecting on these coordinates was the homework approach that I took in this study. Over and beyond this, though, my intention was to disrupt the policy environment of care, gender, labour, and immigration, using what Donna Haraway (in Schneider, 2005, p. 19) calls, 'diffraction.' This practice is like light rays that, in passing through different mediums, create different patterns that disturb the landscape. This is different from reflection that tends to reproduce the status quo with the focus on the same material (Llewelyn, 2007, p. 301).

In this chapter I have laid out the barebones of the research to the extent that it captures, if not the reality of the participants' lives, than at least, the 'homework' with which I was engaged to capture their struggles and those of the research team. Chapter 3 will discuss the wider care industry and how it secured a low-paid migrant workforce of mainly former health care professionals. It highlights a sample of these individuals and the ways that they improved the industry. Conditions in the industry, such as the large amount of paperwork demanded from workers, is profiled, as well as another type of preparation: training. Additionally, personal expressiveness that fits with the Personalization Agenda is also discussed.

Appendix 1 Summary of design and timeline of project

Strand 1: 1/07-4/09—Environmental scan: Literature review, Delphi study, and pilot study (data collecting and analysis)

> Strand 1 addressed aim one, to understand the post-welfare society and its dependence on gendered and skilled migrant care. It involved three phases: (1) A literature review of care, gender, and labour migration issues of 100+ diverse sources, including historical fiction, news reports, academic and policy studies as well as theories; (2) a Delphi study of gathering opinions and forecasts from selected care and migration experts (a total of 64) in the form of questionnaires and then collating their responses; policy-makers, researchers, practitioners in the fields of migration, gender/women's studies, ESOL, care, and workplace studies were interviewed on issues that they ranked as important for migrant care assistants; questions focused on: social, cultural, political, technological, economic, educational, political, policy, environmental, organizational, gender, race, and class issues which were analysed; and, (3) a pilot study, consisting of 50–60 minute taped biographical interviews with 29 migrant care assistants conducted over a nine month period in 2007. Fourteen interviews were transcribed for a thematic analysis of major issues that informed the Delphi study. The intention was to map these 'joined up' forces to inform Strands 2 and 3. This strand allowed for policy changes and other changes through the lifespan of the project (e.g. immigration legislation).

Strand 2: 2/08-6/09—Fieldwork: Panel study, in-depth interviews, observations, informant projects, and documentary analysis

Strand 2 addressed aim 2 (to understand the care workplace), 3 (to develop knowledge of the participants' home, community and work lives), and 4 (to develop a reflexive account). It contained two phases that informed one another. Phase 1 was a panel study of three newly arrived care assistants over a year period and their adjustment, strategies, practices in their community, work, and transnational lives, including technology and mass media uses. Each participant was given an interview that contained open and closed questions four times each to detect changes over this period. The outcomes entailed themes and descriptive statistics about their experiences over time. Phase 2 consisted of 150 hours of fieldwork in various care homes, private homes, and agencies and interviews with 19 participants (13 of whom were also interviewed in Strand 1 and 6 who were new) as well informal interviews with other workers (i.e. domestics and nurses), employers, and clients. Each participant was given three interviews each (taped and transcribed), which were staggered over a year period to develop rapport and to check information. These interviews focused on education, work, and family histories, their experiences in the care industry, their aspirations, transnational relations, and mass media and technology uses. Phase 2 also consisted of documentary analysis of workplace materials/documents, including training materials and inspection reports, photographs of care work environments, and informant projects to understand issues within Poland and the Philippines, including journaling. This phase also included immersion in some of the participants' communities through attending events. Data analysis included: demographic profiles of participants and workplaces, coded transcripts in AtlasTi and from this, maps of selected participants that were used to create portraits. Additional sub-sets of the sample were analysed according to workplaces, nationalities, and professions. The researchers kept journals of their experiences to develop critical reflexivity.

Strand 3: 4/09-3/10—Build advocacy knowledge about the deskilling of migrant care assistants and support their self-determination (deskilling workshop, assessment of issues, phone interviews)

> This strand addressed all of the aims of the research. This strand used the knowledge from the first two strands to develop knowledge about advocacy and support needs of this population. This consisted of two phases. Phase 1 consisted of nine taped phone interviews with migrant care assistants across England about workplace and recruitment agency exploitation. Follow-ups three months later were given to assess their self-efficacy with regard to the English language, immigration and workplace rights, and knowledge of advocacy organizations and networks, and any changes in their lives. The assessment was developed with assistance from consultants and tested on a group of practitioners at a workshop to obtain their feedback. Phase 2 was a workshop that addressed deskilling of migrant care assistants. Thirteen women participants were given assessments (the same as Phase 1) and interviews about exploitation in their workplaces and any problems they faced in England as well as their support needs both during and after the workshop to detect changes. Deskilling was the central focus with the purpose to raise consciousness about it as well as advocate for them. The informant was a key facilitator in this workshop, which she followed with an online forum. The workshop also consisted of recorded group discussions, testimonials, and a short lecture by a guest speaker.

3
Care Industry Needs Skilled Migrant Labour

Introduction

In this chapter I discuss the upgrading of work in the global care industry, with England as a case study. 'Upgrading' refers to adding more tasks and training to an occupation, which, 'may or may not involve greater pay, status and work autonomy' (Rainbird and Munro, 2003, p. 33).[1] Importantly, upgrading depends on the attributes of a skilled workforce: the surplus of former health care professionals from low-income countries willing to work for reduced wages has enabled this industry to thrive. Personalization policies, in tightening regulations and standards, depend on the capacities of these workers to raise the quality of care above the established bar, without much training. Although all participants are included in my analysis, I concentrate on the former health care professionals (nurses, midwives, occupational therapists, and physiotherapists) in this chapter (71% of the sample).

Their recruitment into England's social care sector was precipitated by tough new care standards that were instituted in 2000, to be discussed next. Recruiting this population effectively balanced the labour demanded by the care sector in ways that the traditional workforce could not sustain—not because British-born care assistants were 'unskilled,' as the popular media portrayed them, but because the new conditions privileged skilled migrants. These conditions included demands for: (1) technical literacy to handle the reams of required *paperwork* (such as writing reports on clients), (2) responding to clients' emotional needs through aesthetic labour (*personal expressiveness* such as performing the role of 'good carer'), and (3) attending and passing the many training sessions that were expected of the workforce (*preparation*, which includes training on numerous topics on care for older persons).

The participants' competencies and willingness to fulfil these new mandates within quick and pressured time slots made them valuable human resources to employers in England's modernized commercial care sector. Yet they were not compensated according to their actual worth.

I will first discuss the ethos of personalization in the fabrication of upgraded standards. I show that the person-centred approach, intended to be holistic in its conception, shifted to that of *responsibilization*, whereby government reforms depended on individual clients taking on responsibilities for care just as workers take on more and new types of work. This balancing act became an additional shift of work for care assistants for which migrants adapted well. Next, the discussion will focus on the new training, including its historical absence in the field and the ways migrants excelled in these activities. Then I document the amount and types of paperwork that employers demanded and the ways it advantaged migrants far more than the British-born workforce, who saw this paper trail as antithetical to care. Finally personal expressiveness enabled skilled migrants with their cultural capital to succeed in the sector.

Raising standards: From personalizing care to client and worker responsibility

Personalized acts to produce a personalized workforce

Personalization hailed a 'new type of worker/new ways of working' (Eborall, 2010, p. 3). Staff were seen to need 'different skills to support clients in taking as much control as possible of their own lives' (Secretary of State for Health, 2009, p. 12) with consumer choice driving quality. Meanwhile, care businesses developed 'social responsibility' emphasizing accountability, effectiveness, and efficiency in an era of cost-containment (England, Eakin, Gastaldo, and McKeever, 2007). Government did not disappear, but became a regulatory body through guidelines, codes of conduct, and standards (Walby, 2002). These 'roll-out neo-liberalism' reforms created lean services in England, but also in other OECD countries such as the USA and Canada (England et al., 2007, p. 179).

Not only were care assistants required to have *hard* skills (technical literacy and numeracy skills) but also *soft* skills, such as 'courage, integrity, understanding others, communicating and influencing' (Mason, 2009, p. 5). The goal was to promote self-care, prevention, and self-directed support (Bell, Nash, and Thomas, 2010, p. 57). The new system would 'ensure entry level training, continued professional development and workforce registration to reflect the new skills required in a personalised system' (National Health Service, 2007, p. 4). The state would play a regulatory role. A 1998 report, *Modernising Social Services: Promoting Independence, Improving Protection, Raising Standards* (Secretary of State for Health, 1998), announced that 80 per cent of the care workforce had no recognized qualifications or training opportunities, thus instigating the National Care Standards Commission to produce new procedures and policies. Previously the care sector was regulated through local councils and the Registered Homes Act of 1984, which lacked regulatory enforcements and never mentioned workforce skills or training. The 2000 Care Standards legislation therefore created national minimum standards for staffing, qualification levels, and regulations about entry into the care sector with criminal records checks, supervision, inductions, training, and a target of 50 per cent of care assistants holding vocational qualifications (Cangiano, Shutes, Spencer, and Leeson, 2009; Department of Health, 2000). It was a landmark reform and the foundation of future policies focusing on professionalization and personalization of the workforce.

Making clients responsible

The client had moved from 'supplicant to consumer to active participant' (Dent, 2006, p. 459). The state now depended on older persons to be morally reflexive about their capacities to select care as 'economic-rational actors' who could assess costs and benefits. This new system delegated clients who would self-manage social risks with consequences that they alone bore (Lemke, 2001 in Shamir, 2008, pp. 7–8). These clients were referred to as 'service-users,' a disembodied title that discounted the care assistant's labour; instead older persons *used* a service.

'Managed competition,' as it came to be called, was seen as a way to create higher quality services through increased choices but meant care assistants spent less time with clients. Researchers in one study (England et al., 2007, p. 189), for example, found fewer and fewer 'tea and sympathy type visits' than before. Resources depended on the client's 'voice' and this became a disciplining factor. For example, social workers in this study interviewed clients about their personal toileting rather than deciding what they would need; subsequently fewer visits were requested due to clients' embarrassment over verbalizing intimate matters. The logic of making clients responsible aligned personal conduct with social, political, and economic objectives (Dent, 2006, p. 461).

Person-centred and fast care was viewed as a 'wholesale-shift in perspective' (Eborall, Fenton, and Woodrow, 2010, p. 155); a new public management philosophy that prized individual efficiency looked like McDonaldization (Ritzer, 2008), and downplayed the labour of caregiving. The routinization of care reflected in care plans restricted the care assistant's abilities to negotiate with clients and give them hands-on care with a detailed knowledge of their conditions. It also put clients to work, in having to decide on a host of options and then wait for services.

A responsible care force

To policy-makers, care assistants needed leverage in the market to compete with a large pool of unpaid carers. So health and safety laws were implemented, including training. While entry requirements for the sector had always been low in order to stimulate a large pool of workers, the standards were raised under the Care Standards Act of 2000. These standards (Department of Health, 2000, pp. 5–6) included physical care but also:

> Non-physical care, such as advice, encouragement... emotional and psychological support, including the promotion of social functioning, behaviour management, and assistance with cognitive functions.

This aim was to professionalize the sector with care assistants' educative traits being emphasized in agency marketing efforts to make them seem more competent than informal carers and allow employers to raise their prices (although not wages). One care agency's website, for example, advertised itself as providing: 'professional, friendly, and caring help. We pride ourselves on our selection, monitoring, induction, and continual training of our staff.'

Most British-born care assistants balked at these reforms. In this study, some of them had been in the sector for over ten years. One residential home advertised itself as having 'specialised care' within 'a safe, pleasant, and comfortable environment.' The British-born care assistants in this home were at the time of the study fed up with the increased demands and punitive regulations. They were required to do more work in a limited time, without promotions or pay rises. They were often falsely accused by clients and managers of stealing and, to compound matters, were threatened if they joined a union. They also were subject to more disciplinary actions, including being issued written warnings for things like eating biscuits on duty. They felt they had had more protection against abusive clients when social workers rather than the current business-minded owners managed their home. The social worker was liked because she used to reprimand clients who abused care assistants and requested that they leave. The new business-oriented owners did not shield the workers from abusive clients, making the care assistants feel that they could not 'stand our ground with the residents' as one said.

Their care assistant positions had become unstable and dissatisfying 'Mcjobs' (Ritzer, 2008). They felt that the owners recruited migrants and 'paid more for the ones who spoke better English' as one reported, to further pressure them. They noticed, for example, that 'overseas workers work harder and longer hours,' as one British-born care assistant said. They also testified that there were more expectations of them to produce paperwork and to engage in training that they didn't feel was helpful. The owner of this care home was disenchanted with the British-born staff she inherited when she took over the company and confided that the reason she hired migrants was because:

> The locals are resistant to education and they don't want to go back to school, and they don't register or don't come to NVQ [National Vocational Qualification] training. This is a new home but the staff has been here for a while.

Other employers in the study confessed that the British-born staff were unable to meet the new requirements of the law and were unwilling to accept the extra job demands as it was transforming to a specialist role. So they recruited elsewhere. A national report (Eboral et al., 2010) found that the care sector was more reliant on recruiters than other sectors and that these recruiters said that they looked for skilled and experienced people overseas. When interviewed, the recruiters in this study concurred that the migrants were a better deal. One said bluntly: 'It's not a good paying job. People who are on benefits work in nursing homes for a week and don't stay longer because it's awful... British staff think it's easy money and realize its not.' She knew she was recruiting migrants for, what she confessed was a 'dead end' job. Other studies (Cangiano et al., 2009, pp. 93, 184) found that employers saw British-born care assistants as less motivated and had 'skills mismatches' with the job. Migrant care assistants internalized these perceptions of the British-born care assistants. One participant said:

> They are not treating it as a job, as in caring for people.... They are just thinking, 'oh that's another day, that's another seven hours... at the end of the month, this job pays my rent and I've got a nice flat by this job.' But you don't do this just for that.

Migrants were chosen because employers found it difficult to recruit British-born workers who were motivated and interested in jobs, which were widely perceived as low-status. These employers perceived migrants to be 'a willing pool of labour that wants to work in the care sector, were enthusiastic and set an example to other staff' (Eborall et al., 2010, p. 89). Migrants were also viewed as having 'higher than average qualifications' and were 'very receptive to training and qualification enhancement' (Eborall et al., 2010, p. 89). A major weakness was a 'lack of English' and their 'eagerness "to do anything"' which could cause tensions amongst British-born staff' as well as 'over-qualification [which] can lead to early job dissatisfaction and desire to change jobs sooner rather than later.'

National data pointed to a high turnover rate of this workforce over other occupations (Eborall et al., 2010). Currently, it has one of the highest vacancy rates, over twice the level of all public services, commercial, and industrial sectors. One in four care assistants, for example, leave their jobs within the first year. The turnover, according to a quarter of all employers in a national study, was due to the new skill demands especially technical and practical ones, including written communication and problem solving, which topped the list. Skill shifts and work conditions were often linked to the workers themselves with the British-born seen as lacking. Most care assistants, on the other hand, never mentioned skills as a reason for leaving but were concerned about difficulty in maintaining work/life balance, poor management, poor pay and conditions, and statutory training requirements (Cangiano et al., 2009; Eborall et al., 2010, p. 152). The British-born staff didn't want the qualifications, the multi-skilling, or, the tensions of having to deliver 'specialist' care under increased intensification and job expansion with little bargaining power (Brown and Kirpal, 2004).

Experts interviewed for the project agreed that the British-born staff were disadvantaged by these demands and were 'running faster to stay in the same place' (Rainbird, Munro, and Senker, 2005 p. 47). A social worker interviewed for the study noted that 'care is low paid work—lower than it should be from what we expect from carers.' Another expert revealed the sea change in expectations required of care assistants, and agreed that these should be raised:

> We ask too much of the untrained care sector. I think we should. If you go back ten years, you could roll up somewhere and be one. Now it has gone the other way. You have a criminal record check, lots of paperwork to take on, and now induction common standards.

Then after that there is NVQ training. Traditionally, the people who do care are not academic and now we ask loads. They are being qualified but it is still a turnoff. We lost many older care workers. There is a trend of employing those who are younger and employers are employing people from abroad.

Even though many British-born workers migrated from the newer private companies with poorer working conditions to more public ones with higher pay, unions, holidays, sick pay, and better pensions, they could not escape these new demands. This workforce, traditionally working-class females, were less formally educated and attracted to the sector because it was easy to enter and they could combine it with other caring and family responsibilities (Balloch, Banks, and Hill, 2004; Skeggs, 1997). The new policies exerted the heaviest toll on this population, especially with the increasing focus since 2000 on getting better value for money, topping up training, and increasing requirements for basic skills, and, finally, 'new ways of working' (Eborall and Garmeson, 2001, p. 23). Yet British-born care assistants, who placed a higher value on experience over qualifications, believed the training requirements were not a reliable indicator of care ability (Balloch, Banks, and Hill, 2004). Indeed, induction policies in care companies expected workers to query clients about their situations, something they never had to do previously. The care assistant was expected to clarify details, interpret opinions, and summarize information in their notes. They also had to use industry-specific terminology while following spelling and grammar conventions. One assessor who was interviewed for the study found that these scientific management methods could serve as a type of 'survival of the fittest' test to weed out the traditional workforce. He said:

> Slowly we are whittling out the die-hard carers who are stuck in a rut. You go into homes and they have been there several years and provide the same care. You do get this mindset: I have been washing bums for twenty years and don't need the NVQ. They are not open to it. It tends to be mature staff who have worked in the care sector for decades—they see that they give good care. They are not open to new ideas and if it ain't broke, don't fix it.

Although not made explicit, employers viewed migrants as a good solution to the new high performance and data-driven workplace (Jackson, 2001). They were seen as a 'temporary stock' and a 'labour substitution' for the 'recruitment problems' that the employers found themselves facing because of the resistance of the traditional workforce. Employers and recruiters lobbied to get migrant care assistants on the 'shortage occupation list.' Consequently, this workforce has increased since 2006—most of them being recent arrivals. Prior to 2000, Zimbabweans and Jamaicans composed most of the migrant care workforce, but by 2006 Filipinos were the largest group, followed by Indians. This switch reflected systematic efforts to select recruits from healthcare exporting countries (Cangiano et al., 2009). In this study, there were many former health care professionals (mostly, Filipinos and Indians) who expected to advance into similar if not the same careers. One expert said:

> Some [migrants] are hoodwinked into thinking they will do social work and there are bad practices in agencies, and they are misled into thinking it is other than caring. Employers see them as temporary stock who are not worth training because they will move on to other jobs.

Employers created 'grow your own' projects (to recruit British-born youth) and said they preferred to select from the local labour market because they found that recruiting migrants was difficult. They also lamented the dependence on migrants, disliking the fact that British-born workers would not accept these work conditions in the face of growing public demands for quality services and a government unwilling to fund care at an adequate level. Yet, international recruitment, even with a cap on immigration, was taking place in large numbers with a skills rhetoric that heralded this change (Cangiano et al., 2009).

The fourth shift: Adaptation to a new model of care

Adapting to a personalized workplace involved a type of worker who not only had the skills that employers wanted, but who could also work an extra shift while keeping cool under pressure. This shift required the British-born workers and their families to adapt to their intensified and expanded care work jobs. Arlie Hochschild (2003) developed the concept of 'shifts' to discuss women's paid work outside of the home (the first shift), their unpaid work in the home (the second shift including 'mothering the house') (Hochschild, 2003, p. 9), and the ability of the family to emotionally adapt to the worker's time-usurping first and second shifts (the third shift) (Hochschild, 1997, p. 215). Historically, the British-born workers were able to work the first and second shifts, even if wages were low and conditions were poor. Balancing the two was managed somehow with family members' schedules. But when the first shift changed, these British-born staff wondered if they could juggle the others. The third shift, Hochschild (1997) explains is the emotional work involved in repairing the damage to family members due to 'the compressed second shift' which causes some to combust under the pressure of the work time bind and others to console as a coping mechanism (p. 215). This became difficult for 'the locals,' as one manager explained: 'They don't like change but the owners want to make it more efficient and they need to expand to survive.' In one care home, most of the British-born care assistants left due to expansion and restructuring. One care assistant who had worked for her company over 20 years was upset about her new shift, explaining that she was expected to cook three meals a day for her family—her new schedule was disrupting her family life. They felt that they had to stay in these posts because their families depended on the income and their schedules meshed with their school-age children. Because they had no means to vent their frustrations, they took their ire out on their families and each other. One employee admitted: 'We take it out on our families but they don't want to hear us moan and there is no where to go but us.' The British-born care assistants wondered if they could mesh the newer standardized fast process control that increased their stress levels with their family lives with their older notions of care as a slower, more negotiable, straightforward process. In another case, a British-born care assistant said she was 'ill' from constantly changing her hours and shifting through so many clients. She said: 'A group of businessmen control it and make it chaotic... they slap on the evenings, and they are making me ill.... These companies are bullies and that's why you have Polish workers.'

I introduce the 'fourth shift' to detail the care industry's new standards under time constraints. This shift includes paperwork, personal expressiveness, and preparation that made it difficult for the British-born staff to handle the changed circumstances. Many of the British-born workers resisted these new mandates through conspicuous means, including purposely 'going slow, taking breaks, backchat and bitching' as well as leaving (Batnitzky and McDowell, 2011, p. 196). The migrants who often commented on their work habits knew these tactics. One said: 'It's British: Can I go for a fag, can I take my break now?' The British care assistants also openly defied the restructuring by writing letters to owners, as in one case, where their hours were changed from eight-hour shifts to three-day 12 hour shifts, and their paid meal breaks and bank holiday pay were taken away. In one case, a British-born care assistant told clients what she earned, but understood that when she 'didn't get a response' it was, 'because they pay so much to be here.' She realized that they were unaware that the money they paid to the home was little for her.

Migrants on the other hand, embodied the right 'I can' attitude of corporate care. These migrants passed through these new shifts with some stress but not to the point that it was incapacitating. They endured the stress because they saw it as part of the job itself rather than as part of restructuring. They frequently talked about the stress of their work, but as part of the necessity of handling time-crunches and squeezing so many tasks into restrictive care plans. If something happened that was not in the plan, it was deemed an 'accident' rather than a flaw in the care plan itself.[2] One informant wrote in her diary:

> Mr RM lives far away from the previous one. He needed full body wash, getting dressed. He had an *accident* so I had to change all his sheets. Then me and his wife transported him to the living room, where he spends the whole day. This visit took about 35 minutes, then next 15 to get to the next client. I was running 20 minutes late, very stressful, especially if you don't know a client.

The migrant staff often blamed themselves if they couldn't keep up with the strict schedules for manoeuvring older people's bodies (Roberts, Mort, and Milligan, 2012), like one overworked participant who often fell asleep on her breaks and exclaimed, 'I'm just so bad. I'm really bad... because of the responsibility I've got now, I think I have to be more careful!' Another wondered if she should do even more: 'I do feel that I do need to do more of that because especially when you are tired, so many things in life, I do try to balance it though.' They also rarely made complaints, as they saw these problems as inherent to their jobs. One said, 'I don't complain. The carer is *supposed* to do it.' A willingness to accommodate the fourth shift was done particularly well by those who were former health care professionals. Their balancing act meant juggling these demands (personalization, paperwork, and personal expression) with their ethos of responsibility that fit with the new policies. They did this because they had the competency portability of the new work order and a professional work ethic that they imported to this job, such as, showing up on time, working hard, and saying yes. Unlike the British-born staff, they found the work 'easier'; for example, one said it was a 'piece of cake' compared to her last 'very complicated' hospital post in the Philippines.

The managers in this study functioned as gatekeepers in these migrants' adaptation to the social care sector. But they limited migrants' advancement opportunities by controlling their resources, by keeping them in these low-paid posts, and offering them limited training, with content they already knew. They also discouraged them from taking administrative level courses that would make them competitive for managerial posts. Unsurprisingly, such managers and trainers were rated as most approachable by these migrants for educational information. These trainers and managers were sponsoring a type of worker that fit with the policies that aimed to 'raise the skills of the workforce to deliver the new system' (Department of Health, 2008, p. 24).

Thus, England's social care sector demanded that members of this new workforce, with their expertise and participation in skilled migration care chains, accept these conditions. Once they migrated they had few options. They were recruited because their skills and traits were a cost-efficient solution to complex regulatory and business demands. Yet, as we shall see, skilled migrants did far more than simply adapt to and reproduce the industry's disciplinary aims.

Occupational hierarchies in care

The emerging care assistant

England's 1940s welfare state brought about free care at the point of access with the birth of the National Health Service (NHS) and the National Assistance Act of 1948 (Thane, 2009). During this period, an expanded workforce was needed to deal with the wide-ranging needs of its citizens and this led to recruitment of staff from Ireland and the former colonies, such as the West Indies (Batnitzky and McDowell, 2011; Winkelmann-Gleed, 2004; Yeates, 2009). The social organization of their labour accounts for the emergence of different strands of care but has consistently been governed by conflicting interests of contract, affect, and women's labour (Ungerson, 2004). Notably, women have made up the majority of those who are in paid and unpaid care work (including nursing and social work) (Cook-Gumperz and Hanna, 1997).

Although there are few histories of the 'care assistant,' the role has existed for some time in hospital and community settings (McKenna, Hasson, and Keeney, 2004), but it was not until the mid-20th century that this job category became established in the occupational hierarchy. By the 21st century, care assistant work would merge with the professions through 'role creep' (official upgrading of occupational roles), although in practice the jobs were redesigned to take on practically anything, including cleaning. Care assistants, however, have always been at the bottom ranks of both nursing and social work occupations.

By uncoupling care from nursing or social work, it could be passed down the line to lower level workers (Duffy, 2011); making beds, for example, was devalued and assigned to care assistants. Workload tasks flowed downwards in hospitals being filled by health care assistants who were expected to do more ('task flexibility'). It was not until 1999 that the Department of Health in England formally recognized 'health care assistants' as part of the 'nursing family' to deal with staff shortages and demands for hands-on care. The position ranged from ward assistant to 'bed maker' (McKenna et al., 2004, p. 453). Their presence in the 20th century was viewed as part of a second-level of nursing, and it was also integral to home-based social work as well as domestic work. In the USA 'care work' became a new occupation after the Second World War 'for women who spent years doing family labour.' Social workers established them as 'staff' and it was officially defined as: 'Housekeeper working (dom.serv)' (Boris and Parrenas, 2010, p. 190).

The care system has historically been two-tiered. In the USA, white women traditionally made up the bulk of nurses and social workers while domestic servants were largely African-American women. As the expert sector expanded, in the mid 20th century, care work was passed down and the nature of it had changed as new specialties and hierarchies accumulated (Duffy, 2011). Access to the top caring professions was severely limited by race and class through educational access and professional bodies. Exclusivity raised nurses and social workers' value socially and economically in society. Nursing in particular, unlike social work, was bound to stricter hierarchies.

Historically, nursing shifted from a 'physician's helper' role to a degree-oriented profession. But, like many female-dominated occupations, it was considered by organizational sociologists to be a 'semi-profession' due to the lack of autonomy and authority (Adams, 2010, p. 454). Yet the rise to professionalism was regarded as antithetical to caring (Brown and Kirpal, 2004). The introduction and the growth of the professions through schools and especially hospitals by the 1930s set in place these hierarchies of occupations among women. Practical nurses (those women with no formal training), a number of whom were black and immigrants, were confined to the home. Also attendants in hospitals were predominantly female by the 1950s, a job which grew and became more 'menial' in its reputation for its routinization of tasks and lack of educational requirements. These hospital attendants were not seen as having relational skills akin to nurses or social workers that cultivated middle-class femininity (Duffy, 2011; Boris and Parrenas, 2010).

By the 1980s, neo-liberal policies in health and social care sectors, driven by productivity concerns and market fluctuations shifted individual responsibility from the state to workers. Increasing the rate of production and capital with 'just-in-time' techniques (e.g. shift work, split-shifts, reduced breaks), called 'atypical work,' created intense work pressures (Coyle, 2005, p. 78). Nursing and social work started focusing more on assessing, monitoring, data collecting, planning, and diagnostic activities (Apesoa-Varano, 2007). In many ways, nurses had moved closer to doctors in these roles although they were still ranked below them (Cook-Gumperz and Hanna, 1997). Data collecting was also eventually passed down to care assistants.

In a more recent trend, traditional caring professions have had more role extension with the rhetoric of caring for the whole person (Duffy, 2011). With advertisements for a 'practical mix of skills' and combined technical, relational, and menial tasks (Brown and Kirpal, 2004, p. 234), there are now blurred boundaries and skill mixes between doctors, nurses, and care assistants (Bach, Kessler and Heron, 2012). Many of these professions are said to have a loss of autonomy and occupational decline especially with increasing feminization of, for example, doctors. Meanwhile care assistants take on more complicated procedures, formerly relegated to nurses and social workers (Adams, 2010; Duffy, 2011). The relational work of care assistants, however, has remained invisible as it became embedded into family metaphors (Dodson and Zincavage, 2007). Clare Ungerson (2004) found that some care assistants who were live-ins used the term 'family' to describe their relations with clients. But the family metaphor was a double-edged sword. They were frequently called on to give more care due to their close proximity than actual family members. Moreover, the one-to-one contact, in the absence of other colleagues created emotional blackmail situations. Eileen Boris and Rhacel Parrenas (2010) and Evelyn Nakano Glenn (2010) demonstrate how the 'companionship' law in the USA (exempting minimum wage and overtime to home care assistants) converges with a notion of care as love, making the work informal domestic service rather than as part of formal employment relations.

Migrants move into care

From the 19th century onwards, Irish nurses migrated to England, through the Catholic Church and female religious orders as well as informal networks located in former colonies (Yeates, 2009). These women and migrants from the West Indies expanded the NHS and were involuntary contributors towards reinforcing 'division and disadvantage' (Smith and Mackintosh, 2007, p. 2213); they did not rise through the ranks as easily as the English, and felt they had to be 'quicker.' Migrant nurses were cast as 'others' and their integration was uneasy. Not only that, but they were also disappointed with the poor working conditions they encountered in England (Winkelmann-Gleed, 2004). Moreover, immigration regimes and sector barriers made their qualifications invisible as they were channelled into non-career grade posts, although many hoped that by 'doing domestic they could get landed' (Yeates, 2009, pp. 115–116). While many developed a 'resigned acceptance' of their fates (Batnitzky and McDowell, 2011, p. 196), other nurses reinvented their professional identities to deal with these discriminatory conditions (Apesoa-Varano, 2007).

In this study, occupational slippage was evident among nurses, domestics, and care assistants, as well as other social care staff. Their roles were often interchangeable to the extent that it was legal; migrant senior care assistants dispensed medicine and nurses purchased underwear for residents while domestics doled out emotional care. One migrant domestic believed she cared for the clients without overstepping her role and described interactions with her nursing home residents as caring:

> Sometime they call me. I hold their hand. I go there. 'I love you,' [they say] and I say, 'I love you too'—what they want. I feel sorry for them but pleased because I do for them... I touch, I say, 'what do you want darling?' Sometime they want a drink. They [care staff] are so busy... they like me. I make them happy. I'm a carer.

The slippage was not always viewed as positive, especially when subsidiary roles took over. Domiciliary care assistants, for example, generally did not like to go on cleaning calls. Recently adapted nurses were often asked to do care assistant work and preferred stricter boundaries between the two. One participant described her new nursing home as such:

> Even care plans, they are so nicely organized and they don't mix domestic with the care whatsoever. You'd see the cleaners doing their bits and bobs around there, but carers don't do laundry, carers don't go in the kitchen.

Migrant nurses and care assistants appeared to take on more roles and responsibilities.

Preparation: Training for care assistants

Migrant professionals were prepared for workplace training. With their professional experiences and dispositions, they understood the necessity of attending training in order to be competitive agents. One participant said the training were 'a compensation for low wages.' They knew how to take exams and had the technical literacy skills to engage with the curriculum, increasingly laden with legalese and medical terms.

Holding student visas signalled possible job advancement to the new recruits. The 'student' route further codified training with the emphasis on studying and learning even if it was material with which the former health care professionals were already versed. A number of these participants saw training as a possible route *out* of care work. One participant said about the training: 'I want to develop my skill. I want to do something more and more... because I would like to use more skills, if you know what I mean, to develop myself. Everyday is the same, the same, the same.'

Recruiters, with a heavy supply of prospective candidates, could be highly selective and chose those with the most qualifications, regardless of whether or not these were needed. One participant wondered why her recruiter needed so many qualifications for a care assistant post:

> Most of them got some requirements to come, even if it's not really essential. That's what I thought you know, because they have very high requirements, like, you know, when they took me from my country—in the Philippines, you have to at least have three years experience in the hospital, which is 'hmm, why is that?' You know, and then when you get here it's not really recognized to be honest because you're still given the trainings and all that and then the people that you are going to be working with, which is you know, locals in this area haven't even went to college. So I mean the qualification is just so high.

The National Vocational Qualification system epitomized competency-based education. Established in the 1980s, it focused on flexible learning and industry-specific skills and then developed into a system of standard setting in the 1990s, using models drawn from German vocational education and US competency-based programmes (Hyland, 1998). It replaced a system whereby many workers, especially young people, had little chance to demonstrate their knowledge or training and were unemployed. In 2010, the new qualifications and credit system was introduced to replace NVQs in the care sector and involved gathering units towards a larger goal of certification but was essentially the same. Significantly, NVQs created pressure on the British-born staff who had been in the field for years. In the mid-1990s, only 10 per cent of care assistants took an NVQ and most did not have any formal qualifications (Balloch, Banks, and Hill, 2004). One trainer said:

> One of the biggest hitches at the moment is the legislation that insists that 50 per cent of carers have NVQ level 2 and there is opposition from the carers who say they've done the job adequately and some of them are near retirement. It's not organized opposition, just a general feeling of why should they have the exam.

Mandatory training for care assistants was a relatively new phenomenon. Historically there was on-the-job training and formal training was haphazard. The practical barriers that existed then included release time and payment to train, especially when staffing levels were low, and the shift work nature of care that made training and coverage difficult, plus travel and family responsibilities (Balloch, Banks, and Hill, 2004; Rainbird and Munro, 2003). This training, referred to as 'education on the cheap,' focused on behavioural objectives and developing competencies. Training drew on gendered skills that most women were seen to possess as part of their socialization and the historical gendered curriculum that focused on developing a caring personality (Jackson, 1991, p. 365; Skeggs, 1997). The competency approach to education historically was designed for women's professions to routinize their working knowledge with vocational qualifications that reinforced their gendered occupational segregation and low pay (Jackson, 1991). This assumption was sometimes challenged by participants in the study, although rarely. One British-born trainee, for example, complained to her tutor that 'carers don't get enough money' to which she replied: 'Most people don't come in to care for that reason.' The student retorted: 'But we all care and we don't get enough' to which she was told: 'Then get your banner and stand outside.'

The hidden curriculum

Although NVQs were acknowledged as 'one of Britain's best kept secrets' (Hyland, 1998, p. 369), they had many flaws and have been called 'no value qualifications' because they have not yielded labour market returns for workers (Wolf, 2002, p. 56). Employers were indifferent to the NVQ and unconvinced about its value but were pressed by government officials to offer it as part of the new standards (Hyland, 1998). Yet hidden in the NVQ were values and attitudes that employers sought in skilled migrant women.

While the content was prescribed, its structure was not. In the study, the NVQ was delivered in three different ways to the participants. There were courses offered for a large fee online to those on student routes. They were also delivered one-on-one to workers who were required by their care homes to purchase an NVQ assessment and booklet from a particular training company. Then college tutors in the workplace and in other settings delivered traditional courses. These 'courses' were paid for by the company and students attended one or two induction days with the rest being homework.

After a unit was completed, assessors would come to the site, where the care assistants worked, to test their knowledge. These assessors, short in supply, were often former care assistants and knew the system but there were problems. The NVQ could take much longer to complete in view of the time needed to study for it and for the assessor to come. Usually, migrants sailed through the practice tests in their study materials only to wait for an assessor to come and assess them and these delays were frequent. Units could last up to a year although theoretically participants were expected to be finished between three and six months. One migrant participant called the training her 'own job' because of the time-intensiveness:

> So it's just all about how you provide the care, how you work, how you will deliver the care directly and how will you execute regarding health and safety things, things like that. It's mostly everything that I do here. I started last year but I just covered a little, just a few pages and then we stopped because of running out of people, for assessment. So I stop and then I just started back again. This is like my own job.

In addition, all companies had to offer inductions and health and safety training on an annual basis, and sometimes companies offered specialist courses, including palliative care, dementia, and sight and hearing problems, as well as coping with abuse. Consultants or the companies themselves created the curriculum and 'trainers' delivered the content and skills. These courses were 'symbolic interventions' pertaining to recognition (Lopez, 2007, p. 225). One tutor, for example, in an NVQ course reminded students that the NVQ would imitate the induction training they already received. She said:

> You have to be doing the job to be assessed. You'll not necessarily learn an awful lot, you've done induction—it's all the knowledge

you need. It's something you already do and what you know, it's recognition.

Migrants took these and the specialist courses and asked for more, hoping it would be linked to promotions, pay, and advancement. One participant wanted to do an NVQ3 but her manager told her that 'there wasn't enough funding to do that at present.' While migrants viewed the specialist courses as culturally interesting, they were bored by the mandatory ones and viewed these as monotonous, although they complied and attended them. One participant attended a course about how to dispense medicine, but was disappointed: 'They sat around and talked and I thought it would give me insight but it wasn't a big deal—not a *real* training.' Migrants took any courses that were offered that could help them accumulate cachet and a badge.

One such course was an English to Speakers of Other Languages (ESOL) course that was designed to improve migrant workers' communication skills. 'Effective communication' was the elixir of the new managerialism, framed as demeanour, and 'defined by accent, syntax, semantics, rhythm, pitch, and so on, deemed pleasant to and by customers and employers.' (Lu, 2007, p. 299). One manager, for example, wondered why she should release her already proficient English-speaking Indian care assistants for a 'diction course.' She was in a minority as most employers in the study believed their migrant care assistants needed it. The curriculum model delivered basic literacy qualifications, something they actually didn't need. It prioritized employers' needs in emphasizing, 'listening' and following orders. The curriculum reinforced essentialist notions and maintained myths of these women as 'outsiders' who knew little. Anecdotes, examples, and illustrations that presented information in clinical, task-based, and condescending ways, suggested that migrants lacked skills and expertise. This erasure of their knowledge led them to sidestep these misperceptions in an intimate environment and 'undo' this curriculum. The students relaxed and enjoyed the sessions, knowing they were paid for it, as they already possessed this technical knowledge. They joked about the scripted conversations pertaining to the weather and phrases in the curriculum like 'the tone of your voice—is it polite, friendly, confident?' and 'smile—it will affect the way you sound: Try it and see.' Although policy-makers conceived workplace training of this type as a panacea, and employers complied with limited offerings, the migrant trainees eventually realized that the interventions were more emblematic than real. The same was true for the paperwork.

Paperwork and paper walls

> The people who are carers here before—I've met some of them—and they say it wasn't as complicated as it is now, you know, like all those trainings and all the paperwork. It was nothing like this—you go into care, and that's it.

This migrant participant had heard from her British-born colleagues that times had changed in the world of care. From the migrants' perspectives, this paperwork was seen as a natural part of their jobs and reflective of the larger audit explosion that penetrated a number of sectors (Strathern, 2000). In England's care sector, for example, many activities needed recording with calls for transparency and accountability. These new visible management techniques (Jackson, 2001) reconfigured job roles, skills, and identities, and were not simple additions but reformed the work itself. Yet this new work was not counted towards genuine promotions even though care assistants spent much time on it.

This phenomenon of increasing paperwork has been referred to as the new work order (Gee, Hull and Lankshear, 1996). Now literate workers not only read basic documents but also produce reliable and valid data as evidence of their work. The workplace becomes heavily textualized to ensure quality control and lean production (more with less). The aim is to match talk with text; talk is work and gets translated into texts/documents (Scheeres and Solomon, 2006). These texts exert their own power in making the industry appear to be more professional through the use of technical language. For example, written care plans produce certain conversations that care assistants must have with clients in terms of checking and monitoring their physical and emotional states. Yet there are also 'silences' in these texts as they often minimize the actual interaction (Gee, Hull, and Lankshear, 1996, p. 36). One manager was observed telling her care assistants to write about activities in emotionally distant ways. She advised them *not* to write 'Hannah was rude to me,' as one did, and instead state: 'resident didn't accept food on 30/1/09 at 8.15 a.m.' The emotional labour that the care assistant exerted in the interaction was literally erased as she was turned into a server. The objective language did not capture the feelings or relationships involved in eating, and in focusing only on behaviour, negated the emotional response and visibility of the care assistant ('Hannah was rude to *me*').

The paperwork practices reflected the identity of the worker too. The volume of paperwork escalated in those occupations that were already higher in the care hierarchy—senior nurses, for example, had, what one migrant described, as a 'sickening' amount:

> Well it's such a big part of my job...you get to say 'catheters draining well' every single day...dealing with the same thing and saying the same thing. It's sickening!

The migrant nurses also commented that the paperwork had increased and cut in to their other activities and home life. One senior migrant care assistant who had advanced to a nurse declared that her paperwork load was more tenacious, taking on a life of its own, separate from her care of clients:

> What is different from being a senior carer is you have got the responsibility, you know apart from the paperwork, which is a lot more anyway compared to the care assistant. It is a lot, lot more and a lot more complex.... Care plans are a lot of paperwork. Sometimes you think, if they want us to do nursing, we should be doing the nursing—leave the blooming paperwork on the side and get someone to do only the paperwork. Today was my day off but from 12.00 to 4.00 I was at work sorting my paperwork.

Also paperwork flowed down the chain of command with nurses dictating to care assistants and care assistants to domestics. Domestics often took messages for care assistants while care assistants took instructions from nurses. Officially, while domestics produced monthly stocks of paper in practice, they handled different types of paperwork. Mainly the domestics read (rather than wrote) signs, instructions, and notes. However, they did write in report 'books' that were checked by care assistants or nurses. At the opposite end, nurses wrote care plans, medication sheets, referrals, and multidisciplinary team notes, and senior nurses conducted weekly, monthly, or tri-annual audits. They trained and monitored everyone else's work to the point that it was 'very tiring' as one confessed. Of the care assistants, domiciliary workers seemed to have the most paperwork due to the lack of managerial oversight. Few workers in the social care sector could avoid the cascade of different genres of texts and significant paperwork loads consisting of:

- Charts for: toileting, feeding, fluid, diet, sleeping, elimination, pressure checks, security checks, bathing, exercise, hourly checks, and downtime

- Rotas
- Timesheets
- Client diaries
- Doctor and district or senior nurse or social worker notes
- Menus and choice plans
- Meal instructions
- Schedules
- Driving logs including mileage
- Social work reports
- Guest books
- Announcements
- Reports: day and night
- Training manuals
- Policies
- Portfolios of residents
- Tests/exams
- Care plans
- Hours by schemes
- Health and safety and sick policies and updated memos on bulletin boards
- Equipment instructions
- Family communication book
- Staff communication book
- Letters and cards for and from clients

The paperwork load in social care reflected the routinization of work, although the workers had informal ways of dealing with it, including the use of copying, shorthand, and acronyms similar to the symbolic interventions of training (Lopez, 2007).[3] It was common, for example, to find one-liners in charts written by migrant care assistants that were often duplicated from one day to the next; one such example was: 'Client fine, brkfast, made bed, chatted.' Steven Lopez (2007) defines this practice as part of management and worker collaboration to break institutionalized rules because they do not fit the environment and waste time. In this study, care reports were not overseen or inputted into computers. The charting, therefore, was largely fictitious.

This detailed paperwork, meant to be for surveillance and an instrument of control in the absence of trust, concealed more than it revealed. It was revered nonetheless. Timothy Diamond, in an analysis of paperwork in his book on nursing homes in the USA (1995, *Making Gray Gold*, showed that if an activity was 'not charted, it didn't happen'

(p. 130). Much of the paperwork was about obtaining a good 'industrial streamlined' appearance for visitors and inspectors. The paperwork in this study became a record and in so doing, it erased emotions and emptied the content of relationships between clients and their caregivers. In one instance where a care assistant was hurrying the client suggested 'she not write too much,' upon which she jotted: 'bath, dinner.' In a sense the paperwork functioned more as visual objects, creating a culture of performance and of institutional quality. The migrant care assistants also extracted its physical properties. They used the paperwork, for example, to physically block conversations when clients were seen as overwhelming or difficult or to signal that they needed to leave. And other times charts and logs were even used as door props. Generally, the paperwork did not communicate much about the actual care that occurred.

Yet on occasion the paperwork served as a conversation starter and added humour when clients observed care assistants writing reports of their interactions or told them funny comments to insert. Very few times was the writing meaningful, except when it was meant for family members and was written in 'family books' that were kept in people's rooms (in nursing or residential homes or in living rooms in private homes). These were typically for clients with dementia who could not explain to their families about their lives and how they were doing. The care assistants' notes were important information to fill in the gaps. In one sheltered home, a son-in-law, who lived in Spain confessed how important the book was in letting him know how his father-in-law was doing during the times when he was physically absent. The book sat in the middle of a coffee table in the living room next to other treasured books and was in a different place to the institutionalized care notes in a plastic folder on the other side of the room. The family book helped him to see the types of physical care needs his father-in-law had and showed his steady decline with Alzheimer's disease. The notes also reassured him that the care he was receiving was consistent and, indeed, caring. It was a conversation starter between him, his father, and the migrant care assistant when he visited. He called this care assistant 'a star' and said, 'I feel comfortable leaving him with her.' He would also leave notes in it. These family books were a touchstone for families but they were rarely used. The migrants too selected out paperwork that was valuable from the rest.

Migrant participants made quick decisions about the length, technical language, and rigorousness of note taking and chose the shorter versions to save time for hands-on care at the expense of not recording their labour. As an example, one domiciliary participant who was Polish cared for a Polish client. She was worried about her because her house was a 'pig sty,' and she felt this woman needed more care than what she could afford. Her daughter had recently committed suicide and she was upset, repeating over and over again how she killed herself. The participant listened and reminded her that her neighbours were coming over shortly. Her log, however, noted everything except these emotional interactions:

> Washed up, wiped the kitchen, made a cheese sandwich, meds, toilet, emptied the commode, all well.
>
> (24.02.09, 17.30–18.00)

Mature British-born care assistants tended to find the amount and type of report writing demanding and stressful. Their anxiety was related to the recognition that this paperwork was increasingly becoming a badge of their worth over their hands-on care. Conversations with British-born participants generally showed that they believed that filling in paperwork took away from caring activities rather than contributed to it. This sentiment was also shared among migrants, but only to the extent that the paperwork seemed duplicative, irrelevant to direct care, or was given as a punishment. In this way, they were critically assessing it, rather than disposing of its worth (like their British-born colleagues). Part of the reason for the acceptance of documentation was that in their former professional lives, they were expected to record their activities. One participant found it easy to balance the paperwork with care:

> So I have to do some paperwork for the meantime and at the same time, doing some caring, you know. But then it's not really that difficult because I have gotten used to it especially the caring side—it's every day just a piece of cake you see.

When it was appropriate, they simply copied what their colleagues had done the day before at the same time and checked their writing against the care plan to ensure that what they said was what was stipulated in it. Frequently, though, to ensure that they complied with their duties, they created their own set of paperwork consisting of reminders—often these were carried in their pockets to alert them to problems or schedule changes. In this sense, the documentation, particularly when homemade, functioned as a source of support (Lopez, 2006, 2007). This activity, of course, added to the amount of work they did.

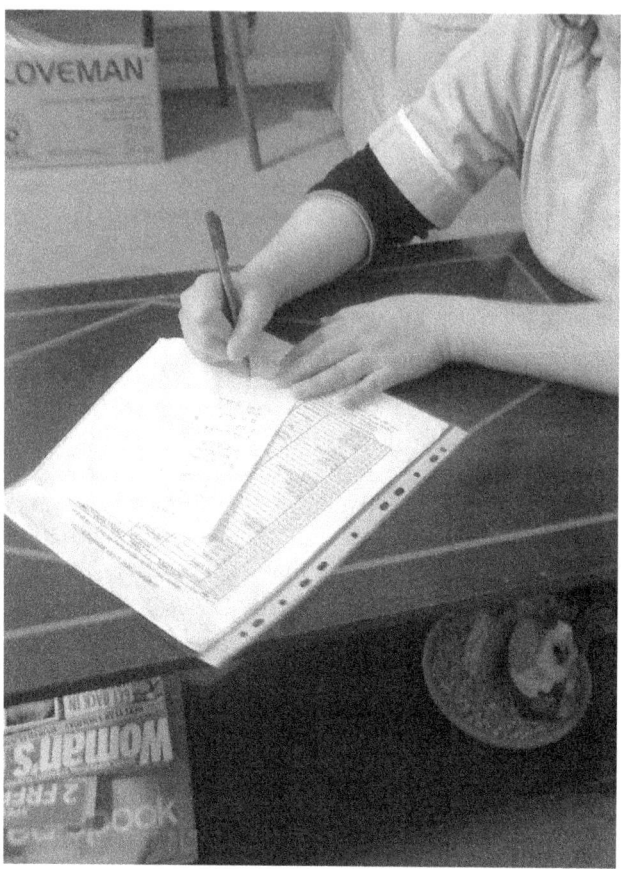

Figure 3.1 Duplicate log

The photograph in Figure 3.1 shows a domiciliary care assistant copying her timesheet on to a piece of paper, duplicating the texts, and adding extra work to her already filled schedule.

Lastly these migrants had the English language technical literacy skills necessary to fulfil company objectives for paperwork. They all engaged in technical writing with ease, hurrying, and writing as they walked from one room to the next. They appreciated the writing aspects of the care work in its reminding them of their former health care professions where recording and documentation of patient conditions was important. They knew the discourse of objective language, including professional jargon, legalese, and terminology. An example is an assessment of a care assistant's report which reflected this value: 'What J. wrote was factual, actual, legible, and complete so that others could read them and she signed and dated these reports as per her role.'

It was surprising then to the migrants when 'the native born ask us for spelling and grammar' assistance, as one participant reported. British-born care assistants, on the other hand, often resorted to oral communication, making hand-over meetings (from one shift to the next) important events for communicating about clients. In this case, they didn't always read out notes about the clients but simply discussed them in layperson's terms. The notes were relayed in an informal discourse of clients' needs. One British-born senior care assistant reported:

> Ella is fine. She was feeling a bit off and was changed in bed. Bob is fine but starting again. Started this time last night. Dahlia is fine. New lady in room thirteen, Nancy Hearn, here for a week respite come out of hospital, she's a slight woman, but all there.

The migrants, while understanding the fictive role of the paperwork, were aware of its underlying legality and its potential to serve as a type of social protection. One participant, for example, called it: 'black and white support papers in case anything goes wrong.' They understood that documenting activities would protect them against false accusations and guaranteed that they received credit for the time they spent with their clients, which translated monetarily. On the other hand, employers could punish employees by forcing them to duplicate every single act of a care interaction, like one migrant who said facetiously that she had to write: 'wrote in logbook.' They also took their paperwork home to complete it.

Personal expressiveness: The aesthetic labour of emotional care

Policies of person-centred care set forth the importance of the client's choice and control but also their emotional and economic well-being. Workers were expected to attend to client's emotional needs and be 'really caring' (Brown and Kirpal, 2004, p. 225). This emotion management was considered to be a personal trait of the worker and was never really specified. While care employers heavily prescribed other activities, they promoted a philanthropic approach (a gift exchange) of care assistants' managing their own emotions and those of clients (Bolton and Boyd, 2003, p. 291). This standard was incongruous and put the burden on the individual worker to figure out what emotional strategy would work best in any given situation. One tutor was observed telling her students:

> If he wants to tell you stories when he wants to, it might conflict with the care plan, but it's his want, so you have ten minutes. Sit down and listen. Most elderly are lonely. What else does he need?

These care assistants were to be shock absorbers of personalization policies; they managed the difficult emotions of clients through their personal expressiveness and relational competence to chat and comfort and defend their 'independence, well-being, and dignity' (Department of Health, 2008, p. 15; Duffy, 2011). Yet training care assistants with skills for handling these needs was both vague and often missing. Company training repeated generic terms to trainees like foster 'respect, dignity and independence' of clients. For this, care assistants had to have personal traits like being 'honest and trustworthy,' as well as 'reliable and dependable.' What was not mentioned was how a care assistant might achieve these ends, or if care assistants should be anticipating more and different needs on a constant basis at the same time as preventing isolation and loneliness and safeguarding clients from dangers. There seemed to be a never-ending amount of hidden skills and behaviours that were required (Brown and Kirpal, 2004). These skills were part of aesthetic labour. This refers to workers embodying the style of service the industry demands including dress, grooming, facial and body expressions and speech, and dispositions that appear as second-nature (Warhurst and Nickson, 2007, p. 789).

Helping clients to manage their feelings well was difficult. One curriculum advised care assistants to use positive techniques to help clients 'raise their self-esteem and confidence' through 'empowering them to take control of as many aspects of their lives as possible' and 'enabling the service users to have opportunities for making their own choices.' This also included helping clients to diffuse and communicate feelings under time pressures. One induction training focused on the principles of care and the duty of care assistants to perform person-centred care but rarely mentioned what it meant to care for someone's emotions other than 'bringing them out.' The trainer began: 'There is a reason we are in care because we *do* care. What is care?' She asked them all. They shouted answers: 'help,' 'support,' 'look after' and the trainer added, 'how about protect and *enable*? Because the opposite is disable. Just because they are 70 or 80 doesn't mean they can't. I want you to make them feel like they *can* do something. Give encouragement. They are often disabled. We see the care plan: wash, get up, feed. Look past the task.' Then she asked more questions: 'How would you feel if some bright thing comes through your door, gets you up and dressed and does everything, and says bye. How would you feel?' A student says, 'uncomfortable,' and the trainer says, 'If you don't *bring them out*, they will retreat and it will take a good carer twice as long to communicate with her. Have you heard of person-centred care? What does it mean?' A student says 'centred around the person.'

Enabling was never defined by the tutor, but depended on the care assistant to figure this out even when faced with contradictions. They were taught in inductions, for example, not to share intimate details of their lives, only general personal issues. Yet while on the job, some of the care assistants used a strategy of telling the clients their own problems in a way that equalized the relationships and even made them 'regain their dignity' as one migrant articulated. One participant said: 'It matters to them when you confide and tell them what's the problem because its like you're giving them, you know, the trust.' This measure of intimacy made a difference in the relations. One migrant care assistant put herself 'down' in order to promote desired behaviours from clients. This demonstrated her ability to engage in complex emotional management with clients even if it made her labour invisible. She explained:

> We have to deal with the people here in a different way because we don't know the culture. We have to please them. We have to put ourselves a little bit down.... We have to level with them, a bit lower than them, so that they could be friends with us.

These migrant care assistants were acting in line with organizational rules, which were also aligned with their own personal and professional ideas of providing emotional care (Bolton and Boyd, 2003; Lopez, 2006). These affective exchanges reaped huge material rewards for the care companies as these translated into client requests for more visits (Bolton, 2009). Francesca Cancian (Cancian and Oliker, 2003) discusses how emotional care may incur risks to workers because of the development of close personal relationships whereby the limits of interventions are unclear (p. 97). These care assistants were what Hochschild (2003, p. 77) calls 'sentient actors,' being conscious and holding intimacy at a distance through their versatile responses. They provided a type of 'educated caring' (Apesoa-Varano, 2007, p. 249) that saw caring as subjective and changing depending on circumstance, environment, and people involved. Former nurses, in particular, understood and practiced this *variability* in their care, especially since there were so many instances where the care plans did not cover client's emotional needs and situations. As care assistants, they made many on-the-spot decisions about how to handle difficulties that satisfied the authority hierarchy and was ultimately cost saving. One participant, for example, said:

> I enjoy going to clients and helping them, and because of the company system, they can't provide enough time to give good quality service—30 minutes—what can you do? Sometimes the client will feel really low. If you wanted to stay and cheer, you will be late for the next client. It's really difficult to leave clients especially when they share your life. It's a privilege when clients share personal things, but I have to rush. I know I am missing a lot.

These former health care professionals did not get involved in the clients' problems and lives to the extent that it significantly impacted their own psychological states. As outsiders in their communities, these former health care professionals often developed familial relationships with clients that enabled them to win acceptance by 'knowing the patient' through close contact as well as particular and contextualized knowledge of their problems (Tanner, Benner, Chesla and Gordon, 1996, p. 203) But these care assistants also wanted to be *known* as one participant said:

> I think and if you are working some years it's easier because the people know you and they don't shame you and they can tell you about their very intimate matters. The first time is always very difficult for them, but at [the care home] it is a small house and we are a family with all the problems.

Many care assistants saw clients as alienated from their own children and performed as a surrogate family to them. One participant said:

> I am sometimes sad, when I see clients—they are alone, they are rich but not happy. One client said, 'You can stay here.' 'I can't stay here my mother,' I said. She is laughing. I knock on her door, 'Hello mother!' 'Oh my daughter!' she says.

The emotional cost to themselves was offset by a highly developed repertoire of aesthetic skills. Often referred to as soft skills, these entail tacit knowledge, which is 'unobservable,' such as commitment to clients (Lafer, 2004; Warhurst, 2008). Most of these skills were developed from their previous professional positions and were not deployed just because they were migrants, afraid of being fired or deported. These participants were extra polite and smiled continuously and spontaneously, when words weren't possible, even suppressing their own feelings. One former nurse described it this way:

> You have to be cheerful everyday. We have to be cheerful to our clients, It's difficult. I have to smile.... Because these clients need you. They feel alone so when you have to face them, you have to be cheerful, even though inside you're crying.

They also knew it was a type of 'game' to be played between themselves and the clients (Warhurst and Nickson, 2007). While British care assistants tended to be reactive with clients when problems arose and often involved management, migrant former health care professionals tended to follow professional discourses of interacting that were more in line with company policies and unthreatening to the power structure.

Former health care professionals transforming the industry from the bottom

The migrant participants who were former health care professionals initiated job expansion beyond the redesigned roles, dictated by industry standards, to not only provide more care than their colleagues did, as some studies have found (Cangiano et al., 2009; Datta et al., 2010; Timonen and Doyle, 2010), but also to qualitatively change the work. Although deemed a low-skilled field that needed to be upgraded by policy-makers, these migrant care assistants uplifted it from the bottom through informal strategies with their commitment to care, the specializations they brought with them from their former professions, and through their abilities to tune in to, and retune to clients' needs as they occurred, over and beyond the restrictive care plans. They also became advocates for the clients. Similarly in a study of migrant doctors working with the elderly (Raghuram, Bornat, and Henry, 2011) migrant physicians were found to transform this low-status field. Due to being outsiders, they connected with clients to create more egalitarian and effective ways of treating them. They did this through diagnostic touching, advocacy against invasive interventions, giving age-sensitive treatments, and seeing patients before signing prescriptions. Their work championed the needs of older persons, which influenced the NHS policies and practices in its earliest days.

The new practices of these former health care professionals stemmed from their embodied cultural capital. Pierre Bourdieu (1986) explains this as 'dispositions of the mind and body' that include gender, race, and class markers, and human capital (skills and knowledge). Its value is contingent to the context and is rated in a type of sphere of worth through rules (Kelly and Lusis, 2006). Using a Bourdieu framework, Beverly Skeggs (1997) saw British-born women care assistants' identities framed through their sense of respectability. This cultural capital was exchanged in their everyday practices with clients and was reinforced through trainings. Similarly, migrant care assistants, as discussed in Chapter 1, developed their own codes of conduct. Yet this 'migrant ethic of care' (Datta et al., 2010, p. 94) was not based on their cultural backgrounds (being from the 'old world') that they leveraged in the industry but their professional expertise. These migrant care assistants didn't just unpack their treasures (former health care qualifications) in a new country but added new practices to existing repertoires of care; the rucksack metaphor neglects the practices that may not be counted by dominant institutions but are enacted creatively and validated among networks, and as such, become new forms of cultural capital (Erel, 2010). In this way, migrant former health care professionals didn't just apply the same rules to a different country, but created a new economy of cultural capital in their new contexts (Kelly and Lusis, 2006). In a sense, by enacting their embodied cultural capital (e.g. professional dispositions and work ethic as well as medical/health care knowledge) in this sector these former health care professionals were increasing their value and 'reworking hegemonic scripts of identity'—that of low-paid, low-skilled workers who give insignificant and low quality care (Dyck and Dossa, 2006, p. 693).

This cultural capital accumulated and operated as advantages in their entry and retention in the care industry. They converted these advantages into 'care capital' (Williams, 2010, 13) that was not officially recognized but used nonetheless by clients and employers. This capital consisted of care practices and resources that they brought from their own countries and converted to this sector. This care capital was like a bond between themselves and the clients who lacked many social supports and counted on the expertise of these care assistants. This care capital was used by employers too; 'Filipino-ness' for example, signalled someone who was caring and reliable (Erel, 2010, p. 649). This positive stereotype as 'caring people' bolstered their image while threatening that of British-born care assistants (Spencer, Martin, Bourgeault, and O'Shea, 2010, p. 41). One Filipina participant said:

> They love Filipinos. The British don't do [for them like us]. Look at that superman [Christopher Reeves]. His carer was Filipino. I never say that because I am Filipino but I heard that they like us. The company knows this fact. It's a big issue with the British carers. They are jealous.

In a sense, these migrants 'bargained' their care capital with clients and between themselves and their companies (Bolton, 2009). This ingrained notion extended to male domiciliary care workers, a rare breed. One Filipino team leader introduced a female client who was nervous about having a man as her primary care assistant. She told the client: 'He actually is a trained nurse. He is used to caring and he worked in a hospital, just like male *nurses*, and they say, "Exactly." They realize that. Just like a male *nurse*.' The participants were, after all, answerable first to their companies, and second to the clients.

Most often though, as discussed in Chapter 2, migrant participants highlighted their cultures, over their expertise, when they referred to themselves as having a 'good attitude' and with statements like 'it is our nature not to disappoint anyone.' And like many British-born care assistants, they saw that being a woman was an asset too. One participant said: 'I feel that women have more edge to the men because I think this job is really inclined to women. Because women are born to be caring and as I say, hard-working and more responsible than men.'

Migrant former health care professionals deployed their care capital, through loopholes in policies and procedures, to help clients. In this way they created healing and nurturing spaces (Dyck and Dossa, 2006). In this study, the participants' care capital was enacted through: (1) giving extra care; (2) dismantling ideologies of 'choice' and 'independence;' (3) re-assessing clients; (4) using pointers and therapeutic touch; and, (5) guarding clients. Other migrant and British care assistants, some of who are mentioned in this chapter, also enacted this care capital. However for the former health care professionals, it was wide-ranging and raised their status on the grey market.

Extra care

Nationality and race have been the primary rationale given in the literature for migrants in giving 'extra care'—to appease clients and reduce negative incidents (Datta, McIlwaine, Evans, Herbert, May and Wills,

2006; Datta et al., 2010; Timonen and Doyle, 2010); migrants reduce 'the cultural divide' by making the clients feel more at ease, with gifts, cooking, and humour as well as relating to them as 'social beings' (Datta et al., 2006, p. 16). They add, rather than withdraw, emotional care to clients, as other research has indicated (Lee-Treweek, 1996). Clients, in referring to them, as 'family members' create pressures to perform additional household activities. These extra duties maintained their long-term employment and connection to the clients but felt like non-stop and bonded work.

In this study, the migrant health care professionals saw their 'extra' care as not just a way to deal with distances between themselves and clients but because they believed it was professionally and morally responsible. In one case, a participant, while driving, saw a client struggling to walk down the street alone. She said, 'I saw her—we are not allowed to give her a lift. I saw her walking. I stopped and ask, "Would you like a lift?" She told me "yes," so I dropped her off at her home and the company didn't know that.' In another case, a participant was given directives by her supervisor to *not* help clients who might injure themselves. She recollected that the staff nurse told her to 'just let the resident fall if you see that they are going to fall down because you don't want to suffer in that case.' When she reflected on this scenario, she thought 'but then that's not good for me. Because I saw that she is about to fall down so I had to save her.'

In these cases, disengaging from a care interaction (not picking up clients on the street or not catching them when they fell) didn't seem like the right thing to do as professionals or as people. So in this way, they were not so much giving 'extra care' in order to receive something (cooperation of clients), as maintaining their own sense of personal and professional ethical standards. In a sense, the term 'extra care' had little meaning, since the actual care plans stipulated the bare minimum of physical care for clients and even British-born care assistants gave this, as a type of 'gift exchange' to clients (Bolton and Boyd, 2009; Hochschild, 2003, p. 76). In fact the companies appeared to depend on all of their employees to do more than the actual care plan mandated. But they especially depended on these migrants' care professionalism to help clients.

Dismantling choice and independence

Care assistants were supposed to be supportive agents in helping older persons sustain their individual livelihoods and make informed choices, capacities which were prized in England's policies. Yet a number of the former health care professionals found that this was not necessarily what clients needed. Many participants, in fact, wanted to cultivate a *dependent* relationship, akin to their former treatment of 'patients' in their last jobs. Furthermore, the constant emphasis on offering clients choices (even from a limited amount of options) was difficult in the face of dementia and depression, and a number of the participants retreated from this discourse. This dependency relationship was not viewed as negative or one of superiority on the part of these care assistants who were once former health care professionals, but what seemed to constitute good care in these contexts. Maria, for example, critiqued the constant questioning of clients' options. She said that while the clients were 'independent and able, some of them had depression' and, because of their generation, needed more than 'prompting' to bathe (which was the lingo of her company). She preferred to do the more labour-intensive showering or bathing, requiring more of her own (unpaid) time but which was considered 'proper.' She explained:

> We're just following the care plans that our managers have made for us to follow. But then there were times that we need to apply what we learned from school, especially when applying cream and giving medication. And hygiene of the clients. But we still need to stick with the care plan or else we are in trouble.... Because in my point of view, because she's wearing a pad overnight, she needs a proper shower, a proper wash. Because you need to check everything on her body, if there's something unusual like bruises, rashes, so, that's the only time that you can check the client's body—if there's something wrong.

In another case, Maria felt that her job was not finished if she left a client who was not 'comfortable' and the place was not hygienic. She said:

> We dump the garbage and clinical waste. I can't leave the dishes. I want the clients to feel comfortable. I saw the care plans didn't include the dishes so I revised the care plans.

Re-assessing clients with new eyes

Policy-driven training encouraged care assistants to listen to clients and to observe them for any problems. The former health care professionals presented themselves as types of researchers, collecting data on clients, in order to better assess their needs. In fact, some of them were so good that the office depended on *their* assessments for determining client care and turned them in to team leaders, even sometimes allowing them to change the care plan. One experienced physiotherapist educator, Marina, knew what to look for. She said:

> So you are the first carer to go to a client, so whatever you are going to find there you have to have a quick look around and, you know, do a reassessment.... If you've been working with a medical background I think you are more vigilant to see things, you know, that needs doing. You know, you are sort of a key observer to things. And doing this care for quite a bit, you know, I think I already know what are the things to look for.

These assessments and reassessments enabled them to understand clients' deeper needs than social workers who made preliminary visits. It was a way to hone the care that they would deliver. Another instance of reassessment was when these former health care professionals went on calls and checked the paperwork against what care assistants said they had done with clients. In one case, Marina examined a care assistant's log to see whether the client actually took a shower by feeling the stall floor and walls. This is a case where the paperwork was taken seriously and the content was actually used. In another case a client who had a sore back but rejected her water bottle raised Marina's suspicions. Marina established that it was made too hot by the last care assistant who visited her and she changed the water. These participants scanned and judged clients' support systems, food, and lifestyle. Marina, for example, in examining the refrigerator of a client thought her food was unhealthy and in looking at her magazines criticized her daughter saying: 'She should not give her gossip magazines.'

Using pointers and therapeutic touch

The former physical therapists (PTs) and occupational therapists (OTs), in particular, could detect movement problems of clients that others could not. One participant, Abigail, said:

> I have a client who is a stroke patient. I know he is capable of dressing himself, because he has muscle strength. But they [medical practitioners] are not doing it. I can't encourage him although I know, as an OT, I can teach the techniques he can use and positions of sleeping so his shoulder wouldn't drop.

Abigail gave her clients therapeutic tips, props, and advice. She said: 'Clients, sometimes I help and give advice, if they would have swollen legs, I would ask them to get exercise to help joint pain, and pain management.' In other cases, she gave pointers that explained to them their medical problems. She said to one client who is

> a stroke patient, he has a hand problem—the joints contract. He holds his hand and it smells bad. When I shower him, I wash the hand and dry it, 'is this painful? I don't want to force.' I check and the word I said, 'is it *painful* to open hand?' But he said, 'It is impossible.' I told him 'it is not impossible.' Slip of the tongue, and he said 'why' and I told him: 'I have patients in the Philippines with the same condition—with proper techniques, you can open it.' He said can I pay you to treat me, and I told him, I can't practice my profession. I can give pointers that can help him.

Often clients asked their care assistants to apply cream, the former health care professionals also massaging whatever body part it was applied, 'to increase their circulation,' as one former nurse explained. They also listened and talked with them while doing it. This type of bodywork added value to an otherwise mundane task by further helping clients with their mobility.

Guardian roles

While the care assistants were expected to protect and support clients, as the training recommended, the former health care professionals went over and beyond this, to actually guard them against problems that could arise and serve as a check and balance for medical and social care professionals, including doctors, social workers, and nurses. They often provided evidence to show clients needed extra and better services. They were the first to find out about problems and immediately reported these, and even nagged the company so that the client was not made to wait. One former nurse worried clients were being ignored and in once case, contacted the office staff:

> One morning I went there, and his legs were rheumatoid.... So he needed more care. It was difficult for him—so I did phone the office and said, 'look guys, the situation is like this.'

They also identified problems to social workers when clients drank too much. Some of these participants saved bottles for social workers to prove clients were alcoholics and needed extra help. They checked for bruising and acted as go-betweens to the company if clients were found to have any that raised their suspicions, like Maria who wanted to check her clients when showering or bathing rather than washing (and seeing) parts of their bodies. They also provided ethical checks on the British-born work force, if, for example, the houses were dirty, as some were, and they were not cleaned. One participant said, 'I noticed they [British-born care assistants] just put water, and dip the plates in and it is ok. But it is not right! Some food is sticking! These are very fragile people and they will use that.' They also became messengers for clients when they could not report their symptoms accurately to doctors, as in one case where a participant became angry because her patient had dementia and could not describe her problems. She said, 'I think they need more attention by the doctors here. We give all the attention for them. We wash them, we take care about them, we love them.... I say to them [doctors], "listen, I don't want to be a nurse here, but like a nurse I can see so many things." ' Lastly, they counterbalanced what the nurses did, if the clients appeared to lack comprehensive care. One participant who said 'we all imitate Florence Nightingale' explained:

> I mean the nurses that I have seen work with us here in the nursing home, they give medication and they will give instruction, they'll supervise, but they won't do the *total nursing care*. So the client is left with the carer to do everything and all that kind of stuff. So their job is the clean one—they don't do—but when you do nursing you nurse the patient as a whole.

Conclusion: Unequal rewards

As shown, the care assistant role is embedded in the lowest grades of feminized occupations in nursing and social work (called 'vertical segregation'). Professionalization and upgraded standards turned care into 'dirty work' producing a higher demand for special workers who could tolerate these difficult conditions. The hands-on nature of this work has also been subjugated to other lower-grade reproductive work, namely the five c's: cleaning, caring, clerical, cashiering, catering that are historically feminized. Many migrants, especially those from outside the EEA could not find any other type of work than the five c's and were often relegated to the two c's: cleaning and caring. Zimbabweans in one study, for example, (McGregor, 2008, p. 801) facetiously referred to themselves as the 'BBC' ('British-bottom cleaners'). This work was expected of them: 'If they know you've been in the UK, they'll ask you, are you a cleaner or a carer,' one said, 'the assumption back home is that everyone is doing that thing' (p. 807).

One expert in the study gave examples of bus driving, a typically male-dominated field, which has comparable training to care assistant work, but where the pay and conditions exceed it. The fact that bus driving, although not seen as highly skilled or valued, has not been stigmatized as 'women's work' frees it from the five c's of low pay and poor conditions. Like care work, bus driving entails risks in safeguarding the public. Yet, care work requires a type of commitment and specialization that bus driving does not; engaging with passengers has different implications than with clients. A bus driver is replaceable to the extent that another one can get a passenger to his or her destination, whereas a client depends on the relationship for his or her well-being. The difference in pay and conditions and image has not been due so much to market failure, where the 'going rate' for salaries is subject to demand, but to occupational segregation: doing the five c's encompasses a number of penalties despite its contributions to public well-being. Also, professionalization trends in nursing and social work have helped to upgrade care assistant work at the same time that it has created glass ceilings in titles and salaries.

The examples in this chapter demonstrate that the industry has secured a skilled migrant female-dominated workforce to implement its reforms over and beyond simply filling a care deficit. The former health care professionals' new practices were shown to enhance a sector that changed its official standards and workload without consulting its traditional workforce (Pyle, 2006). This occurred at the expense of these migrants' 'deskilling' to be discussed at length in Chapter 5. Again, these skilled migrants didn't simply offload their skills in a new country, but modified existing ones, which considerably expanded the quality of care for older persons. The 'care capital' that this workforce commanded upgraded it beyond systemic reforms of personalization with its rhetoric of independence and control. In this sense, these migrants regulated the industry 'from below.' While there is little evidence that the new practices of migrant former health care professionals were integrated into national policies or even into company regulations, their continual recruitment suggests that employers desired their skills and cultural capital. The next chapter focuses on a close-up picture of the community and workplace contexts of the participants.

4
A Place of Settlement and Upheaval

Introduction

This chapter focuses on a microcosm of the worlds of migrant care assistants in elder care and how their struggles to survive created solidarity on the one hand and tightened their hold on the global care industry on the other. Capturing these participants' daily work lives, as well as their mobility and networks, was important in understanding their adaptation strategies and perceptions. I interviewed 20 migrant domiciliary care assistants and drove around with ten of them at all hours of day and night for a year.[1] In this chapter, I profile their experiences of preparing for, and delivering, a new type of care service in Cumbria, a rural region in North West England. I argue that these participants' constant driving and other hidden services they provided, while not included in policy discourses, was an important neglected area that warrants in-depth exploration to understand the local and global position of skilled migrant women in this industry.

As a passenger in these participants' cars as they drove to clients' homes, shopped for them and waited for their calls, as well as an observer in the homes of the infirm elderly that they visited, I was able to witness the hidden curriculum of the provision of domiciliary care by people who were regarded as strangers in their communities and what this meant. This curriculum was not evident in the training materials or courses that I analysed, but it was clear in the fine print of company policies, as well as in the transactions with clients and with supervisors and colleagues. I came to understand how care was perceived, and about the hasty relationships and arrangements that are made within this mushrooming service that is rarely seen or discussed in depth. Finally, documentation that the care assistants, domiciliary companies and clients shared with me complemented the direct interactions and enabled me to understand the routes these care assistants followed and the procedures with which they complied and also sometimes altered.

These care assistants were pressured to provide 'fast care' by private companies that operated under cost efficiency models. These mobile workers drove to clients' homes to deliver care through a pre-determined plan that the company created and contracted out to them. This meant that they had to develop instant familial relations with the clients and swiftly complete their assigned tasks. As homes were spread very far apart from one another, a nagging worry of these care assistants was how to move the transactions speedily and in time with the clock and the care plan. The agency strictly monitored and managed their work by remote control through a strategy of what Cameron Macdonald (2011, p. 92) has referred to as 'puppeteer management.' This management strategy is characterized by one-way communication, low trust on the part of the employer, no shared decision-making, and a lack of autonomy for the workers (MacDonald, 2011, p. 169). It entails rules and informal enforcements that micro-regulate employees from afar as if they were marionettes; one participant used the term 'puppet,' to express how her manager treated her. Due to working in private homes where they were not watched closely by their supervisors, company policies were punitive and rigid including demanding large amounts of documentation from domiciliary care assistants. Unofficial means of keeping these workers tied to their companies included overfilling their rotas (work schedules), which put them on an on-call basis.

The penalties, as we shall see, were higher for migrants because they were recent employees and outsiders in a new area and lacked relational power. This issue of migrant workers encountering blurry boundaries in client's homes, particularly the more vulnerable live-ins, has been highlighted in the domestic care literature (see, Gordolon and Lalani, 2009; Lutz, 2011). Although working in the home, the participants were agency-based (no participants lived with clients) and the companies, as much as they tried, couldn't control everything that took place in the clients' homes. This fact gave these domiciliary care assistants a certain amount of independence from their companies, something that was highlighted in Chapter 3 but has been little discussed in the literature. This chapter focuses on the triple axis of disadvantage these participants faced—of working in domiciliary care services in England, in a rural region, and having a migrant status—but also the ways they survived, and, in some cases, transformed this dynamic. The chapter is divided into four parts. The first part profiles England's domiciliary care service. The second describes the rural area to which these women migrated. Next, a mobilities framework focuses on the participants' physically mobile (although not socially mobile) working lives, and, lastly, the ways their migrant status impacted on their experiences is illustrated with two portraits.

The rise of domiciliary care

Across Europe and North America, sweeping legislation has focused on the economic benefits of deinstitutionalizing services for older persons under welfare reforms making home-based care the most popular alternative and the workers its 'backbone' (Aronson and Neysmith, 1996, p. 61). Recent legislation in England has focused on keeping older people in their homes as long as possible. The mantra of autonomy, choice, and control characterize this agenda with reformers hailing it as an era of 'person-centred care.' Older persons, at the centre of this service, expect care to come to them. A regime of self-assessments, means testing, risk management around budgets, and services for individual outcomes of the 'service user' (clients) implements this reform. Making direct cash payments to clients means, in theory, that they can choose the best care for their needs. They can employ care assistants through an agency (like these participants) or neighbours and family members can also provide paid care. As of 2008, over 73,500 older persons in England received direct payments with 150,000 choosing to finance their own care in their private homes (Wainwright, 2009).

The Personalisation Agenda, named for its individual responsibility ethos, was officially introduced in 2008 through policies articulated in, *Putting People First* (National Health Service, 2007) and *Transforming Social Care* (Department of Health, 2008). These objectives can be traced back to a 1989 Department of Health policy and the 1990 National Health Service and Community Care Act which transferred authority to local councils to contract with care businesses for the goal of independent living (Kendall, Matosevic, Forder, Knapp, Hardy, and Ware, 2003). Policy-makers felt that the social care system needed to be dismantled and reformed, especially funding, but also standards, rules, information dissemination, and services (Secretary of State for Health, 2009). Older people (85 years and over), around 1.4 million in total, were encouraged to stay in their own homes thereby giving rise to home care services, a £2.7 billion growing business (Eborall, Fenton and Woodrow, 2010; NHS Information Centre, 2009). This agenda, in an effort to make older persons self-sufficient, encouraged them to direct their own care in their homes. In developing their care regimens, clients became de facto employers. Yet the system of 'routed wages' (cash pay outs to clients in order to employ care assistants) is problematic in that it is difficult to keep boundaries in the home (Ungerson, 2004). Direct payments to older clients were found to increase expectations of their care assistants, thus creating a perfect storm (Poinasamy, 2009). Related to this, unions have expressed concerns about the exploitation of home-based care assistants in not getting paid the national minimum wage, not receiving sick pay or pensions, and the 'slide in to the informal economy' (Cangiano, Shutes, Spencer, and Leeson, 2009, p. 15).

Because the caregiving happens in the domicile of the client, the workers are called 'domiciliary care assistants.' In other countries they are referred to as 'home helps,' 'home caregivers,' or 'home health aides.' The work that domiciliary care assistants do differs from that of other care assistants in institutional settings. The word 'home' is critical because the client's dwelling is *their* workplace, settings to which they come in and out of up to four times a day in some instances. While the workers are regulated, these 'workplaces' are unregulated; some are small, others are large, and they can be clean or filthy, filled with other family and carers as well as things. They may also be barren. Domiciliary care assistants have to fit their work routines and bodies around these intimate spaces.

As mentioned, working directly in the home, care assistants are in ambiguous territory (Gordolon and Lalani, 2009). The client, for example, may confuse the care assistant with a family carer whose caregiving is perceived as altruistic. Significantly, the care assistant is backgrounded to the client as a type of 'shadow' worker—an extension of the client's body and the face of a private provider. This agenda makes difficult the care assistant's work to support older clients' 'independence'—a term coined by policymakers—since they are clearly *dependent* on their care assistants. This home-based agenda increases the vulnerability of migrants in particular who, as former professionals and outsiders, feel they have to prove their worth, providing extra or 'philanthropic' care (Bolton and Boyd, 2003, p. 292).

With these new provisions, the Personalisation Agenda brings domiciliary care closer to that of personal services and further from the social care sector, its official home. What are personal services? The personal services sector prizes individual entrepreneurialism and is part of the soft tertiary economy that focuses on intangible goods like time and the body, with occupations that range from nail salon work to sewing services to massage therapy. Physical work that is demanded in personal services crosses the formal and informal sector, is historically privatized, and has been done by women, often migrants. This work tends to be hands-on, often repetitive, and with scripted expressions (McDowell, 2009). This configures the domiciliary care assistants as 'carriers' of a pre-packaged care to be delivered on the dot to elderly customers as if it were a 'relational good' (Kendall, et al., 2003, p. 491). The care worker's body and labour can be bought and sold through this policy (England and Dyck, 2011). From the small body of literature on domiciliary care assistants' working conditions, it appears that their work is more intensive because it takes place in the home, and there is limited staff time and energy for an all-encompassing job. There tends to be more women among domiciliary care assistants than in other institutionalized care and, as discussed in Chapter 3, this is mainly because it stems from a history of women's informal work in the home.

A study of domiciliary care assistants in England by Gemma Wibberley (2011) found that her British-born participants often faced difficult situations with many of their activities not being officially counted or included in their job descriptions. The problems revolved around hourly wages that didn't encompass their actual work, including travel time to and from houses, and other informal (emotional) labour that was expected to satisfy clients. The care assistants' internalization of the image of the 'good domiciliary' worker who puts herself second to her client conflicted with the frustration they experienced with their public image—of making tea and doing little else despite their physical labour and skilful negotiations. It was difficult for them to make positive changes in their work lives. Consequently, a number of the participants felt that their only option was to leave their jobs. Wibberley profiles the intensification of labour as a precursor to high turnover in the industry and the care assistants' tenacity and exodus. While there is little evidence that domiciliary care managers, who work in care facilities, target and recruit migrants, it is clear that the high vacancy rate creates a void that migrants fill. For rural areas, in particular, this issue is compounded. The next section discusses domiciliary care with relation to rurality.

National, regional, and local demographics

While numbers of domiciliary care workers are hard to pinpoint because those who are 'on the books' are often enumerated in addition to those providing care to self-funded clients (Eborall and Garmeson, 2001,

p. 14), there are estimated to be over a half a million domiciliary care assistants across England. They work in about 6,000 registered domiciliary agencies, with another 2,400 unregistered ones. These businesses are growing, are mostly private (74%), and reflect the burgeoning privatization of the global care industry itself (Eborall, Fenton, and Woodrow, 2010; Froggatt, Davies, and Meyer, 2009).

Cumbria, where the domiciliary study took place, has a large amount of domiciliary care services over other types of care provision. Local government data sets (in 2011) show that there are 43 registered agencies, most are small, and they provide the largest amount of services in Cumbria to around 40,700 adults. They employ about 1,200 care and senior care assistants, 83 per cent of whom are female, which is higher than other care establishments although lower than the national average for domiciliary care agencies (94%) (Cangiano et al., 2009; Eborall, Fenton and Woodrow, 2010, p. 72). As previously mentioned, males are typically not recruited into domiciliary care because of its domestic image and older women often say they don't want to be alone with them in their homes. However, other factors, such as the capricious nature of the work itself and the on-call hours, with little compensation, may also be inhibiting factors for recruiting and retaining men. Nevertheless, *migrant* male domiciliary care assistants are hired in greater amounts than in the population of male care assistants in institutionalized care suggesting that migrancy trumps gender in a high vacancy service and in rural areas (discussed below) (Cangiano et al., 2009). Domiciliary care assistants do get paid more than most private institutional sites (nationally around £6.50 an hour during the study period), although wages are typically lower in the North West, than in the rest of England, £6.17 an hour (Skills for Care, 2011). Employee turnover in domiciliary care is higher, however (Cangiano et al., 2009), and this trend is reflected in Cumbria with domiciliary agencies experiencing a 26 per cent leaving rate compared to the national average of 19 per cent (Care Sector Alliance Cumbria, 2008). Cumbria also has one of the highest vacancy rates in the North West (Skills for Care North West, 2010). One local Cumbrian survey demonstrated that low pay and unsuitable hours topped the list of retention factors for care assistants and that a strategy to solve an immediate need in the supply was to attract more people to the care workforce pool through overseas recruitment (Care Sector Alliance Cumbria, 2008, pp. 7, 10).

Although nationwide migrants compose about 16 per cent of the domiciliary care workforce (Skills for Care, 2011), they are more of a minority (10%) in the North West. By nationality, however, this region reflects national statistics; Filipinos top the list for the non-EEA overseas group (16%), followed by Nigerians and Indians (11%) (Skills for Care, 2011).[2] Likewise in Cumbria, 5.5 per cent of care assistants are non-British, mostly Filipinos and Polish (Skills for Care North West, 2010).[3] Although migrants are a small but growing population, Cumbrian care force policies rarely mention them.

Study sample demographics

The average age of the 20 domiciliary care assistants in this sample (mid 30s) reflected the larger sample of migrant care assistants (see Chapter 1) indicating that the participants were of working age (Cangiano et al., 2009). Over half of the women were married; 13 of them had children, most of who were living outside of the country. Two of these families were united during the study period. The high numbers of both single women and mothers with children living outside of England indicate that this type of job would be difficult to hold for migrant women with locally based families; Lisette's case will illustrate these dilemmas. Most of the participants came to England through recruiters, which suggests that coming to a rural area may necessitate a mediator although, as Chapter 1 showed, this was a norm. Of those who arrived through other migration channels, such as through spouses or partners, all were EEA citizens—the largest group in this sample being Polish. Some of the Polish participants worked in various low-waged jobs (e.g. au pair, cleaner, hotel maid, factory worker) for a short time in England, prior to becoming domiciliary care assistants. They had highly negative experiences in these jobs and saw domiciliary care work as a better option.

Cumbria as a new place of settlement for migrants

Cumbria, a cultural heritage area, is not normally perceived as a place to which migrants come. Yet migrant workers bolster rural areas like Cumbria in terms of promoting job creation and production, particularly in key sectors such as hospitality, food processing, and care (Chappell, Latorre, Rutter, and Shah, 2009, p. 6). Cumbria's scenic Lake District has been the subject of cultural and literary nostalgia since the 19th century and a Wordsworthian leisure destination. The rustic 20th century guidebooks on Lake District walking and touring, as well as 21st century farming genres, do not, however, capture the experience of migrant entry, settlement in, and exit from the new Cumbria

(Tolia-Kelly, 2007). Cumbria becomes a mini-case study of the ways new migrant communities adjust to an area where there is no recent history of mass migration.

Today, like many rural areas across England and the rest of the world, Cumbria is a new place of settlement for migrants (Massey, 2008). Its ethnic minority populations have increased twice as fast as England on the whole (Cumbria County Council, 2010) with hospitality and care being strong magnets. Since the opening of the European A-8 countries in 2004, Eastern Europeans work in Cumbria's bars, restaurants, in the cleaning sector, and in care homes, sending money home, and saving it for their children's education and future moves. It is not uncommon to see Polish newspapers and stores and flourishing memberships in Cumbria's Catholic churches.

Related to this trend, Cumbria also has one of the fastest growing older populations in England with a higher percentage living within its boundaries than the national average (Care Sector Alliance Cumbria, 2008; Cumbria County Council, 2005); the over 65s compose about 20 per cent of its population (Director of Public Health, 2009, p. 36). Known for its stark beauty, Cumbria attracts middle-class people of retirement age making it a prime place for health and social care and for spending the grey pound. Paired with the very low birth rate and the lack of working-age people—many of whom leave for the cities and to go to university, this had led to the district becoming known as 'Silver Cumbria' (Cumbria County Council, 2005, p. 31). This burgeoning older population makes high demands on Cumbria's limited medical and social services, including hospital admissions and needs for physical daily care (Director of Public Health, 2009) and so without cut-price care assistants as well as other service workers, Cumbria's economy would shrink considerably. Therefore, active recruitment of migrants has helped solve this problem, advancing the service sectors and creating demographic change.

The presence of migrants, according to a Cumbria County Council (2010) report, *Cumbria's Equality Story*, has not decreased due to the global recession but remained steady, with 2,000 migrants coming to Cumbria each year; this is reflected in the rapid increase of migrants into rural areas across England. Yet these migrants, a largely invisible population to researchers and policymakers, have been found to face the general problems of rural northern English communities—poor health, inadequate education services, isolation, and a downward cycle of poverty, with reports of overcrowded housing, workplace safety hazards, and little access to benefits (Ellery, 2006). Discrimination exists and is both overt and covert as this study and other research across Cumbria have shown (Bremner, 2008). An insulated and homogenous local populace that is not accustomed to ethnic, cultural, and racial diversity compounds these problems. Although a multicultural centre was established in Cumbria to assist migrants and ethnic minorities as well as Citizens Advice Bureaus across the region, problems persist. Evidence of discrimination disputes the myth of rural areas (over urban) as community-minded and caring (Cloke, 1999).

Cumbria's geography has been critical to its economic and social history. Situated between the Irish Sea and the Pennine Hills, Cumbria is the second largest county in England and it covers a sizeable, sparsely populated area (half of the entire North West region) and contains considerable geographic diversity. Socio-economic circumstances have changed the economy for its 500,000 residents (Bennison, 2007) and global capitalism has hit Cumbria hard, creating distinct social classes, and pockets of poverty next to wealth. Rural communities have been forced to move from agriculture (in north and east Cumbria), and manufacturing (in west Cumbria), after the decline from shipping to a service economy. The southern coastal areas like Barrow and Worthington are undergoing drastic transitions from sea-related manufacturing. In northern and eastern Cumbria, historically agricultural, farming has declined, especially with the 2001 foot-and-mouth disease outbreak leaving a vacuum for service industries, particularly in health and social care for older persons (Bennison, 2007).

Because infirm older persons tend to be more isolated in Cumbria and have a difficult time accessing social services, domiciliary companies play an important role, especially in an era of personalized care. Two studies of Irish rural domiciliary care reveal critical issues that pertain to Cumbria's situation (Doyle and Timonen, 2009; McCann, Ryan and McKenna, 2005). In these studies, older persons relied heavily on families and social networks for their care. Since loneliness was common, the clients viewed their care assistants, often ones they knew quite well as lifelines, especially when they could talk to them. But these domiciliary care assistants had multiple responsibilities, including informal care for their own families, and didn't have time to really talk to their clients. Although the problem of shorter and shorter visits persists across domiciliary care (McLimont and Grove, 2004), it is more severe in rural areas. Rural road networks were main factors including long travel times that made it difficult for Irish care assistants to spend lots of direct time with clients. Staff shortages were endemic with older persons finding it difficult to find care assistants who could travel such long distances, much of it unpaid.

Major factors which affected the need for domiciliary care services in Cumbria that were gathered from interviews with clients, employers, and staff were similar to the Irish research in that: (1) there were large distances between homes, social services, and shops; (2) there was a minimal amount of available social services for older persons including community centres, nearby hospitals, community clinics, and day care centres; (3) there was a lack of convenient public transport that could easily move older persons from one place to another; (4) inclement weather and road conditions made it difficult for older persons to travel even after transportation was provided; and finally (5) different from the Irish elders who were fairly poor, Cumbrian elders tended to be middle-class with adequate resources to pay for domiciliary care. These factors, and others, appeared to enable domiciliary care services to thrive in this County. At the same time, both employers and migrant staff of domiciliary care companies were impacted by these same rural factors.

The two domiciliary companies in the study provided a range of care services. The primary services involved 'personal care.' This encompassed feeding, toileting, showering, bathing, dressing, and other help, such as cleaning and shopping. Other services they provided were: palliative care, respite care, well-being care (e.g. gardening), night services, and emergency care. The employers sought migrant workers in order to alleviate staff turnover and vacancies, recognizing that their businesses were growing and that they needed more coverage. In one company, migrants composed about 10 per cent of its workforce. Employers perceived their migrant employees as hard-working, liking the training, and complying with company policies and regulations. The problems they experienced surrounded miscommunication issues due to perceived language barriers of the migrants. Also there were problems over driving and assisting migrants with their settlement into the area. These 'problems' again were perceived by the employers to be more personal and 'cultural' rather than related to company policies and the rural context. Employers were also sensitive to British-born care assistants being upset if they were seen to assist migrants with basic necessities with which they also struggled. When migrant employees were said to be abused by or discriminated against by clients, the employers felt there was little they could do other than to give them more training and request that they report such matters, as well as reassign them to other places. The protection of these employees was less of an issue than keeping the clients and making them happy. As an Oxfam report on this issue highlighted (Poinasamy, 2009), legislation has not protected migrant care assistants from their employers or from clients. A conceptual lens enriches understanding of migrant care assistants and their labour, mobility, and persistence.

A mobilities framework to understand the issues of migrant domiciliary care assistants

> Because we have to use our own car, it is bad for mileage... if we have to change the wheels, do the MOT [legal requirement to show that the car is in good working order] buy the tax, change the oil—we have to pay for it ourselves. On the last job I changed the oil in my car and the filter once a year. Here, it is every three months. I have to pay £25 three times a year, so much! Nobody gives me money for that.

Anastazja's story of using her car for domiciliary care work in this rural region reveals the hidden labour and costs in maintaining it as a prerequisite for her work. Through interviewing and travelling with Anastazja and others on Cumbrian roads and by observing their movements in the homes, I could gauge the reach of what it meant to care in a vast rural region.

The bulk of research has focused on care as a physical, task-oriented activity ('caring for') as well as one that is perceptual and relational ('caring about'), although the people who are caregivers often consider these to be the same (England and Dyck, 2011; Tronto, 1992). Where the care occurs is critical too and has been referred to as 'care-in-place' (Milligan, 2009; Milligan and Wiles, 2010, p. 746). That is, care that is directly meted out in particular locations and spaces or landscapes; at a household level, for example, this would consist of the ways care is created and perceived by various actors, including the use of medical equipment and technologies in clients' rooms. At a community level, a care in place model considers the roles and activities of neighbours, friends, and family involved in care provision. It is valuable for highlighting the descriptive elements of care processes in places and the various actors involved in giving and receiving it and their embodied relations and practices (Roberts, Mort, and Milligan, 2012).

Policies, however, tend to focus on, and regulate, care in terms of 'contact hours,' the *amount* of which is assessed and monitored; for example, in a given week, one association found that 'an estimated 4.1 million contact hours were provided' (The NHS Information Centre, 2009, p. 7). Although care minutes would be a more appropriate measure of actual care provision (since most clients are seen in 30-minute intervals), the focus here is on the amount of time the care assistant has with the client irrespective of place and the meaning it has, including physical and emotional, for both parties. Furthermore, care includes other related activities, such as driving and maintaining cars, which are typically excluded in policies.

A mobilities framework offers a wider context for evaluating domiciliary care work in terms of its preconditions (like the rural areas and homes where care assistants work), its *preparation* (cars and driving), and its *points of contact* (hands-on care delivery/provision). Under this lens, care work becomes fluid and embodies physical, emotional, social, and spatial dimensions, as well as the movement of capital, status, and power. Mobile methods (Buscher and Urry, 2009, p. 99) focus on the interplay between migrant domiciliary care assistants as drivers and the roads they travel on in reaching clients' homes, but also their movements in the homes and the outcomes of their actions, as well as their perspectives, within larger socio-economic and political spheres. This perspective on mobilities in workplaces contrasts with Taylor's motion studies of workers intended to gather one model of labour-saving work processes (Ritzer, 2008). By tracking the journeys of these migrant domiciliary care assistants, it was possible to understand precisely *how* domiciliary care services thrived in a measureless and beautiful landscape, even while its ageing population and workers remained hidden from view.

Preparation of care: The role of cars and driving

This section focuses on the ways these workers exercised their labour and agency via cars and care. Driving cars is a necessary part of the preparation for care. In this way, cars are, metaphorically, the 'chains, paths, threads, conjunctions, or juxtapositions' (Marcus in Buscher and Urry, 2009) of the social reproductive work of the personal services economy, especially in recovering rural areas like Cumbria. The important work of driving cars should fill a gap in the literature on the 'body work of care' (Twigg, Wolkowitz, Cohen, and Nettleton, 2011; Wolkowitz, 2006).

The stressful workload, created by domiciliary care assistants' profit-driven companies, often made them feel chained to their cars. The participants used their cars to rush from one house to another in order to get through each designated task in the homes, ones that were paid by the clients on a bit-by-bit basis. Their abilities to care in genuine relational terms, a 'caring about' (Tronto, 1992), therefore was often diminished. One care assistant described her workday, in a diary, as follows, with her driving between homes being a major factor in her schedule:

> Mrs GM lives in the village near to my home, but it takes about 15–20 minutes to get there that's why I had to start the first client a little bit earlier to get there on time. Mrs GM has asthma problems and she needs help getting dressed, making her bed, making breakfast, and washing up. The next client lives in another village so very often we are late having to hurry. Mrs KT can't move very well. She wanted me to make her breakfast, prepare lunch for later on, and get a few things from the shop. Mrs TW lives very close to the previous client, almost no traveling time. We gave her a full body wash, dressed her, gave her a fresh pad. Then I had half an hour time to get to Mrs GM, the same lady that I had been in the morning. I made her lunch during the visit. I had a break from 12.30 until 14.00. The real time of the break is shorter as I have to travel from the last client and leave my house to get to the first client after the break.

This is a case where driving to and from clients' homes is central to the care assistant's workday. Apart from getting to and from clients' houses, driving served multiple other functions such as: (1) mobile offices for sorting and organizing paperwork; (2) 'therapeutic journeys' (Ferguson, 2009, p. 275) for analysing environments and sharing stories about work and life with colleagues; and (3) for doing favours for clients and colleagues.

Alice, a domiciliary care assistant, uses her car for a number of these functions, especially as a mobile office (Figure 4.1). Although it is not apparent, 'a carer on call' tag is on the dashboard to alert community members that her parked car is for the purpose of helping neighbours and she should therefore not be reported to the police. The portability of the materials and technologies, from the pens in her pocket to the mobile phones and log sheets on her clipboard, is obvious and litter the car in designated places. One mobile phone is for her personal use while the other is for the office. The car sounds like a disco when they simultaneously sound with different rings and vibrations. While driving, the office staff text her and call her to switch her rota or convey information about a new client, including information on how to get to their home. She said, 'I like to be busy while I drive.' She has her own GPS navigator

Figure 4.1 Alice in her car

but rarely uses it in Cumbria, as she knows her routes well. Like many of the care assistants who carry 16-hour work shifts, Alice spends much time in her car on any one day. As she sits in a client's driveway, she logs the time of the visits and the mileage so that she is compensated. A young woman pops by her car window and says hello—she is a former colleague who now works in a care home. Alice says good-bye to her upon seeing another car approach the clients' house. She realizes she needs to move her car because the cleaner needs to get in to the driveway.

Alice then takes off. Driving to the private homes on her daily round is swiftly navigated. As Alice circles around the familiar and narrow roads, she scans around, as would the police, and searches for people and any activities in these otherwise quiet neighbourhoods. As she drives through the neighborhoods, she sees other care assistants coming and going from different residences, and acknowledges them. Alice is a mentor to new migrant care assistants and allows them to shadow her when they first arrive. Although they discuss work involved in caring, they also relate personal matters and speak in Tagalog, the official language of the Philippines. Still other times, she uses her car to pick up items for clients or to do favours for colleagues, which are both paid and unpaid. Alice sometimes lends her car to these colleagues when theirs break down or if they don't pass their MOTs. Sometimes these care assistants are afraid to tell the management (which they call 'the office') about this type of problem so they come by her house and ask to use her car. She finds this situation difficult and doesn't like to say no to them and has been training the new recruits to be upfront with management. On this day, she stops by the office and reports events to the clerical staff who create the rotas and liaise between the care assistants and the clients. One issue that Alice is struggling with is finding the home of a new client because the directions in the care plan are not clear and she needs a map, which she looks at before she sets off again. She discusses Cathe, a new recruit, with the office staff and mentions her problems with a recently bought second-hand car that broke down. She recently drove Cathe to see a friend in ice and snow, the two returning home at 4.00 a.m. for their shifts to start at 7.00. Alice told this story to a client who laughed and recommended that she 'change friends.' The role of cars in domiciliary care services then is paramount to working, relating, and caring. Yet their journeys could be blocked through traffic jams, accidents, breakdowns, and bad weather conditions, as well as road work that altered their set routes. Furthermore, many of the participants complained that their backs, arms, and hands hurt as a result of the constant driving.

Care at the point of contact: The delivery of care in homes

While the care research tends to focus on care tasks in the home and policies compute this to time and money, little attention is paid to the workers' movements involved in the personal care of clients' bodies. This bodywork involves washing intimate parts, and silences, jokes, and other verbal interactions that come with this contact zone. Sometimes distance rather than closeness between client and care assistant is more common due to the clinical emphasis, with gloves, for example, that are considered to be professional distancing devices (Twigg, 2000). These bodywork practices form the 'intimate labours' discussed in Chapter 1 that involve the physical movement of care, at the nexus of gender, race, and the market economy (Boris and Parrenas, 2010).

In homes, the participants exhibited movements similar to driving their cars in their orbiting of familiar communities; as nimble dances in the homes, the care assistants circumnavigated the clients and their cherished objects in confined spaces. Their care was executed in a timely manner so that it was cost-efficient for the company and accommodating to the clients in anticipating their moods and their needs. After many observations, these movements were classed as:

1) Taxing and efficient: The care assistants entered quickly in to homes, using codes to get inside, putting on their gloves and aprons and immediately tackling the tasks that were awaiting them, including heaving assorted items, carefully lifting clients on hoists, wiping down counters, throwing rubbish, checking the care plan, and gathering items, some of which were heavy, all the while watching the clock.
2) Fast and tense: Due to the time limits that were dictated and the rushed nature of the interaction (most of the clients desired them to stay longer than they had time for), the atmosphere was hurried and slightly strained with polite conversation, smiles, and rapid assessments of likes and dislikes surrounding medicine, food, and other issues, in order to avoid further favours and questions.
3) Habitual and flitting: In the homes the care assistants' actions were adroitly manoeuvred to make the clients comfortable especially when they were familiar and liked them—care assistants moved around with ease, teased, laughed, and assessed in an informal tone. Additionally, after all of the physical interactions were finished, and at the end of a typical 30-minute session, the care assistants completed paperwork, often scanning and then copying what they did previously and using shorthand for it—what Stephen Lopez (2007, p. 225) refers to as, 'mock routinization' which entails simultaneously resisting and obeying organizational practices (as the examples in Chapter 3 indicated).

The ways the homes were arranged symbolically and materially expressed the clients' identities and aspirations. Often the clients arranged precious items on cabinets that were like shrines to their past lives and became conversation pieces which enabled the care assistants to connect while allowing the clients to reinvent themselves as stronger and more competent people who were connected to their families and the rest of the world. These included photographs, figurines, vases, collectable items (coins or stamps), paintings, and stuffed animals. Many of these were gifts and others were heirlooms. They were carefully displayed in various parts of the homes but were often in living rooms for infrequent guests to see or in their bedrooms. These objects, unlike the gloves worn by care assistants and other medical equipment (like hoists),

Figure 4.2 Miniature bear figurines

mediated the close physical interactions between clients and care assistants and regained a sense of humanity into the interactions (Ducey, 2010) (Figure 4.2).

Contrasted to these treasured items was hoisting equipment that care assistants needed to use for moving clients. These could change a clients' room into an institutionalized clinical space and pressure care assistants to draw on their own resources to create a homely environment. The hoists were used for bathing clients with low or no mobility in their limbs and also if they were very heavy. The bathing involved two care assistants working together, moving carefully around the clients' bed and possessions. An example would be the home Alice went to for a designated 45-minute visit that was in reality about 30 minutes. There, she met Sallie, a Filipina colleague, who helped her with Mrs Greenwood. They first put on their clear bibs and then gloves. It was 7:05 a.m. when they began this doubled-up shift. This client was in her 70s and debilitated by numerous physical ailments and had dementia too. She was cranky and unpredictable according to Alice and Sallie.

A portrait of Princess Diana hung opposite the bed that she stayed in many hours a day. The care assistants were often ready for her repetitive comments and erratic behaviour, such as giving instructions for them to ask her stuffed animals on the bed if they could be moved. Her bed was in the former dining room and next to her open-plan living room, one she cherished. In this room there were numerous stuffed animals and portraits of animals and figurines on shelves that she collected from catalogues. She used to have a beagle and was fond of them and collected many beagle pictures. On this particular visit Sallie and Alice were dressing Mrs Greenwood and the routine became a dance around her bed and objects.

They used a wrapper to lift her body and each time called 'one-two-three' to make sure they choreographed it right so that she didn't fall, and lowered the bed, attached the wrapper to her and lifted her up in the hoist. She hung in mid-air before they lowered her into a wheelchair. They reminded her it was Friday and that they were changing her bed and Mrs Greenwood said, 'TGIF.' They gave her a bowl with water and a cloth and she washed her face and dried herself. The idea was to support the client to take independent action, where possible. Alice asked, 'Can I help you to get off your shirt,' and she took it off while Sallie made the bed. Alice also removed her urine bag. Mrs Greenwood was naked sitting in the wheelchair and said 'I don't have much energy.' Alice washed her back and Mrs Greenwood interjected thanks and sighed; they moved her back and forth as she was getting wiped and she was humming as they washed her. They also made small talk about birds. Alice said, 'I know the tune you are singing,' and laughed. They moved her back to her bed and Alice asked her 'Can I open your legs to clean' and she said 'Yes,' and they cleaned her genitals with soap, and then dimmed the lights. They towelled her dry and put on her underwear. Mrs Greenwood was singing louder. Working together, they carefully slung her over on the other side using the wrapper to get her trousers on, and they repeated 'one-two-three' when they moved her back. Alice said, 'We are almost finished Mrs Greenwood,' and they washed her upper body and sprayed her with deodorant and then put on her bra and sweater gracefully, although she said, 'Ouch' to which they responded 'Sorry Mrs Greenwood.' Sallie prepared her breakfast and then washed her clothes and put others into the dryer. Alice checked the daily log sheet and communication log book. If something important happened, they wrote in red pen. Sallie wrote the day's events quickly with a blue one:

> Hoisted MG washed and hoisted to bed, trousers on and pad. Hoisted to chair, breakfast prepared and changed, made comfortable in chair. [In red ink]: meds prop + 2 leg LPM and WASHER ON.

After Mrs Greenwood had eaten, Alice combed her hair in the kitchen with a mirror in front of her. There was very little conversation at that point and the voices were soft. The water had boiled and Sallie made her an instant coffee. Both left and cheerily said, 'We'll see you Sunday!'

On this day, Mrs Greenwood had moved naturally with the care assistants as they washed, dressed, and prepared her meal but this was not always the case. She, like other care assistants, often asked for special favours, which were not in the care plan, putting them in awkward positions and delaying their other calls. While most saw the client's requests as benign, they also knew they needed to respect the company's wishes. The care assistants, after all, were deliverers of care services and did not negotiate it directly with clients.

To summarize, mobile methods were used to capture the new spaces and places that the care assistants inhabited, and the feelings and senses surrounding the hidden labour that was not counted—travel time to clients' homes and the complex negotiations they engaged in with the clients in their homes under intense time constraints.

Mobility issues

There were many issues that the migrant domiciliary care assistants dealt with that arose from their difficult work conditions and being outsiders. As 'flexible workers' they were supposed to be on call to their companies. Yet as one participant declared, 'I'm a flexible worker but I don't like this flexible work. I prefer to start work and finish work and then have time for myself.' Work conditions were a contentious and sensitive issue for the participants, especially hours; they felt 'on call,' even on their days off. While long hours were common across the social care sector, and especially in domiciliary care, migrant workers felt other factors were at play, including being given the worst schedules, clients, and tasks. One participant who worked 60-hour weeks said, 'I can't plan my time off properly because I have to wait for my rota for next week.' Another major work problem that these participants struggled with was *cars* and *driving* requirements. Much of this, as discussed previously, was unpaid, including travel time from their homes to the first and last client, car maintenance, insurance, and assistance for car breakdowns. Dangerous cars, scheming mechanics, expensive driving lessons, arduous driving tests and, the aches from constant driving as well as petrol reimbursements at the end of the month were also problems for these participants, as will be illustrated in the following portraits (discussed in Chapter 2).

It started with the rota (Figure 4.3). This schedule organized these workers' movements. An analysis of a rota illustrates some of these

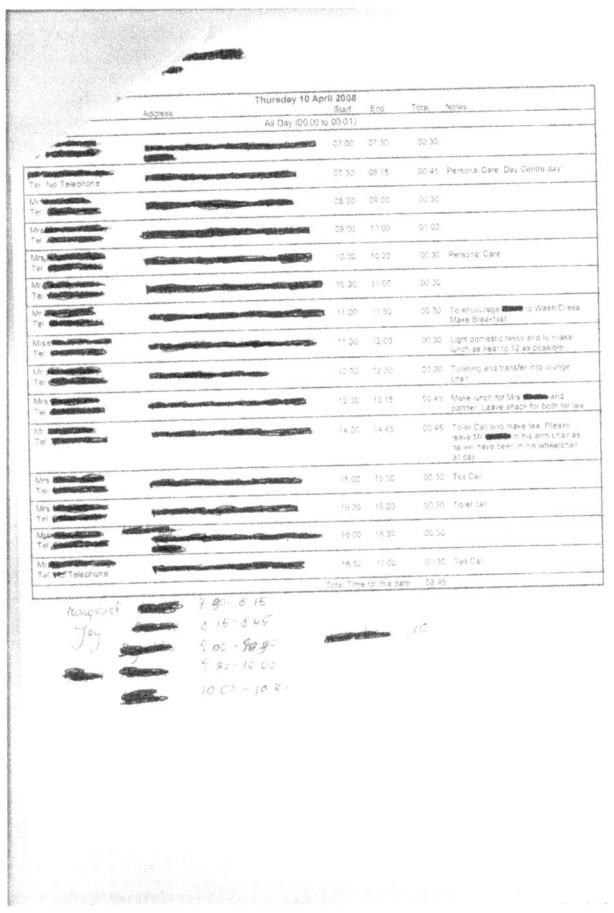

Figure 4.3 Rota

points.[4] This rota demonstrates an intensive amount of driving in a one-day schedule of a migrant domiciliary care assistant in this study. There is almost no travel time between the 15 houses she is expected to visit, except in two cases where there is a 15-minute interval to get from one town to a village and back that was considerably longer in real time. Her first call in the morning and at the end of the day were the longest distances from where she lived and she was not compensated for petrol on these two parts of her journey. She had a back-to-back schedule from 7 a.m. to 5 p.m. (ten hours) with a 45-minute break although the total time she was paid for 'working' was 8 hours and 45 minutes even if she was on call, including her lunch break. The fact that her rota included an all-day schedule in military terms, '00.00–00.01' refers to zero hour contracts and being on-call. One visit was one hour whereas most were 30 minutes. There were five changed times below, written in pencil by the office staff, which the care assistant found difficult to read and which altered her entire morning. Also there were no notes to accompany these changes, making it hard for her to estimate the issues she would encounter once she reached the house. One client who was at the beginning and end of her shift didn't have a phone, which made it impossible for her to call when she was running late. The notes were also unclear, for example, 'encourage [client] to wash/dress make breakfast' does not indicate the emotional labour and time involved in supporting a client to do this, especially if he (as in this case) refuses or indicates he does not want his assistant to wash, eat breakfast or get dressed. Also these are treated as if they are all one activity (wash/dress is separated by a slash).

It also doesn't include the racism or ethnocentrism that infused the interactions. One participant, for example, was frequently told to 'fuck off' when she walked into one clients' home, wishing her good morning, and in another, a male client constantly accused her of stealing British jobs, holding up *The Daily Mail* (a tabloid newspaper) as evidence. Other participants were simply told by clients that they weren't needed and didn't want them to return. Although some clients had dementia, racial discrimination mixed in, creating a complex situation for participants to defend themselves and feel justified in reporting these incidents to their supervisors. Other examples of 'othering' were participants being asked how long they intended to stay in England or inferring that their English was inadequate because they had different accents. They were also sometimes given diminutive names like being called 'little.' One employer called her migrant employees, 'clannish' and didn't understand why they lived together while another told an employee who threatened to leave: 'I bought you from the recruiter' leaving her to feel like an indentured servant, or 'slave' as the participant more bluntly put it. The hours, car issues, and 'othering' made these participants question their situations, especially when they borrowed money and signed contracts, which created additional pressures to stay in companies in which they felt mistreated. As one participant remarked, 'I am not here just to work 24 hours. I am not here to just to have fun either. I'm working very hard and I need some time to myself. That's not fair. I feel that's not right.'

Mobility portraits: Lisette and Elzbieta

The following portraits paint pictures of two very different migrant women domiciliary care assistants and the ways they survived their intensive work in a rural area as outsiders, dealing with difficult conditions. I use a mobilities framework, previously described, to frame the ways they coped with these conditions—the hyper-physical mobility of driving and moving fast at work is paired with the participants' low social mobility of not moving up in their chosen fields. Both women characterized their identities at work as highly controlled, as 'dolls' or 'puppets,' making it difficult for them to change their circumstances. Lisette and Elzbieta's cases reveal these issues.

Lisette

Lisette, 49, and from the Philippines, wanted as many hours as possible to support her husband and 16-year old son, who had arrived recently, and the cost of a new flat. Typically her shifts began at 5 p.m. and ended at 8 a.m. and she admitted these were long, but they paid for the cost of her housing. Yet Lisette's housing arrangements were shaky due to her Bangladeshi landlord demanding additional fees for a TV license and refusing to give her a tenancy agreement. Lisette conjectured that he didn't want to report the flat to the government as income. Her husband tried to reason with him because he used to work in Saudi Arabia and in knowing Bangladeshis, felt he knew how to 'speak their language.' The flat was difficult to afford on her and her husband's salary—£500 a month plus, £150 in Council taxes—plus personal expenses and remittances, so she took in a male care assistant who had arrived recently from the Philippines. She was excited about this prospect because he could be a role model for her son and contribute to the rent. This arrangement worked out well, especially because of the different shifts they all did which staggered their times together and let the young man and son bond, especially over video games. Her husband had recently located a job at a local restaurant where he worked ten-hour days.

Lisette struggled with her son's asthma that flared unpredictably and needed much attention. Previously she was sending money home to him in the Philippines and with her salary in England she could afford it—one month's wages in England equalled her year's nursing assistant salary in Luzon. She had also invested in a college savings plan since he was four. Finally, she decided that as her husband was finding it difficult to take care of their son, the best move would be to sponsor them both to come to England: 'Because my husband is afraid of him having another attack.' Once he got older she planned to send him back to the Philippines and bring over his sister who was eight and currently living with Lisette's sister and mother. Lisette declared, 'I will not spend money in going home for my holiday but rather I will just bring her here.' She also worried about his growing independence and complained that he was not mature enough to cope well in a new country. She said, 'Oh, my son is a bit childish. I bought him a guitar. I bought him a skateboard, and now he's doing that in the park.' She also arranged a volunteer position for him at a day care centre to pass the time because he seemed bored. According to Lisette, he played games with the older clients there, and, when he beat them, shouted, 'I won! I want my prize!' Moreover, she worried that her son's new habit of smoking cigarettes would inflame his asthma and wondered if her husband (or boarder) was capable of dealing with a potential emergency. She said:

> [My son] keeps on disobeying me. If I say don't do that and then he would just say, right, I will not do that, but he is doing that. Even though I am scolding him or I am nagging him, he's just laughing at me. At his age he really he wants to be independent. He wants to do whatever he wants to do but he is not normal you know. I cannot leave him to have an asthma attack outside and because one time it happened so I am a bit scared about that and I talked to the doctor. That's the only fear I have. I don't want this to happen to my son.

Her positive experience with the doctors quelled her fears about her son's asthma, especially because 'they're very supportive' and she felt like he was getting good treatment. Lisette was also concerned about her son's relations with other students in school, particularly girls who called and flirted with him on the phone, one of who initiated sex. She said, 'I think the girls are too aggressive because they are open with that kind of stuff. We are a bit conservative about that.'

Meanwhile at work, there was more stress because Lisette's manager was investigating an abuse allegation and the care assistants were all under scrutiny, including having to document more of their work and participate in individual meetings that detracted from the care. Lisette explained:

> We are being given paper work to write everything we did in the shift, even the minutes, even the hour, so instead of concentrating on the care that we give to clients, sometimes we have this headache of, 'oh what else I've done this afternoon?' Even talking to somebody outside, you should put it down.

Nancy was Lisette's partner for the graveyard shift. She was a British national and in her 50s. They did so many shifts together that they referred to each other as 'husband and wife.' She pointed to Lisette and said, 'That's my wife over there—we used to work five to six nights a week, then we got a divorce when we went on holiday, and now we are back together, again—we have to double up to do night shifts. If we had a falling out it wouldn't work.' Before their shift, they filled in forms in tandem, which Nancy called 'ridiculous' with Lisette writing in her time chart and Nancy composing a night report—these were nearly complete before they left in Nancy's car since they knew the routine by heart, as well as each other. Nancy was a single parent of a daughter who was also a care assistant at the same company. She went on to say, with Lisette nodding in agreement, 'No disrespect to the English girls—they don't want to do care work—there's a lot of lovely people like Lisette and Polish lasses. English girls don't do it.' She added, 'Me and my daughter are the only ones. I don't work with English.'

During their shift, Nancy, who drove the car, directed the show at each house they entered. She even stopped along the road at night to watch a deer eating flowers and both of them peered out of the window in silence. At the first house, there was Mrs Salisbury who broke her leg and was in a stylish cast. She had a fall and her bones weren't healing well. Mrs Salisbury came down the hall slowly in an electric wheelchair when they entered. Nancy said, 'Here comes speedy!' They both laughed. Her husband, also in the corridor, watched the scene. Both care assistants propped her in the Zimmer frame (walker). The two split up and Nancy made her bed while Lisette helped her to get a book. Agatha Christie, *Dumb Witness* was what she said she wanted to read. Nancy walked her into the bathroom while Lisette got her a glass of water. In the large bedroom, Lisette completed a log, and Nancy was helping Mrs Salisbury out of the bathroom. Lisette slowly wrote about the activities that they planned to do. She wrote: 'get up from the lounge, bring to bedroom, change nightie, and commode.' Then Lisette exclaimed, 'Oh it is not lounge but living room.' Nancy brought in Mrs Salisbury to her bed and undid her skirt and took off her shoes. Lisette folded some clean clothes near her bed and Nancy lifted off her skirt and unfastened her bra, with Mrs Salisbury commenting that 'this is not my favourite one.' Nancy put on her nightgown and asked about putting cream on her legs. Lisette filled the 'cream' in on a separate log, as this task was important. Mrs Salisbury pointed to a medicine box and she told them, 'I need 2 milligrams.' She drank water and held the cup with Nancy supporting her. Nancy then put eye drops in her eyes with Lisette supporting Mrs Salisbury even though it was not on the care plan. Mrs Salisbury expected that. Nancy said, 'We have been putting eye drops in the eyes of our children!' Mrs Salisbury claimed she was thirsty and Lisette got her another glass of water. There was no commode so Lisette set it up near the bed so Mrs Salisbury could relieve herself at night without walking too far. They looked at each other and when Nancy said 'Yes,' she hit the remote and the bed raised so Mrs. Salisbury could read. She asked for her glasses. Nancy put the lamp nearer on the night table, and said, 'How is that?' Mrs. Salisbury then told them after they removed her hearing aids, 'I'm out of circulation!'

Nancy and Lisette then drove back to the agency lounge. They fell asleep on makeshift pillows on the couch since the office took out the regular ones (to prevent the care assistants from sleeping). They set the alarms to get up shortly. They knew sleeping was against company policies but decided that breaking the rules meant they could survive these long shifts into the future. Since very few quality standards are actually guaranteed for these workers (Rubery and Urwin, 2011), they often have to create their own informal rules (Lopez, 2007).

Lisette was careful with this relationship because Nancy's daughter once made racist comments to her to which she retorted and the two were not on good terms. Also Lisette didn't have a car and depended on Nancy for hers in order to do her shifts. Driving with Nancy was better than walking, which was what happened a few years back, after she got into an accident in her car in another town. She said, 'Because I didn't have my car and I had to do that work and then you cannot say no because it is in your rota, it's very hard for me.' Lisette wanted to drive again and needed a provisional license as her international one had already expired. Although she was studying for the driving test, the stress of the job, her housing difficulties, her son's problems, and other physical issues were blocking her from concentrating on it. She said, 'I'm not just ready for the test because my mind has to absorb all the things that I'm reading now because I am stressed about what I'm doing now. I keep on reading, but it doesn't... sometimes I feel lazy, getting older. I think, but I have to because the licence of my husband will expire this coming year.' Lisette's sore arm also made it difficult to grasp things at work and a client, who had a similar problem, gave her some advice and told her to go to a doctor. She reflected, 'Oh my god. At my age, at my early age.'

At 49, Lisette's age *was* an issue. She wanted to migrate to Canada originally but she said the government's upper age limit would not permit her to do so and England was the most financially viable alternative. She migrated through a recruiter who was introduced to her by a friend in the Philippines. After accepting her application, giving her tests (including driving), and English language exams, the recruiter processed her migration papers to England. Since her husband had been abroad in Saudi Arabia she felt it was 'my turn,' as she put it. Yet even when the recruiter suggested going to Saudi Arabia too, she said no, because she heard that Filipinas were mistreated there and, 'my husband wouldn't let me go.'

A series of problematic events occurred after she arrived in England. To work, she was required to purchase a car, which her company helped her buy by loaning her the money. However, she got into a car accident soon after starting the job. The experience of hitting another car and working in what she felt was an unfriendly community, which was unreceptive to her care, took its toll. On one of her training days, one client confessed to not wanting her around and another male client, who was a prisoner of war, was fearful of Filipinos, thinking they were Japanese guards. The company moved her to another community. Finally, because of the accident and in having to pay her company £500 for the loan she felt the need to compensate for the loss of income by working more hours. All of this produced stress in Lisette. So she relied on her other Filipina colleagues to help her at work. One, who was younger, noted that Lisette's hours were difficult for her in consideration of her age, and on being granted a scheduling position in the company, she gave Lisette a better rota. Also Lisette asserted her needs with management who believed she would work any shift. She thought:

They just don't care or think about you. It's because you are so hard working. They just think because I'm flexible, I can do it on the day, I can do it in the night.... My time is flexible.

She told her manager, 'I want to change my availability and if you could give me a morning course—I'm not leaving the night—but I'm going to just reduce my hours in my schedule, so they decided.' Still, she felt that this manager was so controlling of her actual work that she felt like a puppet on a string: 'It's just like, the carer is like a puppet to her. She said, "don't do this," and you will stop on this one, and then, "don't do this".' Despite her colleagues' scheduling interventions, Lisette felt vulnerable at work and thought she had to suppress herself because:

I've learned that I am a foreigner here. In the Philippines I'd be treated equally. I have to be *under* to understand people here. You cannot say no. You have to obey first. I am in another country, you must understand them. Before you say no you must say yes.

Although consenting, Lisette didn't always act on this idea: 'First I follow, then change my mind.' Yet with everything that was going on, she felt that she could not pursue her dream of becoming a midwife (her training in the Philippines), as this encompassed a number of steps that would operate as barriers in her life. To begin she had to take and pass the IELTS exam, then, apply for her pin number (a registration with the NMC that allows midwives to practice in the UK), and afterwards, attend an overseas nursing programme. She didn't know if she had the motivation and was conflicted about what to do, given her limited resources and time:

It depends on me if I will, you know, push for this kind of career. I'd like to do it and at the moment I think I'm a bit mixed up if I will do this or not.... That is one of my big ambitions—I'd like to do that. It will not be pursued. It's just another stress of my life.... Or barrier in my career to push or whatever I want to do, because it's a matter of having an allowance or having your money.

Elzbieta

Elzbieta was 24 and from a small town in Poland. She wanted to start over after a string of personal and professional disappointments in Poland and the USA. She had worked for a few years in catering in the USA and after breaking up with an abusive boyfriend there, never wanted to return. Her mother's health was 'fragile' and although her unemployed sister lived with her parents in Poland and helped out, and Elzbieta called her every day, she didn't want to settle there. Elzbieta recounted:

> After I returned from the US, I definitely didn't want to stay in Poland. I didn't feel ready to come back to Poland. For a month I was just enjoying my family, my home, recovering after a few disappointments. Then I started looking for job opportunities in the social work sector in England.

She said, 'I chose England as it is the nearest English speaking country' which was important because she wanted to improve her teaching career in the international market by using English regularly. But when the teaching requirements in Poland were upgraded to a master's level there, she began to question her goals and decided that her 'big dream' was to move to the USA. She also didn't want to teach teenagers anymore because: 'I look very young. So for me, keeping discipline and having authority is just ridiculous with them.' She felt that the social care sector in England would be compatible with her teaching degree and could lead to working in an office in England. Being a care assistant, then, was viewed as a stepping-stone to something better. Although she really wanted to be a teacher, she reasoned that in England:

> The most important goal here was to first of all I wanted to have the experience of doing social work and second of all I wanted to improve my English because my dream is to be a secretary, like a job in the office.

After surfing the Internet in Poland for jobs abroad, she found her employer via a recruitment agency in Warsaw, who advertised the job as 'social work.' She described the recruitment process as quickly careening out of her control:

> The employment agencies in Poland can't take any money for arranging jobs so I had to pay for the training. I really wanted to start my job that's why I decided to pay. The training itself was completely useless but if I hadn't done it, they wouldn't have given me a contract to sign. That's business in Poland.... Just by pure accident I landed in Cumbria. She [the employer] suggested that I live with her and share the rent. I was very surprised by the offer as she didn't know me at all but I had nothing to lose. I agreed.

Upon working as a care assistant, however, she concluded that care work may be the best she could get in England, reasoning that she would at least be 'helping' people even though the work was far from being a long-term career goal. Disappointed that the job turned out not to be anything like social work, she said:

> What can I say because I am helping and I wanted to have this experience and want to help people but I feel deep inside unfulfilled because of the work. I am not using all of my skills. My goal, right now is a one-year contract and maybe in the meantime I will find something better.

Even though she was committed to the job, she felt dehumanized as a migrant at work, as she put it: 'You are just put into a drawer like an immigrant and you don't feel equal.' She was also offended by the number of intrusive questions she was asked by her British supervisor about her personal life and future plans, which, she thought, was uncharacteristic of the English; she felt that these questions were meant to test her loyalty to the company. Furthermore, she didn't like their prejudiced jokes. For example, before Elzbieta left on a short holiday to Poland, her supervisor suggested she bring back friends who would work for 'maximum hours for the lower rate.' She recounted: 'So it was just a joke to say, "Goodbye, have a good holiday," but this kind of joke she wouldn't use you know, to talk with other carers.'

She felt her supervisor tried to manipulate her. She said, 'They treat you like a doll—they play with you.' She was told by this supervisor that she could not break her contract, which stipulated that she would be liable to pay the company £900. This care company felt like a prison from which it was hard to escape. With few options other than to keep working Elzbieta felt 'stuck in this job,' as she put it.

Elzbieta had an unrelenting 15-hour day schedule. She was annoyed at the frequency with which the company changed her rota, according to when, she thought, her British co-workers were ill in the mornings while she herself said that she worked all the time—ill or healthy. On most days Elzbieta woke up at 6.00 a.m. and she acknowledged that she was frequently tired then. While her schedule was often erratic the actual work was routine.

On one particular day, her rota was changed the night before so she didn't know her full schedule, which discounted any possibility of planning something. On her first visit, although she parallel parked her car with ease she said, 'I'm so bad at parking.' She got to her first call a little after 7 a.m. on an attractive street with gardens and gates. Elzbieta said that the last time she had visited this client, she had slipped from her chair and upon entering her house, Elzbieta had to call for help, which was a scary situation. Before she got out of the car, she called in to the office and said 'yes OK' as they loosely rearranged her day with a wide gap in the middle because two British-born care assistants 'went off sick,' but which left her in a situation of being on call. She said, 'This job doesn't have professionals in it.'

Elzbieta went up the steps to Mary's apartment. In the corridor was a long line of trinkets and narrow tables that Elzbieta passed. She apologized for coming five minutes late to Mary who was lying on her bed. Elzbieta went in to the very small bathroom and prepared her bath. Mary followed her naked and Elzbieta said, 'I need to check the temperature in here.' Mary navigated the tub with Elzbieta helping her sit on a seat inside it. Elzbieta told Mary that she planned to go to Poland and that another Polish care assistant, Monika, was coming to visit Mary while she was gone. Monika had been on maternity leave and was returning to work. Elzbieta poured water on her back with a plastic jar and asked her if it was hot. Elzbieta was desperately searching for conversations to make Mary feel comfortable, as she was sitting despondently on the seat. Elzbieta gently scrubbed her chest, and said let me rinse you too. She then poured water all over her body and then scrubbed her legs and talked about the rain, and asked Mary, 'How is your doctor?' She said 'fine,' and Elzbieta said 'lovely.' Elzbieta said, 'Monika is coming back to work' and 'her son is seven months old. I'll have to tell her you asked about her,' although Mary never asked about Monika. Elzbieta reminded Mary of when she fell and attempted to get an expression from her or some kind of retort about that time. But Mary didn't respond. Elzbieta then asked 'Would you like to wash your front?' Then, Mary stood up and washed her groin area. Elzbieta helped by washing the top part of her pelvis and hips. Elzbieta gently helped Mary out of the tub by putting a rug on the floor, taking out her feet first and then legs and then the seat itself. Mary was now standing and Elzbieta dried her while she stood and held on to the sink. The bathroom was small and Elzbieta leaned over and down near the rug to avoid hitting herself or other things. She asked, 'How are your legs today?' Mary responded: 'Not bad.' Elzbieta then asked, 'Are you alright' with Mary responding with a grunt. Mary suddenly piped up, 'There is 20 pounds there for the window cleaner,' pointing towards the living room.

Elzbieta asked, 'Would you like me to dry your toes now,' and she said, 'Yes.' Every body part had a question and response as care assistants were taught that the client needs to feel in control and although Elzbieta, and other care assistants, understood the theory behind it, it appeared like a cumbersome exercise. Another migrant care assistant, who was a former nurse, noted that these questions encouraged older persons to opt out of engaging in hygienic practices, for example, deciding not to take a bath or shower when they seemed to need one.

Elzbieta said, 'I'll put powder on you' with a sure voice and they both put it on and deodorant spray as if in sync. Elzbieta put a towel over Mary and they both slowly walked into the living room. Mary sat on the bed naked. Elzbieta looked at her and said, 'Are you dry everywhere?' Then, Elzbieta put on her bra across her large back as Mary sat on the bed. Mary then seemed to feel more upbeat with this on, and rose up to ask Elzbieta if another care assistant they both knew walked in the Lake District and Elzbieta said, 'Yes, she is very fit.' Elzbieta put on Mary's underwear slowly. Mary again asked about the window cleaner and whether Elzbieta knew if he was coming today. Elzbieta asked, 'Does he know he is supposed to come here?' She said, 'Yes, and the money is in the bag.' Elzbieta said, 'I haven't seen any window cleaners around lately.' She put on Mary's blouse, then Elzbieta said, 'Trousers?' Elzbieta asked, 'How many times does the window cleaner come?' trying to build on Mary's interest in this subject, and Mary answered, 'Once a month.'

They both went into her kitchenette and Mary poured her cereal, while Elzbieta opened the refrigerator. Elzbieta turned to her and said, 'I can do it for you—would you like me to do it?' Mary peeled a banana and Elzbieta watched her. Then Elzbieta prepared a cereal bowl for her. Elzbieta walked her to her table and Mary sat down. Elzbieta said, 'Do you have milk?' She then got it so Mary could eat her cornflakes and bananas. Elzbieta told Mary that the kettle was full and she needed to wait for the water to cool. Everything seemed organized and synchronized, in tune with Mary's morning rhythm. A neighbour drifted into the apartment, and said, 'Hello Mary,' and Mary asked her about the window cleaner.

Elzbieta excused herself and went to the living room to write in the logbook. She wrote: 'assisted into bath and dried and dressed assisted with breakfast washed up, meds prompted nothing else required.' The shorthand text that she wrote to the company didn't describe what she actually did in the interaction to get Mary to feel secure and open up. Additionally the term 'assist' suggested a minor rather than major intervention. Meanwhile, the neighbour talked to Mary and Elzbieta said, 'Nothing else?' and left her house. As she walked out to the car her phone rang and she said, 'Oh no. Mrs Dee is cancelled, ahhhh, I'm not complaining. OK. I haven't been there for four months, no problem,' and she clarified the address of a client whose whereabouts she had forgotten. Since she got cancelled calls that day, she wanted extra calls to fill the time so this rearrangement was a mixed blessing. Elzbieta felt disheartened: 'But I will have to have breaks. I work 30 hours. I have no time for nothing, and no money.' She got back in to her car and added these new calls to her rota.

Elzbieta tried to approach her clients as a familial member so as not to feel like a stranger. As the relationships between her and her clients became more comfortable she felt a sense of success in dealing with them. The significance of this closeness was attributed to a lowering of her expectations along with her emotional labour to reduce the cultural divide between them. She said:

> My clients, I love them, but, how can I say, they are cold. They keep distance. But it gives satisfaction, getting them to accept me, to be welcome in houses because you go to their houses and it's private and finally they must feel like you are not a stranger. Finally, when they know you, they behave more casual and you learn a lot about their life.

She also felt like a stranger in her community, which was compounded by the fact that she was made to work so many hours preventing her from being seen as a genuine member. She said:

> You try to create your own life and it comes every week with something personal and it piles one thing after another–suddenly you are fed up and you just don't want to live here even though the Lake District is beautiful but the people have this kind of attitude and the media creates opinions for people who are not educated. They hear your accent in the store and they change their attitude.

Elzbieta spent a lot of time in her car and worried about it constantly. She had good reason. While Elzbieta was compensated by the company for the petrol she spent to get to and from clients' houses at the end of the month, the actual time she spent driving was her burden alone. It was also hard saving cash to purchase petrol for her work and driving on the left hand side of the road was difficult at first for Elzbieta. But the hardest part was taking out a loan from the company to purchase a car since this put her into debt after she had paid the insurance. Elzbieta was 'grateful' (as she put it) for the assistance provided in getting an old car essential for her work role. She stated that paying back the loan to the company for this purchase was 'just a rule of the company for foreigners;' she accepted this 'rule' and extra costs for car insurance. However, trying to brush the impact away of this indentured treatment, while bearing financial pressures, is indicative of her dissatisfaction.

Worse, after a few months, this car broke down in front of a client's house and she was stuck but did not want to tell her company for fear of being punished. So she called a Polish colleague who helped her move the car to a nearby location from where she could get it towed away. She borrowed money from her USA-based credit card company for this purpose. To keep her job, she bought an old but decent car from her client, borrowing an additional £100 from another Polish care assistant to purchase it. When this car broke down, she went to a mechanic who she believed was overcharging her. The second-hand car she bought also broke down every three weeks and she had to apply for new loans to pay for repairs. This problem was exacerbated by the high cost of living. She said, 'I don't send money home. I took one-month wages and I had to pay rent, food, petrol, some cosmetics, go out for a beer. So it's expensive here.'

She was convinced that the care work damaged her back while the company said the pain was due to not following their safety training. Her supervisor told her, 'You must be doing something wrong.' But she concluded, 'You can't do caring without hurting your back,' and noticed that she seemed to get 'the hard clients' that demanded physical labour. She said, 'I want the ones with the problems and for me to listen to them. Everyone's back is hurting.' Her masseuse in Poland told her, 'You are too young for this,' but the problem persisted because of the relentless physical demands. Despite these workplace problems, she felt she had become more independent in contrast to her friends in Poland who had traditional lifestyles, reflected in conversations that revolved around babies and marriages. She commented that 'we have different lives now' and felt she had more in common with her new Polish friends in Cumbria. Yet she didn't know what her future held in England, despite having taken advanced level English and computer courses as well as vocational courses such as the NVQ. In looking at her limited options, she said 'I'm not living my dreams any more. I see the reality here.'

Conclusion

Alice, Lisette, and Elzbieta's accounts counter the Lake District's romantic depiction. As invisibles, doing the 'back room' work of nation and region building (Duffy, 2007, p. 317), these migrant women are one of many central actors who develop the new service economy in Cumbria. This generation of migrant care assistants bolster Cumbria's stagnant economy while participating in its 'local structure of feeling' (Taylor, Evans, and Fraser, 1996, pp. 5–8). Adapting Raymond Williams' concept, these researchers describe 'structure of feeling' as part of an assemblage of *social practices* (e.g. care routines and tasks) and *social relationships* (e.g. between clients and care assistants) that contribute to a sense (in this case) of northern regional identity. These migrant care assistants also support older citizens to become independent consumers in a competitive regional climate.

These scenes of caregiving focused on the migrant women's experiences of driving and working around Cumbria as part of their mobilities. They provided a glimpse of their 'mobile subjectivities' (Hannam, Sheller, and Urry, 2006, p. 3), which signified the participants' identities, actions, and feelings as they moved around in their preparation of care as well as at the point of contact. As we saw with Lisette and Elzbieta, the preparation for care took up much time but was invisible to their companies even though it was an important part of the caring ritual. Likewise their contact with clients was relational and based on their conversations, preferences, and ways to get along over and beyond the pressures their companies exerted to speed up the transactions.

Although they were often rushed, the participants also experienced independence and solidarity with others like themselves. The cars signified the migrant care assistants as residents (because most Cumbrians had cars) and as 'foreign workers' (because they wore uniforms and didn't haggle with mechanics in their non-standard English). They were referred to in Cumbria as 'foreign staff' and the care assistants often internalized these outsider identities. They mentally cruised to points into their futures, projecting plans and places they desired to be, thereby releasing them from the drudgery of their work. For these women, the trappings of their physical mobility and social stasis is expressed in the car journeys they took, the disappointments they faced as they attempted to improve their lives, and the new responsibilities that entrenched them in their surroundings, despite the tiring work and physical complaints.

Historically linked to domestic servitude in the North West, Alice, Elzbieta, and Lisette's domestic labour is now inextricably tied to the global care industry. In particular the driving and work they do for low pay, difficult conditions, and unsociable hours vastly contributes to developing the economy and subsidizing welfare for older persons. Moreover, their global and local networks enabled them to resolve their problems without depending on formal channels and, consequently, they posed no threat to the region's infrastructure. Saskia Sassen (2002, p. 254) refers to these networks as 'survivor circuits.' Yet while Sassen stipulates these as occurring in city regions, it is clear that the participants in this study formed these in rural areas too. These circuits enabled them not just to survive, but also to create 'healthy spaces' (Dyck and Dossa, 2006, p. 692) that smoothed the bumpy Cumbrian roads and their relations. Moreover, these networks involved not just colleagues and families, local and abroad, but also clients who helped where they could, for example, in feeding back to Alice the boundaries of friendship or in Elzbieta's case, selling a cheap car to her. In a sense, these circuits morphed in to a type of 'care diaspora' with all of its inherent contradictions and difficulties. These diasporic members constructed healing landscapes in Cumbria, which defied the ideology of the new service economy that their competitive companies embodied. The next chapter focuses on the gendered career outcomes for the participants in the study as they attempted to reassemble their lives under difficult economic and social conditions.

5
The Disappointing Journey to Being 'Just a Carer'

Introduction

> I remember there was a time—an incident where this nurse was trying to find the vein of the client and she really pricked and pricked, and I could see the vein. And I was like, we do that in Zambia. But I can't do anything about it here because *I'm just a carer*. They consider us as someone who doesn't know anything.

This care assistant observed a nurse in her residential care home inserting a needle into a client's arm to the point of causing him injury but was paralysed to intervene because she felt that she was viewed as 'someone who doesn't know anything.' Her primary identity, as a nurse in Zambia, was overshadowed by her role of being 'just a carer' in England. Despite her extensive nursing knowledge, she was rendered helpless in England's occupational hierarchy. Her silence was not self-imposed, however, for it was illegal for her to dispense medical advice. In another case, when a care assistant in a nursing home *did* offer guidance to a nurse who had forgotten the amount of medicine needed for a diabetic shot, she was told, 'What do you know, you're *just a carer.*' These care assistants were heavily monitored and prevented from taking action in their institutionalized work settings. This schism in the care assistants' private and public identities triggered internal crises in their retreat from the initial dreams that had inspired their migration.

While chapters 3 and 4 focused on migrant women, many of who were health care professionals adapting and transforming industry standards, this chapter switches the focus back to the participants' gendered identities, motivations, and strategies, and the general neglect of their expertise. I highlight the social and psychological effects of working as care assistants on their careers and lives. I first focus on the socio-emotional, professional, and economic motivations of the women in migrating. These motivations are captured through linking them inextricably to a gendered identity. Then I present the gendered strategies that the women used for advancing, including their investments in education and then migrating as part of a path to a greater livelihood. Upon reaching England and working as care assistants, however, they reframed their plans to adapt to the barriers they encountered. These barriers impaired, but did not destroy, their abilities to advance. Next, I present the issues of some successful participants as each one moved from being 'just a carer' to a nurse.

Gendered motivations

These transnational women's gendered identities were key to understanding their motivations for migrating as care assistants. The majority of the participants who were in feminized professions, such as nursing, physical or occupational therapy, social work, and teaching, were already in a 'nurturing' economy before they migrated. By this, they cared for the next generation (as with teachers), clients with special needs (social work), or rehabilitated patients (as with nurses or other health care professionals). Mignon Duffy (2011, p. 9) defines nurturing occupations as demanding intensive 'relational work that is geared towards improving the personal well-being of others.' This work concerns relational contexts (e.g. face-to-face interactions), attending to personal needs, and emotional responsiveness (pp. 15–16). Duffy traces nurturing fields in the USA to show the ways they became more gender-segregated over time. Evelyn Nakano Glenn (2011) goes further to show how women of colour—Native-Americans, African-Americans, and immigrants—were coerced by policies and laws into low-level caring occupations due to having no other options to support themselves and their families. Not only is the gender contract implicit, but so also is race and class integral to the culture of paid caring. Caring, viewed historically as 'women's work,' is outsourced to female migrants because it is also considered to be a migrant job, one in which 'women from some parts of the world are givers and the others are receivers of care' (Raghuram and Kofman, 2004, p. 95). Care work is one of only a few options for many migrant women who have 'little prospect of using their qualifications in the UK' (McGregor, 2008, p. 802). In one study entitled *I Hate Being Idle: Wasted Skills and Enforced Dependence* researchers found that 80 per cent of respondents, formerly in teaching, clerical, and health care fields, became care assistants (Doyle, 2009, p. 27).

The participants often internalized this gendered labour. Those who were in nurturing fields before they migrated, and even those who weren't, felt that they were destined for some type of care work. One former social worker reasoned that although she was 'just a carer,' as she put it, she felt that she had a 'predisposition for this job.' She added: 'That was my choice a long time ago when I went to school. So it wasn't just like, "Oh, alright care work, it was because I'd like to".' Another Polish participant whose background was in economics felt that there were few other options for her other than care work, similar to her mother who worked as a care assistant in Italy but was treated 'like a servant' and 'hates it.' Many participants were called upon to care by family as a 'status obligation' (Glenn, 2010, p. 6)—an act that initiated them into the global care industry. Like the aforementioned example, a couple of the Eastern European care assistants' relatives were also migrant care assistants. In another case, one participant's mother moved from Poland to Germany on an undocumented basis to substitute for her sister, who was a care assistant there (the participant's aunt), when she was ill and needed an operation. This gave the participant the idea of being a care assistant in England. These examples illustrate the participants' paid care work but as Chapter 6 will show the participants were also expected to care for family without pay.

Sheba George (2005) in a study of migrating Keralite (Indian) nurses found that gender roles and status obligations were key to the women's motivations to enrolling in universities in India and finding work in the USA. These women's families encouraged them to attend nursing schools and to migrate to earn better incomes. This was a family 'survival strategy' (p. 53). Once these women had migrated as breadwinners and sponsored their families to come to the USA, they adopted new gender roles as they became financially dominant in their homes and local communities. However, they also continued to shoulder typically feminine domestic duties like childcare and cleaning. In another study of gender among migrant care assistants, Cinzia Solari (2006) found that the participants in her study, both men and women, adopted identities, either, as 'professionals' or 'saints' in their understandings and practices of care assistant work. 'Professionals' saw their work as public and contractual with a more business orientation. 'Saints' behaved towards clients in more personal and familial ways. While the 'professionals' emphasized their status as 'government workers,' the 'saints' believed it was their calling and that they were performing 'God's work,' which made doing physical care unstigmatized (the opposite of the ways the 'professionals' felt) (pp. 309–310). Interestingly, all the female workers were highly skilled former professionals and many of them were mothers and grandmothers. Unlike the men in the study, however, none of them needed to justify their decision to be care assistants, seeing it as continuous with gendered divisions of labour. But while one group drew boundaries around their care (the 'professionals'), the others found it difficult (the 'saints'). The cultural 'toolkits' that were developed by the agencies in the pre-migration stage fortified these gendered identities: The male 'professionals' found care assistant work to be the most difficult because of its image as 'women's work.' Gendered institutions, therefore, in the pre-migration stage, like former recruiting agencies, family experiences and expectations, as well as former work, were key drivers, as they were for the participants in this study and their entry into the care workforce. The participants' motivations were shaped by these forces, and like the ones in Solari's study, they also adopted a combination of professional and saintly identities to cope with their care assistant posts.

Gendered drivers

Researchers have found that women (Hondagnu-Sotelo, 2000; Menjivar, 2000) are more likely to be economically and professionally motivated to migrate, with family and societal norms also driving their migration. In one study (Hussein, Stevens, and Manthorpe, 2010) of migrant care assistants in England, the researchers found that a number of participants had higher qualifications and wanted to 'broaden their horizons' and 'build on previous skills outside the UK' (p. 93). Therefore professional motivations were strong. Non-EU workers, especially from the Philippines (many of whom were former health care professionals) saw this work as 'stepping stones' for future careers but also as an economically viable option, as their financial reasons for migrating to England were also strong. Their top motivations for migrating were (in order): altruism, better than previous English jobs (e.g. low-level factory work), social care sector easy to enter, and social care as a good career (p. 95). Although not highlighted in this research, these motivations appeared to be highly gendered strategies for many of who were in formerly feminized fields, such as, social work, nursing, and occupational therapy. Similarly in another study of migrant care assistants in England (Cangiano, Shutes, Spencer, and Leeson, 2009), the participants cited diverse and mixed motivations for migrating although economic reasons were the most important. These studies tie migration to employment niches. In this study, too, the two were intertwined. Many of the participants in this study engaged in care assistant work because it was one of the easiest entry points in England's labour market. Yet they also identified with it and their families supported them.

The existence of multiple motivations of the participants challenge individualist and rational migration models that focus exclusively on costs and benefits from an extrinsic standpoint, one which divides economic and occupational reasons from psychological and familial ones (Madianou and Miller, 2012). This study, as discussed in Chapter 1, uses a transnational field model for understanding the motivations of the participants. This field incorporates a number of factors including intrinsic (identity and belonging), extrinsic (networks, households, and groups), and also macro-level factors (segmented markets, welfare regimes, and immigration policies) (Bakker and Silvey, 2008; Levitt and Schiller, 2007). From this perspective, transnational women's motivations to migrate are an 'embedded process' that is linked to local spheres but also larger systems (Sassen, 2006, pp. 635–637). These drivers shape the motivations of transnational women who constantly renegotiate their identities, networks, and roles between sending and receiving countries as they set in place their plans.

The participants in this study also had *mixed* motivations. They were breadwinners for their families and they wanted to develop themselves in socio-emotional ways too. As an example of this mixed phenomenon, one participant in this study, who, on just arriving in England articulated her motivations to migrate:

> My aunt asked me to prove myself—to stand alone. I am a single parent and I came here to give my children a better future and to enhance my knowledge... I have helpers in the Philippines, a maid and nanny. I will do what they do!

Here, this participant desired *autonomy* as a single mother: 'To stand alone.' She also wanted to support herself, from an *economic* point of view when she said she wanted to 'give my children a better future' and finally, she wanted *professional development* opportunities, in her desire 'to enhance my knowledge.' She was operating in a transnational field of inequalities in taking a job in the care sector in England, which would secure for her a higher income, even if the consequences were that it was of a lower status. Like the families that employed her to care for their parents, she had helpers in the Philippines to take care of her family, *before* she migrated. She did 'what they do.' Due to these mixed motivations, many of the participants felt 'swept up' in their migration decisions, as if they *had* to migrate. This feeling was associated with a 'culture of migration' where emigrating from places like the Philippines and Kerala was expected by peers and family but also because of highly personal and social reasons (Madianou and Miller, 2012).

Themes of gendered motivations and drivers[1]

While the motivations of the participants were indeed mixed *and* diverse, it was possible to pinpoint key themes through capturing narratives of their struggles to achieve their desired personal and professional goals within the wider socio-political and economic arena. These themes are: greater professional development; earning a greater income to support family; and becoming autonomous. Narratives illustrate these women's journeys in attempting to move from being 'just a carer' to 'grow as an individual' as one participant expressed.

Greater professional development opportunities: 'More advanced technologies'

Since many of the care assistants were professionals or had just graduated from professional programmes, a key desire was to acquire professional development opportunities. They believed that staying in their own countries would not guarantee a successful career. They viewed care assistant work as an entry-level job while they investigated new opportunities and adjusted to a new country. One participant who was a former university lecturer said, 'I would like to do social work or occupational therapy in the future, so I think I'm on the right path.' Those on student visas were promised good training opportunities. One participant, for example, was told that the NVQ system in the UK was an international degree that was transferable to other countries and therefore valuable. She reflected: 'So I really wanted to learn and to widen my horizons because I think the NVQ here is known to Canada and Australia.'

Yet this qualification is not accepted in other countries nor does it count towards professional adaptation in England. The key to being recognized as a professional again, for those who were *not* EEA citizens, was the ability to pass the IELTS exam, which was demanded by professional associations as a prerequisite to enter a degree programme and to become a licensed practitioner in England (care assistants are not licensed). This was only the first step in the process. Most care assistants were surprised at the amount of retraining that was required to adapt their qualifications, including passing a test that had recently upgraded its cut-off score. Some of the participants took the IELTS exam before they migrated. Jamuna is an example of someone who was motivated primarily by professional development concerns but encountered obstacles such as the IELTS in her career journey.

Jamuna, 29, had been a nurse in India. There was a culture of taking on nursing roles in Jamuna's family with a number of her sisters becoming nurses. She wanted to become a nurse like them, and encouraged another sister to become one. She said, 'I pushed my sister to go for nursing: "It is good for you, you will get a good job and a good career, you'll get a good experience".' In India, Jamuna finished a three-year nursing course; she worked for four years in an intensive care unit and coronary unit in one hospital, and described this as a positive experience. She then worked in another small hospital near her home for a month but seemed to be getting little job satisfaction. She migrated to England in 2005 after a friend suggested to her an agency in India, which issued her with a work permit. She went through an interview and three months later was given a visa. She reflected on her decision to migrate:

> I wanted to work abroad and I wanted to study more because here [England] there is more advanced technologies and everything. I had to work with these old technologies in India, which is why I came here.

Her ambition was to work in a hospital, rather than in a nursing home, where she was employed so that she could build on her nursing skills. Jamuna was not allowed to do injections in the nursing home although she was qualified in India to do this procedure. She thought she could apply her nursing skills if she were in an English hospital setting, functioning as a nurse and remarked:

> We know how to take the blood but we are not allowed to. So, we have no chance to deal with it. We are losing our chance to do these things. I think hospitals can give us more experience.

Furthering her nursing career was her most important priority. She said, 'I have to improve my career. Money is OK, money is important, a very important matter for living standard but my career is also important to me.' Her manager asked her to take the NVQ2 and NVQ3 but she reflected, 'Because I don't need to do the NVQ because my nursing side of it is equal to NVQ3.' Her manager also encouraged her to take the IELTS test again but gave her little practical support such as time off to study for it. As a result of having no time off to review, Jamuna internalized her lack of studying as a personal failure. She recalled that her manager said:

> 'Go and try get that score and then you can do your adaptation.' She will push me but I know I have to improve it a bit more because a score of seven is difficult for me. So, I am very lazy, but what can I do?

She claimed that she felt 'unlucky' because she had taken the IELTS and passed it (before the cut off score was changed) and was registered with the professional association, the Nurse Midwifery Council (NMC) but it had expired. Jamuna explained, 'That time I had a registration with the NMC, and I can do my adaptation but I got only one month. Within one month my registration is expired, so I am *unlucky* to do the adaptation here.' She then declared, 'I lost my chance.' Jamuna was frustrated because she realized that it would be difficult to move upwards without retaking the IELTS with its higher passing score and adapting her credentials and that her nursing home was not improving her skills or knowledge:

> In the nursing home, they don't give us much experience because all of the people are elderly. We don't get any chance to deal with medical equipment. In the nursing home they don't have much equipment.

Earn greater income to support family and provide children with greater opportunities: 'I want them to have a bright future'

Being told that they would eventually earn more money in England was an incentive for the participants to work abroad because of the low wages in their home countries. A participant from the Philippines noted, 'The opportunity presented itself and the value of the pound to the peso is great, very big—I will support my daughter and myself.' For the mothers, making money was often directly related to supporting their children's education, either by saving for their future or by paying for expensive private schools. One participant said about her daughter's education: 'I gave her the best school possible for a good foundation, which is the best school back home. I enrolled her in a private school, which is expensive.'

Upon arriving, however, they became aware that their financial debts and obligations, combined with their occupations and lifestyle, meant that they could barely afford the high cost of living in England, let alone remit enough. One participant reflected on her financial obligations to family and worried:

> The conversion is a bit lower than we expected and it's gone down. I am the provider. I can't give more to them. I'm just getting the same salary as I used to, so the work gives no chance to give my family additional financial support.

Another participant reflected on her daughter's future career, one which she felt she could not fully support, even by sending home half of her income:

> She said she wanted to be a doctor. Which, I know I can't give to her because studying medicine back home is nearly a fortune. It would cost a fortune! But then I'm not going to say 'no, you can't.' I will say, 'OK, but you need to study harder.'

Some care assistants believed that sponsoring children would improve their children's livelihoods. Tina's case illustrates this phenomenon.

Tina, 32, and a former nurse, arrived in England in 2005 from Zambia with her family following in 2006. Being a nurse in England, she thought, would give her the support she needed to advance their lives. Her desire was modelled on her brother-in-law's medical success story in Australia. She also envisaged herself working as a hospital nurse in an intensive care unit but was disappointed at not being able to achieve this goal in the early stages: 'Unfortunately,' she said, 'I came into care work because I cannot work as a nurse here.' Then in 2006 tragedy hit. Her husband, who had been an engineer in Zambia and a cleaner in England, died suddenly, leaving her with three young children. She began to question why she migrated in the first place and resolved that it was for her children. She said:

> And if they never get educated, it will be *my* problem. I mean my husband died. I could have gone back home—what am I doing here? I am here because I want my children to be educated. *I want them to have a bright future.*

She recognized her role as a single parent and the overwhelming responsibility of giving her children a 'bright future' and added, 'I want the best for them.' Her professional journey encountered barriers that made these goals difficult. As a sole provider and without state support, she worked long hours, often during the night, to be able to stay afloat financially. She also engaged in 'side jobs' including shipping used clothing from England to Zambia, cleaning houses, and selling herbal products. Aware of the fact that she needed someone to care for her children when she was working, she secured permission from government officials on compassionate grounds for her niece to reside with her and care for them. This worked for a year but eventually the niece had to return to Zambia, leaving Tina with the same dilemma of trying to support her family with very limited means and having to take 'too many steps' to get stay afloat. She said exasperated, 'There's just too many steps that I have gone through, apart from losing my husband, that really disturbed my career and everything.'

Become autonomous: 'Grow as an individual'

Many participants desired personal development, like one participant who said she wanted to 'grow as an individual' while another said she wanted 'more experience and culture.' A number of the women who were young and single saw England as an opportunity to develop freely, away from their families, and the gendered expectations in their home countries. The desire to be independent from family was strong, particularly from mothers, whom some felt were overbearing. One participant, Sherilynne, said:

> My mother protected me from boyfriends. This country is a free country. You do what you want. I am alone here so no one can see me. I feel free. I have no children, no mother. I never had that before—my mother is strict.

Although liking her newfound independence from her mother, Sherilynne got help from relatives in Europe for food and clothes in an inflow pattern of remittances. She depended on them to send money to fund basic needs and compensate for her low salary and to keep her image as independent for her own children. These mothers often wanted to be positive role models for their children, in spite of a loss of professional status. Another participant said:

> Sometimes you feel an inferiority complex not practising... I always say I have to finish my exam to the children when they ask. It's degrading work, caring. The children are used to seeing me in the hospital. In their mind they think I am a nurse.

For those participants in unhappy marriages in Catholic countries, migration was commonly thought of, as a divorce of sorts. Some of the relationships were physically and emotionally abusive, in which case migrating enabled the women to have more personal freedom and to escape from husbands or partners. This reason for migrating has been discovered in other studies as well (see Madianou and Miller, 2012). Abigail's case demonstrates the effects of abuse on a woman's migration and the desire to become self-determined.

Abigail was 35, and a physical therapist, having graduated and worked some time in her field in the Philippines. She confirmed that care assistant work was intended as a livelihood strategy: 'I will do this work to support my family,' she declared, after arriving in England in 2008. Abigail had partnered with an older man as part of a family arrangement to help her mother's failing business and ensuing bankruptcy. He was already married to someone else. She felt her partner, in his 60s, was using their ten-year-old daughter (they were both in the Philippines) to manipulate Abigail:

> My daughter doesn't know I am suffering in silence. If I tell her about him she would be hurt. When I tried to break the relationship, he used my daughter, to get hold of me. He is controlling. Since I am away he can't force me to do things. The only reason I get in touch with him is because he can turn my daughter's heart against me. He made sure he would get me pregnant when he and my mom were having problems. I was so naïve. He is emotionally abusive.

Abigail's reasons for migrating were highly personal. Moving to England was 'to find myself, to be financially independent, to grow as an individual.' One obstacle that she felt was blocking her ability to become fully independent was financial difficulty resulting from enrolling in a fraudulent training company through her recruitment agency. Since paying £2,500 for her course, she never received training and had no legal recourse to fight the training company or recruiter and felt vulnerable:

> I hold a student visa. We have been paying tuition fees to a training centre but there has been no assessor and no training materials given to us. I tried ringing them and to get in touch but it's only an answering machine. The training centre closed down and we are going to be in trouble if we don't find another training centre because of UK border agency [regulations].

Her partner offered her money but she rejected it so as not to feel tied to him and wanted to leave him. She wanted to become a physical therapist in England but in surfing the Internet, realized it would take much longer than her two-year student visa allowed. She reflected on the job itself and whether her expectations of being independent could ever realistically be fulfilled:

> Before, I can't stand this job. I can't believe I am doing this to myself, this job, especially when clients are grumpy. Why I am putting up with this? The office is ringing me for additional calls. I don't want to upset anyone, so I say yes. Money doesn't motivate me. As long as I am happy. As long as I can sustain basic needs.

Jamuna, Tina, and Abigail's cases demonstrate the extent to which women migrants will go to become autonomous women (Abigail), successful professionals (Jamuna), and support for their children (Tina). These cases illustrate the sacrifices they made, as well as the hardships they encountered as they attempted to achieve their goals. They viewed care work as a pathway to improving their life circumstances and those of their families. But there were a number of barriers they encountered along the way. Jamuna had little practical support to develop a career that was a family tradition. Her manager gave her little time off to study and the professional association had unyielding registration regulations. For Tina, immigration policies restricted her abilities to care for her own children while she cared for clients at work. For Abigail, the training company she signed up with was fraudulent and she was unable to accrue enough resources to become completely free from her abusive partner. These stories highlight these women's gendered motivations and strategies to achieve their goals. The next section focuses exclusively on these strategies and the barriers the participants encountered on their migration journeys.

Gendered strategies

The strategies that the women used to migrate reflected their motivations in that they were composed of a mix of different resources that they patched together from their families and professions. These strategies were sometimes deliberate and at other times desperate measures to fulfil their dreams. Their strategies fit the steps that Mirelle Kingma (2006) listed in her study of migrating nurses. Kingma conceived of these strategies in terms of 'steps' in both sending and receiving countries, that involved: (1) investing in a professional education (e.g. nursing) in the country of origin and gaining professional experience; (2) obtaining a foreign licence, or adapting education qualifications and professional credentials in the receiving country; and (3) obtaining the correct visa or work permits to practice a profession. I adapted Kingma's framework to illuminate the multifaceted journeys of all of the women migrants in this study, in five phases.

The first phase was dubbed 'creating itineraries' to focus on the initial investment the women made in higher education and the various actors who influenced their professional interests. The second phase was referred to as 'venturing out' and captures the initial experiences following graduation, when the women's degrees were tested in the labour market. The third phase encompassed the decision process to migrate and the ways it happened and was called 'making routes.' This phase involved recruitment brokers and the process of being recruited and seeing oneself as a recruit. Then, upon migrating, and starting their positions as care assistants in England, and in settling into these jobs and communities in ways that sent them into a downward cycle, the phase 'reaching dead ends' recognizes the barriers that they encountered. The women became anguished to the point where they felt their identities had become deskilled. Yet this was not the end of their stories. They developed diverse internal strategies for dealing with these barriers. This last phase was dubbed 'reframing aspirations.' At this point they envisioned their futures with limited resources and assessed their options. They often became risk averse. These phases illustrate that the participants' decisions made sense, given their contexts, and that a series of unpredictable events arose once they stepped into the pool of feminized labour. In a social system, where relations are structured by power, politics, and networks (Levitt and Glick Schiller, 2007) these transnational women struggled to find a place.

Creating itineraries

> Becoming a nurse was my ambition. My mother worked as a nurse and I chose nursing as a profession I followed a nurse [her mother]. I had a three-year course in Kerala in a convent. It was a good experience and I mingled with a lot of people. I wanted to go abroad.

In this phase the women took an initial risk to pursue a career by entering a university. This initial investment set in place other decisions and was the first step towards a career. Without it they could not advance (Kingma, 2006). These women chose their degree as a passport because of a mismatch between strong schooling and university systems and weak labour markets in their home countries (Isaksen, Devi, and Hochschild, 2008). One participant commented, 'Teachers don't get exported, but nurses do. Money talks. The amount we earn here is a quarter of what we would get in the Philippines.' Another said, 'If I go for nursing, I got a job... my school worked.'

Family influenced occupational choice, reinforcing a 'culture of migration.' Jamuna, from Kerala, whose sisters were nurses as well as an aunt, wanted to follow in their footsteps. She said, 'My auntie, she was a nurse. When I was a child I liked this career—that's why I chose it.' Parents were also key influences, as for one participant who said, 'I always wanted to be a nurse, but my parents wanted me to be a teacher so I got a teaching certificate and obeyed them and went to college.' In other cases, the location of a university could open up opportunities and lend status (in a city). One nurse moved from a small town to a metropolis, which entailed meeting new colleagues and launching a prestigious internship:

> I moved from a rural area to a city, New Delhi, which had the highest rating and I worked with critical cases there for nine months. I did in-service training one year abroad. It was a dream of some of my friends to go and I was selected and went to Riyadh.

Many participants said they dreamt of their future fields with their universities as a gateway. One participant said, 'I had this opportunity to be a nurse, to be able to work in a hospital so I took a nursing course. I had a privilege to work in a hospital because when I was a little girl I was dreaming to be a nurse.' Some participants received government subsidies that enabled them to continue. One nurse recalled that she paid 'a little amount.' She reasoned, 'If you went to a private school it would cost you really a fortune to finish that that course.' She made friends in her programme, 'because you're going to have a group,' which was important for support. These university experiences also activated networks, which endured well after graduating as a source of emotional support in new countries. One former physiotherapist was inducted into a cohort that continued in England. She said, 'My colleague from university, I was a witness to their wedding last January. They are just so nice—the family has welcomed me and his sisters who are in different parts of England.'

Other professionals from non-feminized fields had unclear pathways and less direction, support, and resources. Marcelina, who was Polish and a single mother with an economics degree, decided to pursue her master's but could not locate a job afterwards because of 'my small town.' But there were other factors related to her degree and opportunities to practise:

> In economics college, I wasn't sure about the future—to be a police, fireman or nurse. My parents said I could work in banks or offices... six months after finishing I couldn't find a job, so I wanted to try to go abroad. I pay for my daughter's education. In a bank, tax office they haven't any places for me.

Marcelina's case illustrates the dilemma of having little support to pursue a career in a non-feminized field and how this catapulted her in to locating work abroad. Marzena's case is similar and highlights gender segmentation in the earliest stages. Aged 32, and from a small town in Poland with one technical college, she earned an engineering degree but could not locate sustainable work in this field. She originally wanted to go to nursing school like her sister (who was a nurse) but at 15 didn't pass the exam and realized she had to take a different direction: 'I have to put my certificate to different school you know.' Engineering was not her 'choice' as she stated but she 'had not enough money to go to a different town and study in a different direction.' She realized there were few options to study and work as a woman there:

> When I started university, not a big choice to learn. The school where I was, it was typical technical—the directions of school, mechanic, for men. *For women, nothing.* Typical men's school, technical university, where I went... It was difficult to find a job. Everyone wants to have a person with degree and experience. It was difficult as a woman.

Marcelina and Marzena's experiences signal the difficulties of pursuing fields less popular than the nurses who had more institutional and family support.

Venturing out

The second phase involved volunteering, applying for and starting jobs, and staying in them for several years until it became too difficult or they reached a threshold and could go no further. A number of participants experienced setbacks in this phase that induced them to migrate. First-time jobs were ones where the participants' endurance and sense of ethics were put to the test. They often experienced disappointments in the actual work that was required of them. Others were overworked or overlooked for promotions, or they were made redundant. Still others could not locate anything and concluded that they were not employable in their local labour markets, or were working in fields that were substantially lower than their degrees and were not sustainable. Race, gender, and age discrimination were cited as prevailing factors in exiting these jobs and sometimes their professions, like a social worker who was laid off because she was told she was 'young and single' at which point she waitressed. A paramedic was a victim of a new law that stipulated that women could not lift over 20 kilos. She said, 'This is why women can't find a job in the hospital or in ambulance.' In another case, a Thai participant who had a degree in business administration worked as a gym receptionist in Bangkok and could not advance in this international company, she felt, due to her skin colour. Some workplaces abandoned employees. For example, Gertrude, a Polish human resources specialist, was laid off in one job only to be propelled into another that was not viable:

> I was an HR officer—a pretty serious job but this company collapsed. Three times bankrupt and they sold it. It was like communism collapsed—this sector disappeared. I lost my job. I very quickly became an IT payroll specialist for an English company in a year... It wasn't paid good enough. It was a really hard job to do. I decided to go to England. To be honest, I had no time. After this accident I just gave up.

In Gertrude's case she worked for a British company, which launched her migration directly to England. The poor conditions of these former jobs often triggered migration in this phase (Yeates, 2009). One Filipina participant said, 'I grabbed that opportunity [to migrate] because there in the Philippines you are only earning very small amount.' The long working hours, in conjunction with low or no wages, and staff shortages during internships (in-service) periods and upon graduating, appeared to be strong push factors for migration. One nurse said, 'I am a nurse in a government hospital for five years. We work really hard—we handle 50–60 patients in a ward.... Not paid well.' They searched high and low without success, like another nurse who said, 'In India, there is no salary and opportunity... I searched for a job in India for a month.' International jobs were regarded as 'a stepping stone to going to Europe or the USA,' as one Filipina participant claimed. She first went to Singapore where she was a staff nurse because: 'In the Philippines I was working in a small hospital and it is hard to raise kids, as I do it independently.' Even those who worked in other countries experienced difficult working conditions there too. Flora, a Filipina former nurse, contracted back pain from lifting heavy patients in a Saudi hospital. She further explained:

> I got my professional licence and then you know in the Philippines they are not paying. And there is an opportunity. There is one agency there and my friend is working there and she told me that, and I try and the agency called and told me I am qualified for that because I am a volunteer in the hospital in the Philippines. After eight months they call me up to work in Saudi. In Saudi, it's not very good... I don't really like it. Yeah, that is why after my contract I will really go home. I have had enough of this place.

A number of participants could not locate work in their specialism but took posts in lower-grade positions, for example a midwife and nurse who worked as nursing aides in hospitals. Most of the participants' professional identities, therefore, were tenuous *before* they migrated. The only way they believed they could make their lives work was to migrate.

Recent college graduates who were single and in their 20s desired the *experience* of going abroad. A recent business graduate from Poland, Katarina saw migrating as part of a list of personal and professional goals but cared little for the type of job: 'My first step,' she said 'was to finish university in March, and after that I have no idea what I will be here.' Katarina was systematic:

> I made a list of what I would like to do in the future since ten years. So every time, I am checking my list and I've done it and very proud that I done it. Cause that's what I have: Finish university, get married, find job, go to England.

Only a minority of the women had positive experiences working in their first jobs but thought they could enhance their careers by migrating as a care assistant and even make it a learning experience. Mei-Li, from China, who entered on a student visa, said she was motivated by professional development opportunities with her 'dream to study abroad.' These positive first jobs drove them to further venture out to cultivate more good experiences through migration.

Making routes

The women made 'routes' to migrate. This involved a series of steps, starting with consulting friends and colleagues about *how* to migrate for work. They often discovered a recruitment agency to help them migrate in their countries of origin. Sometimes these agencies were employment or travel agencies rather than strictly for migration. Yet once they were matched to this recruiter, they were bound to the agency's procedures, for documentation, financial commitments, and training. Family, locally and abroad, backed the new recruits through sponsoring bank loans and directly loaning money. The process could go quickly, as with many EEA citizens. But for the rest, the longer it took the more money they owed. The women believed that the jobs were a 'stepping stone' and 'grabbed' the opportunities as a number of participants explained. The supply of recruits was so disproportionate to the demand that recruiters were highly selective. One occupational therapist was surprised when her recruiter said that a university qualification was required for this job but in knowing that she:

> was selected from so many people who applied for this, I said, 'OK I would like to go.' So then I came. I only thought of doing it for a few years, and I said, I would like to try and go back again to occupational therapy if I would be given the chance because *I think this would be a stepping stone.*

Another former English teacher was surprised at the amount of steps involved in the recruitment process, including training and 'checking her English.'

Dorina, from Romania, migrated to advance her nursing career and to improve her financial situation. She worked as a nurse in cardiology for five years in Romania. Dorina migrated to England through an employment agency. Her father helped her with the expenses needed. She recollected that the agency staff told her she would earn 'seven to eight times better than Romanian money. It cost £2,000 and my father borrowed it from the bank. The bank charges £500 for that amount.' Dorina was rushed through the steps by her recruiter: 'I didn't have time—so many things to sort out.'

The recruiters, who dealt with groups of migrants controlled the pace, amount and types of paperwork and money the candidates owed them. The process could be delayed for non-Europeans with the recruiters blaming postponements on English immigration regulations. A Filipina participant recalled how at each stage the recruiter demanded more money and she borrowed nearly $8,000 from her extended family. She was not given receipts or 'even acknowledgements that they received our money' and hoped to recompense the amount:

> You see in the Philippines they are recruiting. My agency told us that they are going to have student visas for us, so we grabbed that opportunity because they are telling us that after adaptation you are going to be a RGN [registered general nurse] here. That was our thinking—that we can work as a RGN here after the adaptation. So after that they processed our papers and we paid $2,000. That is the first payment we've paid for that agency.... Then I wait for that one year and three months before giving another payment because our agency in the Philippines is asking 3,000 US dollars after my working permit was released. The $3,000 US dollars is again from my sister. Half of that from my sister and half of that is from my brother-in-law's sister. She's here in London. That's why she's asking me 'Why you are paying that much money?'

In another case, a Keralite participant said, 'My dream was to work abroad.' She went on to say, '90% of nurses go abroad. If you have someone leave and send money back, you become richer.' She borrowed all of the money from her sister to migrate. But the agency did not treat her fairly, and even after protesting, she was not fully compensated for her loss:

> Costs around £6,500. No receipts and I paid them in cash, £5,500 and the rest was air tickets and medical check ups. I paid money for adaptation and was offered the post. The picture I got was of nurses—you don't have to work long, getting a job at the NHS was easy. I'm still working as a carer. The agent is under police investigation. I went to his house when his family was there and his child opened the door and let me in—he tried to hide from me. His mother-in-law was there. I told him I want my money back. He said he would give me £2,000 and I waited three to four months. We had an argument. I said, 'you will suffer!' He told me that amount but gave me £1,500. I was lucky.... Many nurses are being exploited and they think the future will be bright and they take bank loans. They have no peace of mind.

Recruits were told that paperwork was the main reason for the fees and a few of the recruits were asked for cash with no receipts and told to 'trust' their recruiters. One participant who paid too much money to an agency was soon abandoned without a place to work once she arrived in England. This participant, Nina, recounted:

> I was unlucky. I tried to speak to the owner but couldn't get through because the owner of the agency is in the US. The nursing home didn't accept me, as it was a new manager and said they'd stop hiring.... The owner moved to the US and I couldn't locate her. I reported her to immigration, and I wasted my phone cards. I don't have a receipt. 'You need to trust me,' she said. The agreement was, 'you trust me, 50-50.'

During this period, few recruits were informed about the real situation of work in England. These participants believed the recruiters when they told them they would receive professional development opportunities (training for new careers in England). Yet the vocational training did not progress their careers, as the examples of Abigail and Jamuna illustrated. An informant for the study returned to the Philippines and posed as a family member of a prospective recruit. A recruiter told her that NVQs that emigrants earned in England would translate to higher degree qualifications and was evasive about the steps. The promises of the recruiters, including the long waiting, or conversely, very short waiting periods, signalled 'greener pastures' for these care assistants although they were more like red flags.

Reaching dead ends

After a short time working as care assistants, many of the participants realized that they were engaged in a sector that was widely known as an 'occupational dustbin' (poor pay, image, conditions, and promotions). One participant said clients 'treat us like slaves—it's your disease—they call us cleaners and slaves.' Binding employment contracts were major barriers. The English employer who recruited Gertrude directly from Poland through a newspaper advertisement bound her to a contract through loans, making her feel that she had to comply with the relentless care work schedule:

> They borrowed me money for the first deposit. But the contract said that minimum was 12 months. If you leave before that period, you have to pay £1,000 for flights, accommodation and basic food.... I had no imagination of how hard this job can be. They can give you ten residents to look after.... You can't sit down. Buzzers go.

Another barrier was the poor salaries which barely covered their costs of living and left little for savings or sending money to family. Most of the women commented on the high cost of living, including housing, energy bills, phone calls, and the costs of transport, paired with their minimum wage jobs. One participant expressed the kinds of sacrifices she made on minimum wages: 'We need to work harder.... You have to save. Little by little we will. We need to be wise on what we bought. We don't really buy things we don't need. We don't go out.'

Immigration policies were one more barrier, particularly for non-EEA migrants. The short student visas, in particular, threatened to end their stays before they had a chance to establish themselves and find new work; they could not complete studies that would enable them to advance into the professions. One participant from India said her dream was: 'To get a good job and to help my family and my parents.' But eventually she found that she 'cannot go further, I cannot proceed.' She went through adaptation and passed her programme. However, due to being on a student visa, she could not locate a job in a hospital. This barrier set in place many other hurdles. She could not pay her loan back to her family without a nursing salary and she subsequently did not feel eligible to be married: 'You don't have the job, they can't get you married.' She felt so overworked as a care assistant that she didn't have time to research nursing opportunities. She said, 'Because always busy, busy. I don't get time.'

The most difficult barrier, however, was the long and cumbersome qualification pathway towards adapting credentials that was unresolved by governmental efforts to harmonize qualification systems between countries (to be discussed more in Chapter 7).[2] Tina said she would have to completely retrain and estimated that it could take her up to five years to become a nurse again in England. She recounted, 'I really want to get this, but it's painful doing the things that you have been through already.' Other participants felt that the routes to adapting their credentials were unaffordable, given their survival salaries, as for one participant who explained: 'I mean you're wasting your money. It's an uncertainty and I can't afford to waste anything.' The IELTS was a major hurdle as Jamuna's narrative illustrated.

For those migrants who tried to adapt their qualifications, there were many logistical hurdles, including problems with mentors, unsupportive managers, and expiry dates of the NMC (see also, Kingma, 2006). One woman paid a recruitment company for an adaptation course that never transpired. She explained her problems:

> When it's my time to do the adaptation, my mentor left, so we asked the management, 'can they do something about it?' We were there a year. We did a care assistant job and waited to do adaptation as well.

It didn't happen. I asked again to the company managers. They were just making excuses. I'm still a carer at the moment.

Additionally, there were not always professional pathways for participants to follow. For those former professionals who were *not* in health care fields, there were few professional adaptation (retraining) programmes, or, like the nursing pathways, those that were available were drawn-out and complex to the point of making people give up before they started. Many of these A-8 European participants were told that they needed to convert their qualifications first through an agency called the National Academic Recognition Information Centre (NARIC), which compares academic qualifications and skills from one European country to another and gives credits and advice for a fee. One former teacher assessed her degrees and experience against the UK NARIC system to learn that her qualifications had been downgraded and that she would need to completely retrain to practise again. She exclaimed:

I'm still stuck in this job. You are just not moving forward. You are not developing yourself. I know it's difficult. It's going to last awhile... I'm so tired working these hours.

A more blunt comment by another participant was: 'I don't want to be *stuck* as a carer,' which reflected the resolve of many who had reached dead ends in their time as care assistants. These participants had become disillusioned with recruiters' promises and treated their situations as if they were caught in a bait and switch operation, especially for those students whose training never occurred. They felt that these dead end jobs were deskilling them permanently. One participant who was a physical therapist perceived her deskilling as akin to not being able to use her expertise. She said, 'I've been stopped to do the things I'm quite capable of doing.' The obstacles that the care assistants encountered made them feel defeated. The longer they stayed as care assistants meant the less they felt they could develop themselves professionally, like Mei-Li (profiled in Chapter 1) who had little support in her nursing home to cultivate her career. She said, 'My manager knows I'm a qualified nurse but she didn't help me.' Another care assistant described her deskilling as forgetting her former skills and being out-of-the-loop: 'I have training as a nurse, graduated as nurse but we are here as carers. We forgot something. We are not updated and we miss the hospital setting.'

Another stressor was that the vocational skills that they developed as care assistants would not translate back to their countries, as there were no such positions. One participant claimed, 'If you have *unusable skills*, you can do nothing really with them. In Poland there simply are no such things as carers, just nurses. To be a nurse you have to finish nursing college.' As a result, the participants felt ambivalent about their futures and confused about what to do, leading them to feel paralysed to take action. They had few resources to advance and there were numerous obstacles to overcome. The feeling of being 'stuck' in the job was entrenched; as one participant said, 'Still stuck in this job plus taking the course, plus not having anything else by doing it. I'm stuck!' Without formal support to make changes, they felt they were alone, like one participant who said, 'I have to change my life *by myself*.' She added that her manager 'didn't care about us—we are from another country.'

Reframing aspirations

Unable to overcome most of the structural barriers to advance, most of the participants reframed their aspirations, creating *internal* (perceptual/attitudinal) strategies to deal with their disappointments. They assessed their options and looked towards their futures matter-of-factly, not wanting to take big gambles, considering their limited resources, time, and energy due to these barriers. Some of them did complain to agencies, such as unions or other advocacy organizations but they stayed as care assistants; these interventions were too weak to make a difference due to the lack of legal enforcement. Their cognitive reframing of their problems helped them to come to terms with their decisions, like one participant who reflected:

> My attitude I think changed. I was kind of thinking that maybe it will be as easy as in Poland to progress or look for a job... *I changed my approach to my life*. And that's why I chose to be here so I can't complain really.

This strategy was not a solution. Nor was it uncommon. Beverly Skeggs (1997) found that the care assistants in her study internalized the idea of a caring personality and created a sense of 'respectability' to compensate for the poor image of care work. This strategy, however, did not buffer their disappointments of doing work that was not fully appreciated or reciprocated but such internal changes in self-perception facilitated their search for positive valuation (1997 p. 72). The internal strategies that the participants in this study developed were: (1) refocusing on family relationships and making a new home; (2) finding deeper meaning in care work; and (3) seeing care assistant work as a temporary situation.

1) Refocusing on Family Relationships and Making a New Home

Those participants whose children lived with them began to see care assistant work as a way to spend more time with them, using the unsociable hours as an advantage. One participant with a master's degree said that she would prefer to 'pursue something on the professional side of things, the intellectual side,' but in the meantime, as a care assistant, she could spend more time with her young son. She said, 'We have really good quality time as a family because of the hours I do.' Another participant 'had no plans to do the adaptation, it's very expensive and I have children to support.' She felt that her 'brain is already stagnant. I never used my skill. I forget so many skills. I'm just looking for work only for my kids.'

Other participants developed relationships with English partners and friends and decided to settle in England. One participant in her 30s decided that she should find a British partner in order to support her family. Entering England on a student visa and knowing that she had limited time before it expired, she invested all of her energies in this venture, explaining, 'I am Filipina and I want to bring my children here. I put my real life on [this match making service] and I said I am separated and have three kids and they [two men in their 40s and 60s] are interested in me and I give them a chance. The reason is because it is hard to stay in England.' Although not marrying, pursing this course of action gave her a sense of control and promise. This tactic is not uncommon. In a study of migrant women in the Canadian Live-In (domestic) programme, Deirdre McKay (2003) discovered that some of her participants decided to marry their employers due to their limited options and because they were aware of the conflation of good wife with good domestic worker.

2) Finding Deeper Meaning in Care Assistant Work

Some participants began to value the service ethic and the kinds of skills that were important for determining clients' needs. They wanted to care more for clients, rather than less, like one participant who 'expected that there was more caring' and complained that she lacked 'time spending with people.' She described her job as 'just service—washing, cleaning, feeding, that's it.' Another participant tried to cut through the red tape to care: 'If you sort of spend a lot of time with them and really try, you will try yourself to understand how they are and what their needs are and you know, how they live their life.' Some participants acted as 'saints' in their care of the elderly:

> This kind of job of mine *is like a mission for me* because when I was back home, I told myself if I will be given a chance to work abroad, it will be a mission, you know. I like doing it with humility, with your whole heart.

By growing the meaning of their work, they were able to embrace the intensive hands-on work of 'caring for' while at the same time were able to 'care about' the people that were in their charge (Tronto, 1992). This didn't mean that these 'saints,' like in Solari's study, found it easy to care. One participant, in wanting to be seen as a 'good carer,' was constantly questioned by a more senior British-born colleague. The participant exclaimed, 'This is *my* call, why is she asking me about this?' Another participant left a care facility following a disagreement with management, but said she 'loved' the clients: 'They were really good, all of them, I loved all of them, all 16 of them' and felt that she put her 'heart and soul into the job.' This deepening of care enabled participants who left their jobs to feel that they gave 100 per cent in caring for clients and in linking to the professional ethics of their former careers, and in performing as both 'saints' and 'professionals,' did not feel that they were abandoning them.

3) Seeing Care Assistant Work as a Temporary Situation

Some participants thought of their care assistant work as temporary in order to cope with job difficulties and before they trained for new careers, moved to other countries, or back to the country from where they emigrated. Some participants desired to train for other careers in the helping professions although they were unsure which one. They adopted a professional identity to deal with this crisis:

> I would like to go to school, but I don't know where I can. I would like to specialize in disabilities, or counselling, or group therapy. I would like to have the option to advance myself. It's a burdensome job as a care assistant. Where can I go to? What universities can I go to? This is my wish and my desire.

Others wanted to change careers completely although they knew it could be difficult. One participant wanted to become a police support worker. She realized that her goal was a way off because it was hard to break out of a care assistant niche:

> Like I say that [is] just long, long way because you know it might be you know a few months to exam and then another interview and, so you know it might take ages... they don't want to give you anything,

just care homes. I really don't want to do that anymore because they are all the same.

Still others, intending to return to the countries where they originated, so reconciled themselves to tolerate the conditions because it was a short-term experience. One participant felt she needed 'a break' and planned to return temporarily to Poland to be with her family:

> I need a break.... My future is unknown for me, very unknown.... It's not easy when you have to work all the time with people who have dementia, Alzheimer or other mental problems.

Finally, some participants wanted to migrate to other countries, as they had given up on England as a place for advancement as one participant said, 'If I finish, it's easy to go to other countries, and be anything.' These participants often wanted to migrate to Canada, Australia, and the USA, as they perceived these countries to offer better opportunities and extended family lived there. Most participants, however, moved to care assistant posts in other companies in England. Kingma (2006, p. 13) describes this syndrome as a type of 'carousel.' Many participants adopted a resigned attitude to a fait accompli, like one who said, 'As a human being, you become weak. I really accept what happened in my life.'

Stuck in care stepping stones

The barriers altered the participants' motivations and strategies by impeding their abilities to move forward with their original aspirations and plans. The concrete barriers were:

- Immigration laws that linked employment to immigration status thereby limiting occupational mobility and advancement.
- Recruitment brokers and employers that, early on, locked migrants into inescapable situations.
- Poor workplace conditions and salaries that made it difficult to accrue enough relevant resources to advance, thus creating a system of bonded labour with a lack of social protections and enforcements.
- A lack of viable and economical professional pathways, including problematical labour market tests, little or no access to higher education, and a downgrading of qualifications.
- Few social services aimed at women migrants that could provide genuine support and advocacy.

Apart from other penalties, such as gender and race, discussed in Chapter 1, it was these tangible structural barriers that led to their deskilling—an inability to practise or use the skills that they had learned in universities and in their workplaces. Subsequently, the participants revised their plans. They decided to build their families and find greater meaning in care work, and they viewed these jobs as temporary. In a sense, they put their careers on a 'slower track' to deal with these intractable barriers (Rubin, Rendall, Rabinovich, Tsang, Oranje-Nassau, and Janta, 2008, p. 83). Women, in general, tend to maximize their lifetime earnings and have slower income growth over their lifespan (Jacobs, 1996).

The participants' internal strategies did not remedy the deskilling that they experienced in these jobs. These strategies did, however, soften the blow of being in low-status and difficult work and, like the participants' inter-ethnic supports (to be discussed in Chapter 6), did not compensate for the lack of social protections, but buffered their difficult experiences.

Discussion of deskilling: Lost in translation

Deskilling can be defined as a mismatch between the skills of workers and the workplace. Migrants' qualifications and experience are not validated and they end up working in poorly paid vocations that limit their capacity to use their expertise. But it is not only the jobs themselves. Staying longer in these jobs makes it harder to advance a career and locate good paying positions, in view of not being able to accrue enough capital and knowledge. While some studies (Cangiano et al., 2009; Dumont and Monso, 2007; Rubin et al., 2008) indicate that length of stay, particularly after ten years in the destination country, *decreases* the likelihood of deskilling because newcomers are less reluctant to discriminate in employment take up while long-termers accumulate human capital, this study challenges those findings (see also, Boman, 2011). In this study, which takes place over a two-year period with migrants who had a range of entry dates, the longer participants stayed as care assistants, the less likely they were to find work as professionals because of forgoing a higher education, a topic to be discussed in Chapter 7.

Deskilling also refers to the loss of human capital to the migrant herself and the underutilization of her skills in the labour market often leading to 'contradictory social mobility' (Madianou and Miller, 2012, p. 34). Although she is highly skilled and has migratory mobility (Urry, 2007), upon landing in a new country, her skills are lost in translation with 'information asymmetry' (Dumont and Monso,

2007, p. 143), when she encounters structural barriers (e.g. immigration legislation that limits her job prospects). While these women invested in expensive higher education to leverage their geographic and demographic disadvantage in low-income countries and then migrated to high-income countries, they often ended up in lower paying jobs that became end points. This trend is worrying because those women who are more highly educated are also more likely to migrate (to be discussed in Chapter 7). One of the direct causes of deskilling rests on the ways that qualifications have been translated in destination countries using approaches that are ambiguous (such as classification systems, labour market tests, and standards, as well as self-reporting) and degrade or do not acknowledge the sending countries' higher education systems. Few multilateral agreements or worldwide systems exist for the portability and codification of skills and qualifications.

This leads to over-qualification among immigrants, especially those from outside of the OECD (e.g. India, Philippines, and China), vis-à-vis the native born (Dumont and Monso, 2007). Although the reliance on education as a marker for selecting migrants began in the 1970s (Miller, 2008), 'having a higher education degree does not specifically protect a person from over-qualification and indeed tends to *increase* the risk of mismatch between education and job' (Dumont and Monso, 2007, p. 146). The politics of not recognizing qualifications is pronounced among women who are viewed as 'unskilled migrants' and face special difficulties and risks in the destination labour market (Jubany, 2009, p. 2). The country where qualifications are obtained signals to immigration officers and employers that migrants lack social and cultural capital, reinforcing the myth of deficient language proficiencies (as discussed in Chapter 1).

The concept of deskilling is often conceived of as an inevitable part of a capitalist labour process (Braverman, 1998). In this scenario, the bargaining power for workers is weakened by management (or other external controls) that reduces barriers to entering a field but then lowers skill levels (by routinizing tasks), so that knowledge-production is diminished thereby reducing the workers' human capital and potential. As chapters 3 and 4 showed, normative controls such as bureaucratization is pervasive in the care sector (see also, Wibberley, 2011). The NVQs are an example. These exams are cast as 'training' to increase knowledge but are really assessments of basic job tasks that workers already have and do not lead to professional careers. On this view, skills exist along a vertical ladder and are polarized within an hourglass of high end jobs that have upskilling potential and are knowledge-intensive and low end jobs that are at the bottom with low-skills and repetitive routines (Jackson, 1991; Warhurst and Thompson, 2006) and very few in the middle.

The 'low-road' strategies, of low skill, low wages, and low trust work (Grugulis, Warhurst, and Keep, 2004, p. 4) characterize deskilling, which is viewed in opposition to reskilling and upskilling. Yet in one study (Carey, 2007), agency managers experienced covert forms of deskilling in the guise of upskilling; for example, new requirements to complete paperwork which was duplicative—an issue that the participants in this study faced too. Reskilling and upskilling (Warhurst and Thompson, 2006) happen when employees are encouraged to share and learn new knowledge through technologies, education, and training; these forms of advancement are aligned to the knowledge-based economy. But they may not always be cast as true knowledge work especially with regard to trainings in aesthetic (soft) skills in personal interactive service work (Warhurst, 2008; Warhurst and Nickson, 2007). In this case, the 'skills' are really personal and moral attributes that are shaped by family socialization and become proxies for social class (Warhurst and Nickson, 2007; Warhurst and Thompson, 2006). Likewise qualifications are not true estimates of skills or knowledge but are substitute measures as well. For example, when degrees are rebadged for previously sub-degree work, a process referred to as 'qualification inflation,' employers simply raise the entry tariff with increasing demands for credentials to deselect candidates in a particular sector (otherwise known as 'credentialism') (Warhurst and Thompson, 2006, p. 792).

Reskilling and upskilling are often discussed as one in the same in the literature, although distinguishing between these concepts assists in analysing migrant women's situations. Reskilling was illustrated in instances when participants were offered workplace training that actually helped them to understand a new culture and sector; for example, specialist training in topics such as palliative care. Upskilling referred to the higher educational opportunities (adaptation) that increased the participants' human capital worth on the national labour market enabling them to pursue professional positions. These were, however, often unavailable to the participants. The participants had access to workplace and vocational training, but it was neither interesting nor valuable for the professional market. Yet this training was promoted as 'upskilling' as if it were making, 'silk purses from sow's ears' (Hyland, 1994). There were some participants who were able to access higher education, or convert their degrees, although it is unclear whether this was upskilling or just upgrading, considering the jobs they obtained.

Advancement or carousel

Eleven per cent of the participants progressed from being 'just carers' to paid nurses in England.[3] They viewed this advancement as part of 'stepping up' in the world of care like one newly minted nurse:

> I feel relieved because it meant leaving here [the care home where she worked]. It meant getting a better job, *stepping up*, you know, moving on, whatever you want to call it. It meant that. Basically that's the reason I left home at the end of the day, isn't it?

They also viewed this move, according to this nurse, as 'a chance to have a life.' These new nurses, however, found it difficult to manage all of the work that was expected of them. One new nurse summarized her work life by saying she was called on to do 'anything':

> I have to do anything—carer work and as a nurse. And as a nurse I have to work and when the manager is not there we have to be in charge of everything... we have to do the same as they have to do. It is difficult.

Another nurse rationalized that she worked like 'a mad woman' because she was new and didn't have many outside commitments:

> If anything arises, I will be there to pick it up. And there's another thing, they know that I haven't got other commitments, so they'll just jump at the opportunity and just ask me first thing and they know I'm always there to cover, so that's the problem.

One care-assistant-turned-nurse, Anya, from Romania, was in her early 50s. She was given all night shifts totalling 42 hours a week, part of which were care assistant duties to fill a shortage in her care home. She said, '42... I think that's enough for me, I'm getting older!' She felt uncomfortable about having so many responsibilities that were over and beyond her nursing role with colleagues that did not always follow her lead. It was overwhelming:

> When I am in charge everybody say 'oh, you are a boss.' For God's sake I don't like to be bossy and I told my colleague and my colleague

say, 'sorry, we are colleagues, mate.' What can I say? Except when I am in charge with a big responsibilities I have to respond to everything that happens in the nursing home, you know. It's a big responsibility.

Her family in Romania became more supportive since she had become a nurse in England. She reported that she was 'very happy because I progress now and they are more support for me now and my friends from Romania as well... Before they said, "why are you a carer, or something?"' Her former colleagues thought it was a 'shame' that she worked as a care assistant. But she retorted by telling them: 'It's not easy... and they understood, finally.' Anya had to make major accommodations for her nursing post, including applying for it without any workplace support, dropping her English to Speakers of Other Languages (ESOL) course, which she could no longer attend due to working in a new town, and she had to leave her family for long periods of time. It took her nearly an hour to get to work and the bus travel made her sick: 'Travelling by bus is killing me, it's a sickness travelling.' Although Anya had moved from being 'just a carer' in a residential care home to a nurse in a nursing home, her work life was substandard. Only two new nurses in the study got jobs in hospitals and these were private. Kingma found that the global elder care industry depends on the labour of migrant nurses to such an extent that it is often referred to as a migrant ghetto from which it is hard to escape. Other studies have concurred that being a nurse is hardly the end point in integrating into the labour market or host society (Winkelmann-Gleed, 2004).

The act of becoming a nurse was difficult and the length of time it took to convert qualifications was relative to the country where the participants were trained. For the European national participants, it took between one and two years to convert their qualifications, which involved extensive translations of documents and bureaucratic wrangling with professional associations in both countries around obtaining and making legitimate their degrees and experience. Also the rationale for the amount and types of documents that were demanded from the participants was not clearly explained, including confirmation letters from top officials and doctors in their countries that they had indeed practised and that the documents were authentic. Anya, for example, waited nearly two years to finish the process, and asked why 'in England we have to wait and they ask for a lot of documents and I don't know why.' As part of this process, she frequently travelled to Romania. She saw this process as part of 'fighting' and she solicited her Romanian colleagues to help her transport the documents and get signatures during their holiday trips. She felt the process was punitive because she was a citizen of a late-joining member country of the European Union, one which was filled with people who were perceived as undesirables (Romanis or 'gypsies'):

> My country was the last country, and Bulgaria, who came in the Union Europe, you know. And in my country there are a lot of gypsy people. They are doing a lot of bad things you know, and we are suffering.

These participants were then issued pin numbers (a professional validation from the NMC that enabled them to apply for jobs as nurses). For those participants from non-EU countries (only two in this group), it was necessary to undergo a costly and labour-intensive process of: testing, adaptation training, mentoring, licensing, and then, with visas, a process of locating work. These steps involved, if they had at least three years in a nursing degree programme, first, taking the IELTS exam and passing it, applying to the NMC, and if accepted, enrolling in an overseas adaptation programme through an accredited university (of which there is a small number) and which consists of 20 days of protected learning time which is about 150 hours plus supervised practice. Then they were allowed to register, which means they earned their pin numbers only to be subject to a fickle market. These nurses paid their recruiters a lump sum that included payment to the nursing home for mentoring. One successful nurse described the process:

> I paid £1,500 for adaptation, £2,000 for agency and £1,000 for nursing home. I spent 20 days at the University. Teaching is set up with classes halfway and clinical assessment is here [in the nursing home]. B. is my mentor. The programme leader came here to assess and my mentor, myself, and manager did it. I sent the paperwork to NMC and got the declaration form for £76. They sent it back and then I received my pin number.

This nurse was lucky whereas another one could not locate a position, once she obtained her pin number. Jayanti was 26 and in England for ten months working as a care assistant. She migrated to 'do adaptation— that was my main ambition and to get a pin number to work as a nurse and after a time being I thought I can do some master's and that was my ambition.' She began her adaptation in April at a university over a two-week period but completed the process in November, which she referred to as 'a long time' with 'many things we had to do.' After returning to her nursing home and completing her mentoring she created a portfolio that included an essay of 2,000 words. She had it signed off, sent in her materials, and had to wait for them to publish the results. One month passed and they made the declaration, after which she received her pin number, by 'God's grace.' Jayanti went to the library on a daily basis to use the Internet for job-hunting but without success. Her visa needed to be renewed and she worried that she would not locate a job and did not 'want to make trouble.' She reasoned that 'she still has a job' and would stay in it until she could move up. Kingma (2006) discusses the delaying tactic of nursing professional associations and programmes as part of exploitation. Meanwhile, Jayanti felt that working long hours as a care assistant while undergoing adaptation was 'too difficult for me—morning to night, 8 a.m. to 8 p.m. It's hard work.'

After undergoing all of these hardships, the participants who had located nursing posts reinstated their professional identities and were adamant that this move reaffirmed their initial migration decisions. It improved their images too. One participant felt she had 'arrived' in nursing when she 'could get my job again' as a nurse. Their newness, however, made them feel as if they were in entry-level positions. This nurse went on to say, 'I'm going back to square one practically.' Most of these new nurses in England felt that it would be difficult to get a job at a high-paying NHS hospital and were hesitant to apply based on the fact that they were only just certified. One nurse wondered, 'What are the chances of me getting a job as a nurse in the hospital now, when I wasn't actually a nurse in the UK?' The NHS seemed impenetrable to these new nurses. The Indian participants, for example, found jobs in private hospitals. While their waiting periods to migrate were long, their initial entry visas that allowed them to live and work in England were brief, compared to the European nationals. This situation propelled them to adapt as quickly as they could, taking whatever hospital nursing post that was offered first. They also endured much discrimination.

Conclusion

The primary identities of the new nurses were restored when they moved into these positions, despite the difficulties they faced. They saw themselves in entry positions willing to do whatever it took to prove themselves in their new roles. But only a few of the former nurses advanced and while they became 'integrated' into the systems of nursing in England, their own knowledge bases did not count (Raghuram, 2007). There were no straightforward or economical professional pathways for the other professionals to follow beyond care assistant. Former teachers, for example, would have to take 'top up' undergraduate courses to lift their original credentials (Miller, 2008, p. 21). These participants decided that they could not afford the time and cost to overhaul their entire careers. Plus many of them were in a type of debt bondage that further tied them to their employers. This issue went beyond the critique of the positivist culture of 'measuring' qualifications (Miller, 2008, pp. 22–23). It pointed to a real deprivation of these women's livelihoods.

For the majority of participants whose occupational role never changed from that of a care assistant, they clung to their former identities as professionals in order to preserve their sense of self-respect and dignity. This group never referred to themselves in the past tense, for example, using the term 'former' to talk about themselves but claimed that they *were* professionals, a fact which they hid from others with who they worked. One participant said: 'I don't tell the district nurse that *I am a nurse.*' Some of these participants adopted a type of martyr or saint role as care assistants (Pratt, 2004; Solari, 2006). Or they turned their attentions to their families and carved out a bigger role for them in their schedules, or built lives with new partners. They also viewed their care assistant work as a temporary situation that would at some point be recouped, either in England or a new country. The double-consciousness that the women participants in this study expressed towards care work—seeing it as essential to society but realizing they had become 'locked-in' to a downgraded occupation affected their aspirations. This double-identity was conflictive (Haour-Knipe and Davies, 2008).

This chapter showed the ways gender regimes shaped these women's trajectories with the mechanisms of the global care industry tracking them before their actual migration began (Yeates, 2009). As women, many embraced the culture of service and working in helping fields *before* they migrated—with traits that were carried over from their feminized professions into their current work as care assistants. Eighty per cent of these women were in some type of nurturing field prior to becoming care assistants. These participants often saw caring as central to their professions, although they recognized that the hands-on part of it had little worth on the career ladder. They also saw care as central to their gender identities and status obligations in society.

The participants in the study viewed care assistant work as a type of survival employment while they gathered together their resources. These jobs were introduced to them as stepping-stones by recruiters, but they functioned more like 'trampolines' where they bounced around rather than moved up (Warhurst, 2008, p. 79). These types of short-lived jobs were not sustainable for their long-term employment and livelihoods in view of the poor conditions. These migrants appeared to be sought for this overtaxing type of work and when they figured this out, they revised their plans. These jobs were not 'safety nets' either, like those for British-born students bussing tables, who draw on the resources of their middle-class families because of the low pay. The participants were not told by their recruiters about these obstacles, a finding which is not uncommon. Susan Maybud and Christiane Wiskow (2006, p. 223) claim that, private recruitment agencies:

> Invite the loggers-on to explore a myriad of opportunities. Go ahead, they entice, just click on this website and you are one step closer to a better life.

The barriers that the participants faced, which were structural and gender-based, affected their motivations and strategies. These barriers emerged as soon as they enrolled in their universities (in the itinerary stage) with their subject specialties and were exacerbated when they entered the labour pool (the venturing out stage). Upon migrating into an entry-level employment niche and a country with short-term visa arrangements and severe professional standards, they were forced to adopt a strategy of slow tracking their careers by putting their dreams on hold while they laboured in low-level care work. Few of them could accumulate enough resources to advance out of their situations. Eventually they either reduced these hurdles (a minority of participants) to advance, or they cognitively reframed their aspirations to align with their circumstances. For the minority, they progressed through on their own, while the majority withdrew from their dreams. Significant deskilling resulted. This chapter illuminated the mechanisms for this 'race to the bottom' of the care labour market (a concept which will be discussed in depth in Chapter 7). The historical precedence of this downward trajectory is clear for women migrating to England (Yeates, 2009). This situation, however, was also subjective and therefore contradictory, as many of the women concluded that the difficulties they faced as care assistants developed their character as if it were a 'silver lining in the cloud,' as one participant said. Their redemptive narratives emphasized being a 'good person' and 'mother' as they had

> become more strong. This is the first time I sent money for my children. No one help me—independence. I like that I enrolled my

children on my own money. I sent 85,000 pesos to her [her mother]. I had nothing left. How many years they support me. 'Just once, can you send money,' my mother asked. That was the first time my mother asked me. That was last week. I felt good about it... I am so happy and I become a good person and mother.

Many of the participants, as independent opportunists, saw their education as 'passports' and became immersed in a 'global treasure hunt' for a better life long before they migrated (Kingma, 2006, p. 182). One nurse imagined:

> What I want most with the nurse is their uniform! When I was young I really wanted to be a nurse because I look at them and they are really clean and when I get older, I still liked to be a nurse because I want to go to other countries.

The next chapter turns from the participants' idealized career aspirations and challenging work lives to their families and discusses the informal care that they provided and exchanged. These interactions operated as both supports and pressures to the participants as they entrenched them further in their roles as caregivers at the same time that they propelled them into being change agents.

6
Caring in Transnational Networks

Introduction

This chapter presents the innovative strategies that the participants used in caring for their families and friends amid tensions they experienced with their paid care and its effects on their sense of belonging and identity. While Chapter 5 discussed the problems that these women experienced in developing their careers, this chapter gives a closer glimpse of their worlds apart from their workplaces and outside of England. For this, I analysed a subset of 22 participants in Strands 1 and 2 who engaged in in-depth interviews up to four times each between 2007 and 2009.[1] These interviews, staggered over time, and covering many issues surrounding technology and media uses as well as social support exchanges, enabled me to gauge the function of care in the participants' transnational relationships—also referred to as, transnational caregiving (Baldassar, 2007a, p. 387), which includes childcare, eldercare, and the maintenance of family and friendship ties.

Deborah Bryceson and Ulla Vuorela (2002, p. 3) define transnational families as living apart from one another yet holding together and creating feelings of collective welfare and unity, namely 'familyhood,' across national borders. I will first focus on the transnational caring of family and network members and the issues that arose for the participants. These interactions were also the basis of diasporas that preserved, shared, and transformed practices that gave the participants a sense of belonging. Next I will discuss the technologies and the digital practices that facilitated care exchanges and the development of network capital. Lastly I will examine the rewards and strains of caring from a distance and locally. For this, I will focus on one case, which illustrates the preceding themes. Throughout the chapter, 'scenes' of caring for 'others-at-a-distance' illustrate the worlds that the participants physically left behind but in which they were still immersed.

Importantly, I will highlight these participants as 'pioneer migrants,' mentioned in Chapter 1.[2] These migrants are the first generation in their immediate families to enter an employment niche in another country and to endure the consequences of neither receiving information nor support provided normally by migration networks (Lindstrom and Ramirez, 2010, p. 54). As Chapter 5 showed, these migrants used agencies to migrate to become care assistants, which was a risk when the staff fallaciously presented it as a route to advancing into the professional arena. Still the participants stayed and channelled successive migrants to follow them, a flow that was made possible through phones and computers. Pioneers, typically high-achieving and resourceful, play a critical role in migration streams, making it easier for followers by providing shelter, information, and jobs, thereby decreasing barriers to adjustment (Lindstrom and Ramirez, 2010). A number of the participants, for example, sponsored spouses and one brought her sister, nearly all of who became care assistants, creating a solid base for local networks. Another example is a participant's sponsorship of her brother as she felt responsible for him because 'I am the only family he had in England.' Although he had some medical training and a BA in business administration, his sister advised that he take care assistant training in the Philippines. But when he arrived on a student visa in England the training company he had enrolled in and paid for folded, making him vulnerable for deportation. She found him a new training company, helped him move to a new city and care home, and asked her British boyfriend to further assist him. In turn, with his business background, the brother helped her navigate a divorce so she could marry this man.

As this example shows, pioneers take risks and although they may bring over their support networks, they are never fully protected from larger problems; Tina, in Chapter 5, for example, could never have counted on her otherwise healthy husband dying from an illness a year after he was sponsored by her. Like these other pioneers she had to recover and reinvent her livelihood as one of many 'new faces in new places' (Massey, 2008).

Transnational family and social networks: Childcare, eldercare and friendship ties

Many participants migrated without their children. Their care assistant jobs were not family-friendly and laws discouraged family reunification.

Furthermore, as Chapter 5 highlighted, these mothers put their own professional careers, ones established in their native-born countries on hold, when they migrated to England. They hoped, however, to sponsor their children to migrate and remitted with the goal of giving them the best education and opportunities they could afford.

Their breadwinner status, however, worked against them as mothers from the perspective of agency officials who saw 'left-behind' children from 'broken homes' as a burden on society (Parrenas, 2005). The Episcopal Commission on Migrants and Itinerant People (ECMI), for example, pronounced: 'The absence of the mother is felt more than the fathers, why? Because mothers are the normal point of reference for children in situations which requires consultation' (cited in Ogaya, 2004, p. 180). Although government officials try to keep mothers from migrating, they glorify them as heroes for their remittances (Lutz, 2011).

Another view sees transnational families sympathetically, highlighting rather than degrading women as mothers *and* breadwinners with a strong will to survive under globalization pressures: They migrate due to poverty and overcompensate to their children with gifts and deeds as part of assuaging their guilt for not being the 'light of the home' (Parrenas, 2005, pp. 57, 103). This is because they give their love to those in advanced economies in exchange for 'gold' (Hochschild, 2002, p. 15). The ones back home, however, are emotionally deprived as a result due to the 'pain of family separation' (Parrenas, 2001, p. 361). *Caregiver*, a popular film, encapsulates this view. It is about a Filipina teacher who migrates to London as a care assistant. Her plight in dealing with the emotional problems her child experiences in the Philippines is viewed with compassion and is moving, although it reinforces the view that children are a type of 'luggage' that burden the mobile parent (Orellana, 2001 in White, Laoire, Tyrell, and Carpena-Méndez, 2011, p. 1162). This analysis does not consider the new emotional grammars (rules regarding the display and performance of emotion) that form across the miles between family members (Nussbaum, 2001, p. 149).

Both of these views produce conventional accounts of transnational families losing 'care resources' when a member migrates (McKay, 2007, p. 177). First, women's migration is focused primarily on their mothering role rather than as daughters, aunts, sisters, friends, and colleagues. Subsequently, women without children, sibling relationships, and eldercare are downplayed (Baldassar, 2007b; Yeates, 2009). Second, the 'stay-behinds' are viewed as passive and immobile in the migration process. As one study (Goulbourne, Reynolds, Solomos, and Zontini, 2010, p. 7) showed, there are 'wheels within wheels simultaneously turning' that change transnational families' situations and children are active participants (White et al., 2011). Due to what has been conceived as a downward cycle in a 'global care chain' (Hochschild, 2000, p. 130), the care these children receive 'back home' by 'helpers' is viewed as unstable and wanting because these stand-ins are not seen as fully available or competent as mothers. This conception also assumes that the meaning of care in lower income countries in the 'global south' carries the same meanings in high-income countries in the 'global north;' in some countries care is based on obligation and reciprocity and a combination of economic ties, social contracts, and support, not market relations alone (Kofman and Raghuram, 2009). Third, neglected in conventional accounts are pre-existing family and work complications in migrant women's countries of origin; the participants' stories, particularly those who were laid off or experienced partner abuse, are missing. This leads to the last point. Emotional labour (especially for the emigrants' family) is viewed as a limited monetized resource like raw materials that are extracted from poor countries (Hochschild, 2000). This implies that migrant women can only emotionally support their employers or clients and few others (McKay, 2007). Yet participants in this study showed again and again that they formed resilient networks with friends locally and simultaneously connected and communicated with family abroad too—sending both money and love (Baldassar, 2008; Fresnoza-Flot, 2009; McKay, 2007) and where possible, sponsoring them. Mirca Madianou and Daniel Miller (2011, 2012) found that, historically, emigrant Filipinos crafted care and compassion in innovative ways that fostered different types of relations in their communication through audio tapes and letters. This communication continues in different forms in to the 21st century. I will provide examples and argue that participants challenged conventional depictions with multiple ways of transnational caring.

Rearranged dynamics in transnational families

Newer studies on transnational families focus on family rearrangement through emotional, financial, and technological connections bridging the distance rather than family abandonment (Fresnoza-Flot, 2009; Goulbourne et al., 2010; Parrenas, 2005). These involve wider networks of support and resilient bonds. Mothers, for example, may engage in both 'natural' and 'social' collective approaches to childrearing (Lutz, 2011). Importantly, these families and communities work on their relations through innovative means. One small-scale study (Graham, Jordon, and Yeoh, 2010) found that transnational children miss their mothers because of their hands-on care, although they had frequent daily contact with her and that 'other mothers' mediated their level of happiness. They found that children's control over the contact and their own ideas around mothering were important factors in their well-being. Loretta Baldassar (2007a) showed that transnational families care for one another in similar ways to proximate families, including personal support (hands-on caring), practical support (from gardening to advice-giving), and emotional and moral support. These care exchanges happened through extended visits, phone calls and texts, gifts, audiotapes, letters, email, and new media computer/internet connections. These supports are shared across the miles as an 'emotional gift exchange' (Hochschild, 2003b, p. 84). Visits become opportunities for 're-emplacement' in family and community rituals, and are ways for emigrants to recharge batteries and check on the effects of being away (Fresnoza-Flot, 2009; McKay, 2005, p. 75). These exchanges are shaped by histories of commitments between family members, that is, obligations or cultural expectations, as well as their capacities to enact them in addition to 'the license to leave' (approval of kin to migrate) (Baldassar, 2008, p. 249). The family and community, after all, are important mediators in women's migration as they are involved in a continuous and complex process of decision-making and nurturance (Ryan, Sales, Tilki, and Siara, 2008).

Women tend to develop network and household strategies for migrating (Boyd, 2006; Mahler and Pessar, 2006) that create stronger embedded systems, including long-term relationships based on emotional bonds and obligations (Ryan et al., 2008). These networks also reinforce women migrants' traditional gender roles as nurturers especially when it comes to maintaining these dense ties (Parrenas, 2005). As 'mothers-away' (Parrenas, 2005, p. 120), for example, they are often expected to remit more to children for basic needs as they are considered more reliable, and cheap airfares and technologies may increase expectations that they communicate and visit more often (Boyd, 2006; Fresnoza-Flot, 2009). Yet other research suggests that women experience liberation from gender norms upon migrating (Boyd, 2006; Hondagnu-Sotelo, 2000). This may lead daughters and mothers to have more open communication about intimate subjects (Fresnoza-Flot, 2009) or, on the other hand, alienation from kin due to not wanting to be ensnared in 'old ways' (Baldassar, 2007a). Idiosyncrasies within transnational families and personal networks are the norm and will be discussed in the next sections. This perspective is different from the self-sufficient male migration model (Kofman, Phizacklea, Raghuram, and Sales, 2000).

Multiple ties

For those participants without children, their roles as daughters and granddaughters often took precedence. Cielo is an example of a daughter and granddaughter, breadwinner, and caregiver. Illnesses defined much of Cielo's intergenerational and transnational care in her family and personal network. Raised by her aunt in a suburb of Manila, she was a 24-year-old single nurse from a well-off family. Cielo's mother was a nurse in Austria who had returned to the Philippines when her husband, working in Saudi Arabia, became ill. After getting lung cancer, the father came home to the Philippines to be cared for by his wife and daughter and died at age 53. Cielo was a key support since her brothers worked in Saudi Arabia like their father. Although Cielo initially enrolled in medical school, when her father returned to the Philippines, she dropped out to care for him. She pursued nursing due to the lack of funds to return to medical school. Upon graduating, she worked as a community nurse while caring for her father and, after he died, decided to work abroad. Her mother, however, 'told me not to go because of her own experience, that it is very difficult.' When Cielo arrived in England she was still grieving for her father and was homesick, crying nearly all of the time. Her mother and boyfriend in the Philippines were her main support system and they called her at first every other day due to their 'worry' and she chatted with him daily in the mornings through her housemate's computer. But then she started to make new friends locally. She said, 'I can handle problems without my mum. Because I used to ask mother when I first came here, but now I have [names of four friends]. Maybe now I am confident.' The content of her calls to them continued to consist of trading sentiments of closeness and checking on one another. She said, 'I was excited when I called my mum. I always miss her every time. I just talk. I cry and sometimes I don't want to talk because she or me is crying: "I miss you. 'I miss you,' she says." Cielo also texted with her brothers, the whole family communicating from afar by phone and computer. When her new life settled down, her grandfather suddenly became ill and was put into hospital. While she wanted to return to see him for the last time, her schedule and resources would not permit it, despite her sense of duty. Her new friends and flat-mates in England consoled her and asked her critical questions, as family would do, that made her closely assess the situation. Her friend asked, 'What if your grandpa dies, are you going back?' 'And I am thinking about it...but we don't have the ticket and I don't have time for my holiday to go.' Cielo and other migrants in their 20s had young parents in their 40s and early 50s, which did not rule out the fact they might not be in good health.

Family members found ways to care for one another despite the distance. For Eastern Europeans, hands-on caring for parents was less difficult due to the proximity and ease of visiting, as, for example, two Polish sisters. Both in their 50s, they traded off caring for their 70-something year old mother in Poland and relieved a third sister who lived with their mother. One of the sisters said, 'When I go to Poland I am only going to my mother's. She [the other sister] needs a rest from mother because she does the caring for her. She comes here once a month.' The sister's trips back to Poland, therefore, were not vacations but additional care work. Once returned, they claimed they needed a 'holiday.'

Sisters were important to many of the participants. They depended on their sisters to care for ageing family members and exchanged support with them by listening to their problems and giving advice. One Polish participant praised her older sister for caring for their mother who was in poor health as well as her 85-year-old grandmother who depended on her granddaughter for 'cleaning, shopping and giving her a bath once a week.' Her sister, she thought, 'was amazing.' Although the participant's sister had a degree she could not locate work in Poland and settled into a family care role. She confessed, 'I am so lucky—I am her little sister so she feels responsible for me as well!'

Spouse or partner relations, however, could be fraught with tension especially when living apart. Maria, a 40-year old Filipina tried to divorce her sea-merchant husband of 11 years who she had not seen since he left her and their ten-year old daughter. Since then he had 'married' another Filipina in a Gulf state but had already 'divorced' her. Due to his complicated situation, she felt 'it won't be a problem' to get the divorce papers, although it was difficult in the Philippines due to law and also 'because it's been a long time' since they saw one another. But when she asked him to sign the papers, he demanded that she sponsor him to England and finance it too as part of the deal. Through her family's help, she got him to cooperate. It was not uncommon for participants to have partners in England, like Maria, whose boyfriend wanted to marry her. A Romanian woman, Doriana also had a British boyfriend and wanted a divorce from her husband in Romania. He was unwilling and because of the law, it was made more difficult. 'You have to have very specific reasons to divorce,' she explained. Before leaving, they lived in the same house but had separate rooms and did not argue for fear of upsetting their daughter. This created more difficulties in securing a divorce without evidence of problems. She said:

> This is what I said to the judge, 'so you want me to come back here with bruises and you know, shouting that he bite me or what else do you want me to do? There's a child there and she can listen to us when we're arguing and I don't like to.' I'm not that kind of person to argue.

She returned numerous times to Romania to see her daughter who lived with her mother and even once found work while she was gathering documents to prove her case. She felt that she was mismatched to his farming family, which held traditional ideals for women as 'suffering—they have to stay with the man because of being married and they have to raise children like a 100 years ago.' This contrasted with her 'modern' ideals of 'freedom and more civilization' which prompted her initial migration. While she supported her young daughter's expensive private schooling, her ultimate dream was to 'take my daughter here [to England].' She also planned to sponsor her mother for her childcare. She wanted to flee her small Romanian town, 'to be so far away from these people—I'm just fed up with them' although she wanted her daughter to live in the small town in England where she resided because 'it is more safer for her to live in a small town.' It was even harder to sponsor partners or friends due to the strict immigration controls. Dahlia, a Romanian, invited her 'best friend' to England. Although he was a computer engineer the only jobs he could locate were in industrial cleaning and fast food. His misfortune caused the two to argue and he returned to Romania within a month.

Maria, Doriana, and Dahlia's examples demonstrate the persistence of gender in the participants' roles not only as mothers, but as daughters, sisters, and spouses/partners, and also the ways they circumvented these roles. It also indicates the fluid nature of 'family' in including non-biological members (Goulbourne et al., 2010).

Mobile and engaged mothers and children

Most participants in this sample were mothers. Most of their children lived in their country of origin, except for those who were eventually sponsored and several participants (four) gave birth to children in England. The children were highly mobile. One participant returned to her natal India to have her baby and then brought her parents-in-law to England to care for the infant during the initial maternity period. Upon the birth, she sent her colleagues photographs of her child by email, naming her daughter Diane, but with an Indian nickname, India being a hub of national and transnational communication during this period. This also reveals the case of 'travelling grandparents' who ameliorate difficult times (like having a baby) for their adult children. These grandparents often created the necessary support within the household as it adjusted to a new member as maternity leave was granted by the workplace (16 weeks normally) but free childcare was not.

All of the mothers timed their emigration in line with life course events. A few of the participants had adult children, one of whom migrated to work at the same care home as his mother. He wanted to be closer to her, having been raised by his grandmother in the Romanian countryside, so his divorced mother could work and live in Bucharest. He was used to caring for his grandmother too, enabling his mother to migrate and he migrated a year after his grandmother died. He said, 'I just stay in Romania because it's better to stay with my grandmum.' The children therefore were active participants in their mothers' migration, influencing their decisions. They often encouraged their mothers to return for holidays, in which case, the non-Europeans often took month-long visits each year. During periods of being apart from their children, it was common for mothers to contact them daily by phone or computer. In this sense, they were not 'distant mothers' but were 'mothering from a distance' (Parrenas, 2001, p. 361). Their connection was important in letting the children know that mum was still 'here' although not physically present and that being in a transnational family was OK. This contact was more than 'intensive mothering' through technological management of family members from afar that created a 'semblance of intimacy' (McKay, 2007; Parrenas, 2005, p. 103), but was of great emotional support to everyone. One mother paid £50 a week in phone call fees to the Philippines to communicate with her children daily until she began using a friend's computer to chat with them (on Yahoo messenger and Skype) as well as share pictures. She said:

> For my break, I open the laptop and I talk to the children and show them England and tell them, 'this is England!' I miss them so much. My youngest daughter told me 'Mama, the time is quick, now it's March' and she is full capacity and speaks positively: 'I am here for you Mom and don't worry and don't cry.' She is eight years old. I don't cry.

Tensions could arise however when teens began to question their live-in caregivers. In one case a teen, raised by her grandmother, asked her mother, Joy (a participant), 'Mama can you come home,' when the two had problems. Joy then requested that her ex-husband intervene. She also had friends to check on her daughter and her other children:

> My friends in Philippines are in contact by Internet. They help me by sending photos and telling me what happened to my children. They are near in my heart. If I ask them, 'can you look after my children and go to their home' they can go and check. They give me information about them.

Joy's mother, who lived in Germany and cared for Joy's sister's children there, also gave her advice. Joy was assured that the care that her children received was good and reliable, being guided by extensive support through transnational family and friends. Also, their phone calls, texts, and computer connections became small but important interventions that helped maintain an emotional equilibrium.

The technological connections were not just means for sustaining intimacy and obtaining information from far away but could prelude sponsorship. Some mothers put off sponsorship until they felt their children were ready. One mother sponsored her teenage son so as to monitor his medical condition but kept her daughter, half his age, under the care of her mother and sister in the Philippines. She did not think it was wise to remove her because if she sponsored her, she would only return soon after with the older brother 'to finish their studies.' She felt in control of her sponsorship decisions. However, many mothers worried about their children losing their first languages, after they had been sponsored, especially if they were to return to their natal country, so ensured that the native language was used in the home. Once the children were settled in schools though, it was more difficult for parents to return. One Romanian who brought her husband and two children to England said, 'My children don't want to go back to Romania. They really like it here. They like the school, they make friends there.' While she took her one child back and forth to Romania for medical care she wanted to stay in England for at least 'five to ten more years.' She taught the children Romanian at home so that their adjustment would be made easier upon their return.

The issues of sponsorship are rarely discussed in a literature that focuses more on children as 'left behind.' The sponsored children in this sub-sample (a total of ten children) had a number of issues to contend with including adjusting to a new type of schooling, after school care, and conflicts in values between home and community. As Chapter 4 showed, in the case of Lisette, her son was tested by his peers, and smoking, sex, and other family morals were called in to question. In one case a 20-year-old niece was sponsored to England for childcare but caused distrust in the participant when she exposed the three children to content on the Internet as well as television shows that challenged her beliefs. She said, 'These things I don't want my children to be listening to. I was so cross, and I said [to her niece], "I don't want this anymore" and she's doing this again.' Some parents specifically did not sponsor their daughters for fear of breaking mores. Lisette was worried about sponsoring her daughter, she said because of the 'drugs, and they are open to all sorts of alcohol, cigarettes you know.' Another mother decided to put off her daughter's sponsorship because: 'I'm just against the way children are brought up when it comes to sex education because back home, we still treated children like children.' Many of the participants preferred private religious schools where their daughters were enrolled and excelled. They wanted to sponsor them when they were more mature. They spoke British English to them as a way to prepare them for this time. One participant said, 'I spoke to her and she said, "wow Mummy you speak English fluently" and I asked her if she would like to come over and you know stay for a while.'

Pre-migration pushes: Home and work stresses and familial incentives

Nearly all of the participants were breadwinners prior to migrating and they balanced work shifts with home life for most of their adult lives. As examples from Chapter 5 revealed, migration was precluded by stressful events that had become intolerable to the participants in the home and the workplace, with its impoverished work conditions and management pressures, sexism, and limited opportunities to advance. On a macro level, it was also due to restructuring and neo-liberal policies for which women's jobs and lives were made vulnerable in conjunction with deficient or non-existing social and health care services, as was discussed in Chapter 1. For example, the remittances were sent for basic amenities including medical care, housing needs, and schooling. One participant said she remitted for her daughter's 'schooling and food, you know, *her basic needs*.' Another participant migrated to afford the cost of her son's medicine and noted that generally medical services were increasingly expensive over the past 20 years.

Migration was key to surviving these difficult family conditions. Saskia Sassen (1998) theorizes that capital-rich nations create unstable markets in emerging countries' urban centres, producing large-scale displacements from the countryside. Women move to these jobs but they are insecure. Once women are engaged, they are more amenable to follow markets and enter permanently into the short-term economy in advanced economies. Although Sassen focuses on factory work, a similar situation exists for care work for source countries of health care professionals (Kingma, 2006). Once in hospitals, these overworked nurses looked for other ways to carry on their care work that would lift their incomes even if it didn't raise their status or careers. This situation was also apparent for those who were non-health care professionals. Economic upheaval tends to lower people's threshold levels until families can no longer bear them and they are compelled to take risks to migrate (Bryceson and Vuorela, 2002). The participants discussed the difficulties related to poverty that preceded their emigration. Nearly all of the mothers felt that it was an economic necessity to migrate. As one Romanian said:

> Because in Romania life's quite difficult and hard in every way, school, food, house, clothes, medication, everything... so here with my wage and my Mum's help, I can afford to raise her [daughter].

Stressful work lives meant these mothers had even less time to spend with their children and didn't communicate as much as they would have liked with them. A couple of mothers noticed that their communication about difficult and deep issues had actually *improved* after they migrated with regular phone calling and more open communication. This happened as their children grew older and adjusted to their transnational situation. For those women who had been in other countries prior to migrating to England, their children (and other family members) accommodated and attempted to find an even ground to forge better relations across the miles—the distance permitting more emotional communication (Fresnoza-Flot, 2009). One mother bought her daughter an expensive mobile phone 'because I need to hear her voice you know I want to hear how she speaks' even though she noted, they couldn't 'cuddle' each other. Her constant calls smoothed her roles of being a breadwinner and an away mother—voice, rather than text becoming an intimate medium (Madiniaou and Miller, 2012). She said, 'Because I'm away, I tend to be more active and involved with her because that's the only way that I could be, you know, a mum.

Although I'm away.' She acknowledged that the physical distance made it tough though, 'Because we're not seeing each other personally, only through the phone.'

In other cases, close transnational relationships further led some women into a pattern of serial migration. One Polish woman met her Australian boyfriend in the USA (where she was working at the time). He intended to move to London but was then transferred temporarily to South Africa. After waiting for him, she decided she was 'done' with the relationship and migrated onwards. Other women migrated first to countries like Singapore, Israel, and Saudi Arabia prior to migrating to England where they knew family members and were informed about the job, culture, and other issues. As one participant said:

> Because most of my family were working in Israel—my aunt my cousins and some of my distant relatives so, for me it's not difficult, I mean to deal with Israeli people because I was informed ahead of time.

Few of the women had family in England and of these they were more distant relatives who they hardly saw or expected support from. Transnational family members in other countries (e.g. Australia, USA, and European countries) would also assist with migration to England even if they didn't live there and modelled living a transnational life for those who were uncertain about how to do it. These relatives would help them mainly through emotional support, information, and advice. In a sense, these dispersed family relations could 'care about' in ways that could be considered a type of 'cultural or social remittance' (Goulbourne et al., 2010, p. 84; Levitt and Lamba-Nieves, 2011). The frequent contact enabled the participants to keep the family together amidst difficulties and distance (Bryceson and Vuorela, 2002, p. 14).

Emotional care to and from many in local networks

Family relationships and friendships were important, particularly for emotional care. Some clients and relatives of participants had a give-and-take emotional relationship. One participant, for example, went with a client's daughter on holiday trips abroad in a non-work role. The clients of the participants, most of whom were also women, were also former nurses, teachers, and nannies, as well as wives and mothers. One client was a former nanny of a wealthy family in England and had had a difficult experience with her employer, the children's mother who ordered her around. Years later, this one-time employer called her. 'She rang me up and said, "You must look after me I am dying."' To which the client responded, 'But I said, "No, I can barely take care of myself"... we kept in touch and the children still come and see me.' This former nanny—now a client of a care assistant herself—didn't want to repeat that behaviour since she said her home was 'very friendly' and she understood the complexity of long-term care. Hence, she tried to forge a good relationship with her own care assistants who said they appreciated her. This client also had much support from her grandson's wife, a social worker, who located the care home nearby to them, so they could visit on a regular basis. This family support lessened her dependence on her care assistants, enabling a courteous relationship to form. Other clients exchanged advice and other supports with participants. In one case, a client who was a former solicitor advised a participant about a complicated divorce, which she appreciated. Others asked about their children demonstrating sensitivity to their lives outside of their immediate care environment. Often these occurred during intimate moments where there was a mutual sense of needing support and strength. One participant testified to this type of relationship:

> My favorite client, she has cancer. She is strong. We talk about our personal life. I tell her about my children and she tells me, 'everything will be alright.' After a month I saw her, thin, because of weight loss: 'Can you tell me will everything be alright?' 'Yea,' she said, and I said, 'everything will be alright. You need to be strong.' I said to her, 'you told me my children will come.' I encourage her to eat so my children will come and see her.

But not all of these relationships were emotionally close and ended well. In one case a participant thought a burgeoning friendship between herself and a former client could further develop but ended badly when they went to a bar for a drink and she became drunk and offensive. And pity for clients could take over when they were seen as 'big babies,' as one described: 'I try to make them more happy, but I pity them. They live alone the whole day. I feel sad for them.'

In other cases, neighbours and church members as well as British flatmates and colleagues would offer emotional support to participants, although the relationships were oriented around physical proximity and a sense of common membership rather than an overriding sense of duty as with a close (or kin) relation. Church members could fill important gaps that could not be met by social services for which they were ineligible. One Zambian participant Tina was resilient. She counted on her church friends to take her children from school and pick them up as well as to help her make weekly budgets. She said, 'The church really helps.' These members also donated enough money to repatriate her husband's body to Zambia and provide a guard to oversee his grave. In another case a Mormon participant discovered, through a client's son, that there was a Mormon church nearby. These church members became a type of fictive kin that helped her integrate into her community. She acknowledged that in finding the church, she 'met people with the same belief—it is comforting. I am far away from my family and the next best thing is to be near church.'

Inter-ethnic friends and colleagues, however, were most important for emotional support. This was especially so for old friends who had migrated; they were looked at as kin. For example, one 'loved' a long-term Polish friend who lived in Ireland and was regarded as a 'soul mate' who would be there for her if she needed. New co-ethnic friends were also sources of emotional support, especially upon arrival when there was a greater need for it. Yet as their networks widened it could threaten relationships. Two participants who were recruited at the same time by an agency called and texted one another during the two-year waiting period. They lived together once they arrived in England, with one describing it as: 'husband-wife and [we] are now on a honeymoon.' The 'honeymoon,' however, did not last long when one moved out to share a home with more settled migrants of the same nationality; this was a jolt and the other felt abandoned when 'things changed.' Other co-ethnics, however, could be viewed, at least initially as competitive and distrusting (Ryan et al., 2008). Filipino participants had a term called 'crab mentality' to describe this feeling. A Filipina participant's brother warned her 'there are Filipinos who make life miserable: crab mentality—the crab goes up, the others will drag you down.' Overall, however, co-ethnics received and exchanged emotional care in the form of listening, sympathizing, and trading secrets and advice, and they exchanged material supports when they could (sharing computers, lending money, phones, etc.). This also extended to hanging out, buying and cooking food, sharing similar media, and speaking the same language (to be discussed in the next section). Most importantly, this emotional caring here contributed to a sense of belonging.

Diasporas for transnational belonging

While diaspora is referred to as a foundation by which dispersed people identify with their ethnic group and nationality (Brah, 1996), these participants also formed, 'labour diasporas' that manifest as an economic expansion of the migrant's homeland as well as when, as a group, they become locked into a subordinate status (Cohen, 2008). These migrant women participants formed an employment niche in care through their 'ethnic economies' (Rubin et al., 2008, p. 64). This diaspora, then, was characterized by both cultural allegiance *and* labour movement. This diaspora concept should be used with caution so as not to be so deterministic as to exclude certain behaviours and practices that do not fit within typical 'cultural boundaries' (Temple, 1999). This point is important because these participants were pioneers on a frontier in opening up the care industry, as Chapter 3 showed, to new practices. This chapter reveals that these participants also developed new familial and network spaces.

Nearly all of these participants risked their livelihoods and careers to migrate under precarious visas. Deborah Bryceson and Ulla Vuorela (2002, p. 11) define these migrants as 'frontiering' at the interface between two or more contrasting ways of life. Also the intimate domestic spaces that they worked in became contact zones for clashes of cultures and histories of colonial servitude, such as with Indian care assistants working with elderly British clients some of whom recalled their earlier days travelling and living in India and having servants. The labour diaspora also refers to the gendered nature of the care that, along with selected nationalities who work in the industry, created a 'diaspora space' of marginalized women. Diasporic space or transnational space (Brah, 1996, p. 242) was a base from which these migrants achieved a sense of belonging that they then cultivated. In this study, relaxing, talking, and sharing food were the main means by which these migrants carved out these shared spaces apart from work. These were informal relationships that flourished in the local homes, which they shared with one another, rather than public spaces such as bars and community centres. The private shared space enabled them to let down their guard, and separate themselves from the roles they played in other people's homes where they had to act deferentially and 'know their place.' In their own homes, they could speak freely and share resources, even at the expense of their employers' perceptions that they were 'clannish' as one claimed.

Getting together in houses/flats was key to not just sharing stories, but also cooking food and speaking in a familiar language as well as sharing media. They socialized at home because they had little spare time in their work schedules and were often on-call. Socializing at home meant they could sleep while waiting for friends to arrive and because their schedules were at times that most institutions, including pubs would be closed. These private spaces were the best places aside from cars, as discussed in Chapter 4, 'to get together nightly to hang out' as one said. When asked what they did in their leisure time, the most common answers were: sleeping, watching TV, cleaning, and cooking, as well as talking to family and friends. One participant said, 'I only have one day off, so we clean the flat and cook, we don't go out. We don't go to the pub.' It was also hard to find mutually agreeable public spaces to meet and they grabbed whatever moments they could to socialize and exchange goods and intangibles in a domestic, familiar, and safe surrounding (Brown and Talbot, 2006). This space was part of their 'grounded attachments' to their new dwelling places (Blunt, 2007, p. 687; Procter, 2003) and became a terrain for a collective sense of belonging (Fortier, 2000). In addition, there were few public services specifically aimed at them other than for specific purposes (e.g. visas) so the public space was, in a sense, not theirs. When they could not socialize at home they often phoned one another to check in and establish their schedules for when they could meet. Getting together enabled the participants to build a second 'home' in a new country.

Language

English was spoken at work for the most part, aside from times where co-ethnics needed to give quick organizational pointers or help one another. Employers required English but care assistants also wanted to prove they were competent communicators, albeit second-language speakers, because as one participant testified:

> Some of the elderly think that Filipino girls are domestics/helpers or even slaves, had a very hard life and that they came to the UK to serve the British people. People were surprised that there are Filipinos who are professionals, and can speak and understand English.

Many participants quickly learnt local dialects and one participant claimed that clients thought she was a 'British girl.' At home, however, they spoke their first language if they lived with those who came from the same region. They also mixed this with English, for example, Taglish (English and Tagalog, the official language of the Philippines). Taglish was also used by mothers to linguistically transition children who were in the Philippines to life in England. But for those who were born in England, using Taglish for oral purposes was rejected as an inadequate version of Tagalog. One mother explained: 'because it creates confusion and does not promote proper speaking of the language.... If you want to speak in Tagalog, then do it right to avoid confusion.' She felt strongly about this, in large part, because language schools for her children were unavailable so speaking Tagalog in the home was a way to preserve her first language.

Food preparation and cooking

A number of the major stores in cities stocked ethnic products. In more rural areas, ethnic stores opened up and became a place for purchasing food and meeting others. Cooking was a way to share stories and involve oneself in parties, rituals, and events with new friends. In one case, a participant cooked every Friday for her friends. Another Filipina wanted to cook a traditional dish for her European housemates and so she contacted her Filipino friend in Italy through the webcam for advice on how to cook it. Sharing food compensated for the shock that many new migrants felt in adjusting to a new environment but it was also for self-nurturance. The first three months could be a difficult period for participants who had few resources, as one newcomer said, 'I am craving food because I can't buy it.' Those participants who had 'helpers' cook their food for them in the countries where they were raised felt unprepared to undertake cooking, as a participant said, 'It is difficult to do everything yourself like food preparation.' Women made the crucial decisions about food preparation but couples, especially those who were both care assistants and had difficult schedules, often took turns cooking for their families (see also, George, 2005).

Christmas was often a difficult time for non-European participants who couldn't return home and had to cover for both British-born and Eastern European migrants who left for the holiday. But they also had more shifts and could earn more money. They often celebrated with their *local* family and friends. Several participants who lived together in a house had a party 'for all of the Filipinos' in her town, in which they each brought a dish and exchanged gifts for under £10, as one guest commented. The party was drawn out due to the invitees' work lives because 'they're on duty... so they're going out, coming in, going out, coming in.' Children's parties were also a way to share food and celebrate, but also to cut hair and sing. These were kind of 'everything' parties where a number of bonding activities took place, and were often for nationals of a particular country and their spouses.

Watching/listening/reading the media

The participants did have time to sporadically read women's magazines, crime books, or tidbits in the local newspapers that were available at work, free to the public, or ethnic media sent to them by family and which were used mainly for relaxation. But as one woman said, reading was not habitual. She said: 'I don't have the habit for if I have a habit, I'll find some time and read.' Print dictionaries were used the most but books were not easy to finish with their busy lives; as one said: 'I could get books but no time to read.' If they did read books, it was for learning, such as studying for tests or for their children. One mother bought books and received Polish books from her parents for her children. Another read crime stories that she found in the lounge in the care home where she worked 'because someone told me it was the best way to learn English.' Still another donated her Polish books to the library, which had a very small collection.

TV watching was convenient and easy for the participants. One said apologetically, 'It's radio and television... I'm sorry I don't have time to read papers.' The participants seemed to spend more time watching TV within the first three months. In one house where participants lived, 'the TV was always on.' It was easy to turn the TV on and off in between busy schedules and it was used for leisure and learning. One participant said, 'The movies here are very good for the eyes, and I understand it and it helps me to speak. I'm watching TV for the accents.' Many clients constantly watched television, and this was a medium for the participants to connect and converse with them about England. Access to TV was often through friends' computers, which were used not just for communicating, but also for infotainment or to check the stock market and news in their hometowns, and still others had large TV sets with satellite and hundreds of channels. The mothers monitored their children's TV both locally and from afar, worrying they were not spending enough time on homework. One mother said:

> She watches too much TV and hasn't finished schoolwork. I would check the school diary, the students bring it home... I want her to keep good study habits.

The participants used multiple media sources for diverse purposes that fit with their work lives and diasporic spaces. They could be considered 'cosmopolitans'—people who use multiple means for interacting with their social environments as well the wider world.

New support networks that bridged and bonded but did not link to services

As the above examples showed, these migrants had rich emotional supports that were acquired principally through their *bonding* with their immediate and extended family and co-ethnic friends, both local and abroad. These ties were for socializing, intimacy, and exchanging information about jobs and basic life issues. These were strong ties, which contrasted to their weaker ties to other nationalities, through a process known as *bridging* or ties to heterogeneous social groups. These weak ties, considered important for building social capital (norms, networks, and relations that have socio-economic value), were limited to a few select people in the participants' personal networks, and were not significant supports (Goulbourne et al., 2010; Granovetter, 1983; Iosifides Lavrentiadou, Petracou, and Kontis, 2008; Nannestead, Svendsen, and Svendsen, 2008).

Nevertheless, the participants needed more than weak ties to advance their lives and careers: what these migrants crucially lacked were *linkages* to gatekeepers such as professional associations and networks, career services, and advocacy-based organizations. They did not lack information about career upgrading as Chapter 5 showed. Indeed these women had knowledge and skills to search for information they needed in order to advance their careers, but they lacked critical resources, time, and support from gatekeepers. As Chapter 5 revealed, they found it difficult to leave the care field due to larger structural barriers. Not being able to activate these critical links to public services meant that advancement became challenging. The participants were incorporated into the service sector as care assistants but not into the knowledge economy as skilled professionals (Raghuram and Kofman, 2004). Their ties in bonded and bridged network systems did not reach far enough to encompass critical services that could advance them. They were situated well within these makeshift diasporas to survive but they lacked gatekeepers who could sponsor them for higher paying and professional posts. Newcomers in the study were the least likely to use services. Within their first year, they stayed within a safe comfort zone of friends, house-mates, and transnational family to adjust to their new situations, rarely venturing outside of their immediate localities for support unless they were forced to do so.

Why social support is important

Social support is what people give and/or receive within their personal networks, such as emotional aid, instrumental (or material aid), goods, services, and information (Antonucci, 1990). Members can enact and mobilize these under duress (Barrera, 1986). The level of supports and the direction of their flow often occur as a result of a life event or crisis, such as migration (Thoits, 1982). Mapping the participants' social supports in the post-migration stage revealed the social resources in the here and now; what participants perceived to be available to them through their current connections. It highlighted the diverse and relevant resources that were available and those that were lacking.[3] The purpose was to gauge the extent to which the participants had enough and diverse types of supports through their networks and access to services to advance out of the social care sector. Mapping also tracked reciprocity between members of their social support systems (Antonucci, 1986) including emotional support (*Em*, assertion of affective needs), informational (*I*, knowing about services), and material support (*M*, aid or acquiring tangible resources). These are important social resources that 'provide differential opportunities to realize interests, manipulate others and gather information' (Campbell, Marsden, and Hurlbert, 1986, p. 97). Furthermore different ties elicit different resources with most relationships providing specialized support (Wellman and Wortley, 1990), such as when women provide emotional aid to others. Yet not all social supports can have positive effects, even if they are well intentioned, since often exchanges are governed by unwritten codes/rules and where receiver and giver have different power levels. Additionally, a broader perspective of social support is needed to encompass macro-level issues. Rarely, for example, is educational support part of this system. Yet it is a key resource for advancement. Therefore it was included in the mapping process in terms of participants connecting to educational institutions and agencies for professional advancement (*Ed*). There were educational 'brokers' in this study, as Chapter 3 revealed, who steered the participants towards vocational, rather than professional qualifications, which in this case was a support to stay in the industry rather than leave it—not an ultimate aspiration of the participants. As the map of Alice's support system will show, good educational brokers were a key missing link to the services that could assist them in advancing their careers.

Support exchanges serve as a type of support bank (Antonucci and Jackson, 1990, p. 178), whereby members maintain an ongoing account of incoming and outgoing sources (locally and internationally) and which determines expectations. This support bank can also help individuals cope with their own declining resources. Cultural norms, age, social class, and gender dictate types and levels too. Remittances are a good example; many daughters were expected to financially support their ageing parents. This norm could determine remittance rates and involve considerable sacrifices for the participants especially with their low salaries. But shared among siblings, they could meet their expectation of fully supporting parents. One Indian participant said:

> When we are working in a nursing home, we won't improve our career. We will get money to live, but we can't improve our career. My family and my husband's family, we are middle class families, so our parents they are dependent on us. So we send some money for them, to live. My sisters, they also send money to my parents and my husband has one brother and he is working abroad as well and his wife, they all need to send money for the parents. I think we have a right to look after our parents.

These pioneer migrants were 'anchored' in many worlds (Hondagneu-Sotelo, 2007, p. 152); in entering through agencies, they were bonded to their employers and clients but also to their transnational families through obligations. They also developed, albeit to a limited extent, their personal networks to support future members. The map of Alice's support system (Figure 6.1) illustrates that she had many emotional

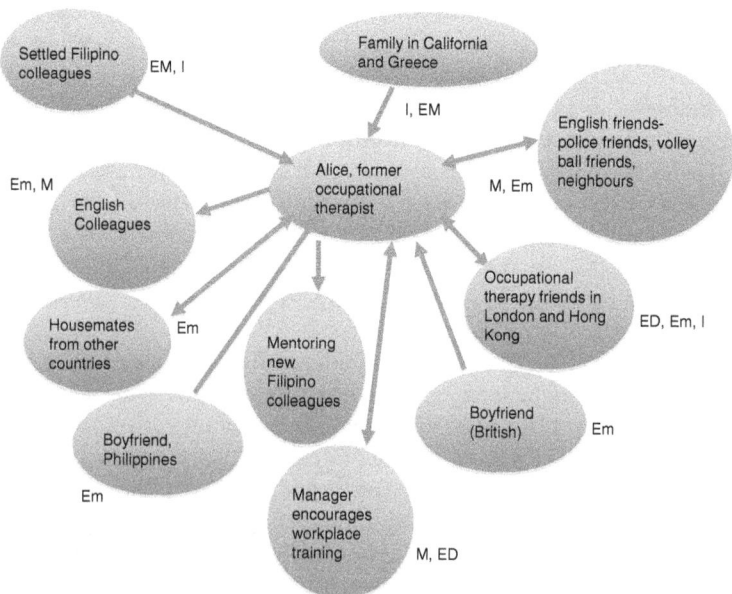

Figure 6.1 Alice's map (for meanings of abbreviations see text)

supports and bonds from within her dense personal network, including her new Filipino colleagues, relatives in Europe, and family across different continents. Her bridging capacity was revealed through supports she exchanged with housemates from other nationalities, in a sports club, and her community. She crucially lacked, however, educational supports in order to advance as an occupational therapist in England. In only one instance was she given advice from her occupational therapy friends in London and abroad about adaptation. The other supports helped her to survive in the workplace and adjust to her community, with many of these being reciprocal exchanges. Few of them focused, however, on her future and her aspirations to become an occupational therapist again. Alice was single and without children. Her map was significantly wider than other participants who had children and spent more time connecting with them, like Sarah, whose case I will soon describe.

Sharing resources was one way that she and other Filipino friends could manage and remit to their families. While she lived with people of other nationalities, most participants who worked for the same company lived with inter-ethnic colleagues or in the same block in houses they rented and sublet to each other. Newcomers often migrated through one of these homes and then started their own nearby. They taught one another about purchasing basic goods and services (e.g. mobile phone stores and internet services) and about remitting. Perhaps the biggest type of remittances was social—norms, capital, social identities and practices distributed to their families and communities abroad (Levitt and Lamba-Nieves, 2011, p. 3), through information and communication technologies (ICTs)—they prized this most upon their arrival.

Digital transnational relationships and care

These pioneering migrants' high digital literacy skills combined with their access to technology to communicate with family and friends at-a-distance contrasted sharply with their work environments which, aside from mobile phones, lacked ICTs thereby not giving them opportunities to showcase their expertise. The digital interactions within their interpersonal networks enabled them to exchange supports and maintain closeness between members and generated 'network capital,' meaning novel exchanges in different places with 'others-at-a-distance' (Elliot and Urry, 2010, p. 10). This includes material supports to enable people to cross borders (visas, qualifications, and economic remittances), mobile communication devices (phones and computers to arrange connections and make arrangements), and people at-a-distance (who offer invitations and encourage visits). Those with high network capital are highly mobile and demand that others be available as they continuously share information and have very connected lives.

Normally the global elite, such as 'executives,' are considered to have high network capital with their many resources (Elliot and Urry, 2010, p. 22). However, the participants, with their limited resources, acted as cosmopolitans with their media-saturated lives and constant on-the-go communication with their portable computers and phones. These devices enabled participants to engage in the 'third shift' of managing their families' emotions due to their difficult and time-intensive jobs at-a-distance (discussed in Chapter 3; see also, Madianou and Miller, 2012). They also invented new ways of interacting because of ICTs' advantages of permitting talk, texts, travel, and time. These new migrants shared ICTs: they split phone and computer time between themselves to communicate with their transnational families and friends. Using these devices became 'the social glue of migrant transnationalism' (Vertovec, 2004, p. 219). They used these technologies smartly (optimizing all of their features like emailing, texting, and talking) because they were social necessities. They depended on these technologies because they moved around and couldn't afford disconnect fees. Consequently, they bore a larger financial load with their low salaries. This network capital created a type of circulation of ideas and feelings that further cemented their transnational and local relationships, but it did not link them to professional careers or services that could have enhanced their social and financial assets. It was mainly for bonding and bridging.

The constant communication was also preparation for sponsoring family members as well as onward migration. Not only were participants' families spread across the globe as the examples showed but also 'families' were seldom in one household or town. For example, Cielo expected to sponsor her boyfriend and both planned to move to Canada at a later date where her relatives lived. Nearly all of the participants intended to bring their children to England at some point and a number of them did so during the study period. Electronic communication precipitated that transition rather than being used simply for maintaining home life, 'back there.' The technology enabled them to keep in touch and forge bonds at the same time that it expanded their networks in non-place-specific ways. But as Madianou and Miller (2011) warn, it is critical not to hype the new technology in the same way that corporate sponsors often do, as the only ways for transnational families to stay in touch. While being aware of the danger of hyperbole, I recognize that these ICTs still mediated these relationships and assisted in new types of transnational communication.

For one, the participants used the Internet as a 'passionate affinity space' (Gee and Hayes, 2011, p. 70) that was fuelled by wanting to share feelings and experiences; sharing pictures for visual impact was important like one participant who said, 'Every time I go home [from work], I open the Friendster, to see my children.' These virtual spaces expanded relations at work although they didn't alter power relations on the job. One participant became 'friends' with colleagues and her supervisor on Facebook. She said:

> My manager—I invite them and they respond on Facebook, and T. invite me as well to join Facebook, it is surprising to me because they are in higher positions. They put their subordinates on the same level, to reach you.

She also used a virtual matchmaking service in England to look for men to marry, one of whom she met on the Internet but began calling on the phone for support: 'He sometimes asks me about children, I give him advice as well.'

Women, in particular, tended use ICTs to maintain their motherhood status (Parrenas, 2005), even to the extent of 'micromanaging' household relations, time, and budgets through ritualized calls that they initiated. As Sarah's case illustrates (in the next section), mothers tended to be heavily involved in all family interactions and dynamics despite their 'absent presence' and as a way to deal with tensions related to being mother and breadwinner (Gergen, 2002, p. 227; Madianou and Miller, 2012; Thomas and Lim, 2011). Furthermore, children (from the mothers' perspectives) appreciated her frequent contact. In this sense, the mothers became even more present through their absence. In this study, by frequently talking, texting, and emailing, as well as sharing photographs and through annual visits, these mothers could see their children growing up and, in responding to changes, constantly assessed when bringing them over would be right for their own development. The visits, however, were crucial. One mother who had to delay one due to her immigration status felt 'so sorry that I wouldn't be able to be with my daughter at you know – that age is difficult time at the moment.'

Aside from visits, talking on the phone and communicating via the Internet was a touchstone for nurturing emotional relationships, managing family matters, and growing personal networks (Thomas and Lim, 2011). Other text-based media were also used, such as sending letters. Like Madianou and Miller (2011) Baldassar (2007a) found that emails tended to be used for daily matters while letters were used for elderly kin and for important news or information—none of which replaced the other but which sped up the communication and increased expectations for more of it. Mary, a Polish woman in her 30s, lived with a family who she called her 'spare' parents or 'English parents' but made few friends in England, according to her, because of living in a rural village and a packed work schedule that didn't allow many hours to socialize. She said, 'Sometimes I feel here very lonely, without family, friends... I don't know any places where I can meet people. I don't want to go to the pub or the disco.' So she frequently stayed inside and spoke with her sister on Skype. She called her parents 'because my parents have no computer—I ring to my parents every weekend—and just I speak with my sister on Skype.' While her parents 'know nothing about computers,' her sister told her about how to use Skype and she eagerly signed up. She relied heavily on the Internet, especially one website which had 'everything' on it and she 'could spend all day on the Internet.' She added, 'I sometimes talk to my sister by computer or just really read everything on the Polish websites you know, about Poland so I can everyday know what is going on in Poland or you know my town.' She concluded, 'So the computer helps me to live here. I keep in contact with my country.'

Participants constantly checked their phones and the Internet as a world they might miss as well as for information since they did not often have books available to them, as one said. ICTs had penetrated participants' families to the point where it was a type of 'new family member' (Bacigalupe and Lambe, 2009, p. 15). The text and talk facilitated a type of co-presence in their relationships and an exchange of care that worked both ways including giving good and bad news, and it helped these women to nurture their family life from afar through daily connections. One woman said, 'We don't talk long, just say hi and hello, how are you.' As pioneers, they could manage the impressions of themselves from afar (Rybas, 2012), making their situations look better online than in person ('netglow')—they didn't actively lie so much as withhold details about their problems; for example, a number of the participants didn't tell their concerns to family so as not to make them worry and focused instead on issues 'there' (see also, Madianou and Miller, 2012). One participant said, 'I don't usually tell my mum or my daughter or my brothers and sisters about my problem if I have to because I don't want to worry them.' Local networks were often more useful for resolving the problems that they encountered after they migrated.

While participants in this study took turns and shared their computers and connectivity, it could be difficult for those on the other side of the world who lacked these resources (Madianou and Miller, 2012; Thomas and Lim, 2011); as Sarah's case will show, Internet connectivity could be a problem and so a number of different forms of communication were needed. Madianou and Miller (2011) found that texts were relied on more from the Philippines because of the costs of calling and were used for different purposes including birthday messages and coordinating further contact through Skype. Telephoning was important for this and real-time personal contact, making the migrants 'feel and function as a family' with everyday kitchen-table discussions (Vertovec, 2004, p. 222), but could also increase the sense of physical distance; some participants, for example, became sad after their phone calls (see also, Thomas and Lim, 2011). Phone costs could also be high. Sharing computers and connectivity wasn't possible when the participants lived alone. One participant set her computer up in an unstable position in her apartment just to get a free wifi signal from an unknown neighbour.

The digital media itself was a delivery system for language: 'a system of conventions about how to make meanings that can be expressed or delivered in different ways' (Gee and Hayes, 2011, pp. 15, 35). This is nowhere more apparent than for today's labour migrants in utilizing social and media networks. The participants were not 'digital have-nots' or even 'digital immigrants'—lacking skills and knowledge that are relevant to today's 21st century media and networked communication society (Gee and Hayes, 2011; Prensky, 2001), even though they were marginalized in English society. Although some of these pioneering migrants were not networked their entire lives through ICTs, they embraced the new technology quickly. With their high digital literacy skills, the participants spurred the development of digital competencies and code-switching from one language to the next in their networks too (Lexander, 2011). These migrants were articulate and with their necessity to communicate for social support and a sense of belonging, they used this technology, including talking and texting, and sending and receiving data, rapidly, frequently, and creatively for social bonding in the 'new floating world' of absent presence (Gergen, 2002, p. 234). This was not, however, without tensions.

Managing contradictions of being here and there: The case of Sarah and transnational sense of self, family, and community

Emotionally managing family dynamics from abroad produced 'care strain' in these mothers as they helped their children adjust to this situation, while expecting themselves to be ideal migrants of ideal families (Baldassar, 2007b; Parrenas, 2005; Rostagaard, Chiatti, and Lamura, 2011). Sarah's story illustrates the tensions due to juggling many roles and responsibilities. It also illuminates her feelings and actions as well her practices and the ways her children were active in negotiating the relationship.

Sarah's case

Sarah was 35 when she arrived in 2007 in northern England from Luzon, Philippines. As a domiciliary care assistant for the first eight months she was on call up to 90 hours a week, starting around 7.00 a.m. and ending around 11 p.m. She was frustrated, however, because she only actually got paid for nine hours of her 17–hour-days, due to irregular hours, breaks in her rota, and client cancellations. She wanted more paid hours so that her time away from her children was worthwhile: 'I leave my children for this job so I really want my day to finish with meaning.'

She was constantly tired but felt she had to 'keep on going' even though her hours were challenging and she despaired at the difference between what the client actually paid her company vs the amount she received—a fact that was made clear to her in the paperwork. She wanted to present herself as available for her clients because they depended on her but which was emotionally difficult because her children needed her too. She said: 'Even though you feel bad, you have to be cheerful.' She rationalized her decision to migrate: 'If you want to lead a good life for your family you really have to work in another country. If you aren't born rich there's no chance for you to really change your life if you stay there.' She said she migrated to England as part of a 'career move,' leaving her five-year nursing post in a hospital in the Philippines because she was overworked—handling a titanic amount of patients 'in a ward with only one nurse' and was not compensated. She couldn't support her family on this income, with three young children, the oldest being 12. In her nursing job she worked 40-hour weeks on day and night shifts and said she never had a 'real rest' but was 'used to it.' Furthermore she cited the economic situation in the Philippines as worsening, thus giving her 'no choice' but to migrate: 'Unfortunately we have a bad situation in the Philippines,' she said dimming the hope of any further career advancement there. Her view of nursing as a passport was a means of escaping this dire situation: 'When I was young I really want to be a nurse,' she said, 'if you are a nurse you have a big chance to go to other countries.'

Although she became a care assistant she despaired that she was not a nurse in England, saying she was 'sad because I worked hard to graduate in nursing.' Still, her dream was to become a nurse again, as she claimed, 'I *am* a nurse, so I want to work as a nurse here,' and she felt her profession was 'always there' for her. After she had her children, she felt ambivalent about leaving them but didn't want to miss a career opportunity (see also, Madianou and Miller, 2012):

> I'm a bit confused about them because I could feel that I can't leave them. I can't imagine myself leaving my kids. But I think when the opportunity comes, you have to take the chances so you have to grab it.

This sense of ambivalence hung over her; although she felt she 'wanted to give her children the best,' she also said, 'Most of the day I feel guilty.' She questioned her mothering role even though she knew her mother was a good caregiver to them: 'It's not fair to them. Even though my mother took care of them, it's different—a mother's different.' She sensed that her role as guardian was even stronger. Knowing everything about their daily lives and advising them verbally compensated for not being able to physically care or protect them from harm. She wasn't just managing them but she was

> trying to be their mother even though I'm here. I'm still trying to do my role. I'm still trying to talk to them about their every day, everything, schedule, especially in school, how they are doing in school. I'm actually always asking them how they feel, if there's something hurt or if they feel any pain, actually everything I ought to know.

She was torn because she didn't feel that she was providing 'enough' to them as their mother who was 'not supposed to leave them,' although she felt she had to offer them the 'best.' She said:

> A lot of things come on my mind because it's complicated. You have to give them the best but you can't do it when you stay with them.

And you can do a lot of things to them but you have to live there. It's difficult and you have to work here.

Her family's problems further reinforced her ambivalence and guilt especially when they argued. Her mother was 57 and struggled to maintain Sarah's standards for childrearing. Even though she told her 'nothing happened,' Sarah still worried, especially when her youngest pleaded, ' "Mummy, please come home, can you stay here...what about my papers, can I come?" I cried and cried. He is asking now.' Sarah's high standards were in part due to wanting to change the way communication happened from when she was a girl. She said:

> My mother was busy, when I was a child and I don't remember conversations. We never hugged and kissed—I was the oldest of five. I always talk to them. Conversation is the most important thing especially when you're away. I didn't get it as a child.

Sarah was proud of her eldest daughter, in particular, who, she sensed, 'understood the sacrifices' and appeared to be maturing to the point where she could 'count on her.' While Sarah wanted to have 'peace of mind' that they were OK, emergencies jolted her confidence, especially since she wasn't there to physically help. When this happened, she called many times a day to 'be with' her family:

> My second daughter got a urinary tract infection and she's been hospitalized and that is so hard time for me...the minute you heard her crying saying, 'mummy I don't like this, mummy come home,' oh, its like, I can't describe the feeling. It's really hard—the feeling that you want to help her and be with her, comfort her and you can do nothing but cry.

Getting the correct information, even 'any bad news,' from her children was important especially about their health care. For example, her daughter once told her that there was a 'car crash' when in fact her aunt had 'scratched the car,' and Sarah was persistent in learning about any hidden problems as this meant doing her 'part with them.' She told her mother: 'Please tell me anything that happens, bad or good. I just want to know, especially with the children. Don't hide anything because *I have to know.*'

Sarah was the only one who asked about the children's welfare, since her husband of 12 years who worked as a merchant sailor came home once a year and was only financially involved with the children like a number of men in transnational families (Parrenas, 2005). Sarah relied on her mother who lived with her and took part-time care of the children while Sarah was at work and when she left for England it was her 'mother and sister who took full-time and good care of the children.' Sarah also had a 'helper' who did domestic duties as well as took care of her father who was paralysed. This helper planned to do this job for a year, although Sarah admitted domestics were hard to find because 'they move around a lot.' Sarah knew that 'there are lots of poor people there who can't get an education,' which is why they did domestic work. But even in the Philippines she said this was not limited to those without formal education as she added, 'Even if you finish a degree it's very difficult to get a job.'

Sarah supported all of her family members, as the eldest of five siblings and the only one who migrated. So while Sarah's salary in England paid for daily items for the household of eight (three children, her sister and brother-in-law, her parents and a domestic), her husband's salary paid for 'savings.' The fact that she was away from her children gave her the opportunity 'to work a lot of hours here compared to when I am in the Philippines' but she continuously found it hard because, 'as a mother, you still think of the children. You can even have a free day but you can't really enjoy it because your mind is with them all the time.' She did so for the 'money,' as she said her salary was staggeringly high compared to the Philippines: 'You have one month here, it's almost one year in the Philippines.' This was important since she felt 'the needs of the children were getting higher,' including their education, which she said was 'expensive in the Philippines and I want to give them a better future—to send them to a better school.'

A friend told her about this type of care work and took her to a recruitment agency to sign up. She knew the job would be different from nursing, and 'had an idea, but I don't know really how it is.' After applying, she told her family and colleagues only after she was accepted and recalled that her 'mother is very supportive with me and she assure me that if I leave my children with her everything will be alright.' Sarah also told her eldest daughter 'that everything is for them, for their future. Then, she's alright.' From the moment Sarah arrived in England she called the children 'every day' to develop a sense of closeness and bought them mobile phones for this purpose: 'Just to check the children's alright. I want them to hear my voice and I also want to hear their voice.' She also shadowed them day-to-day 'to make sure about everything' including being sent to and from school safely and that they had enough food to eat. She wasn't 'settled without knowing and without talking to them... just to hear them say they are alright.' She also monitored their academic progress, especially their homework and sometimes intervened by talking to their teachers to ensure a successful outcome:

> I just have to encourage them and motivate them more and by talking to them. I've always got a good report from them and from my mother and from their teacher. I also talk to their teacher and they are doing good.... They even save the test paper so that when we are home they can show it to us.

She could do this because 'I know their schedule.' She even hung on the phone to hear them discuss what they would buy at the shop: 'I am still there... "oh you get these things for your brother, you get that," you know, things they like.' Additionally she monitored their free time and texted them about their food, their friends, and their whereabouts. She asked her daughter, 'Have you had your snack?' And Sarah confessed that 'I text her more when she is out with her friends. Really, because I miss my eldest. She is a teenager and she sometimes goes out on her own.'

Since there were sometimes problems with the connectivity in her children's house due to a problematic telephone line (although they had Sky cable for the television and the children had computers), she asked them to go to the local Internet café to talk during which time she relayed news about her house in England. When she showed them the house, the children 'were excited to see their rooms,' and the youngest, 'ask me too about his bed—he want his own bed, not really on his own but with us, me and his dad, things like that—so I showed him our bed upstairs and they are very happy with it. My eldest daughter is asking already about what kind of [school] uniform they have here.' The house Sarah rented was empty when she arrived with her colleagues. After a year she moved in to it from across the street where she lived with a settled Filipino family of four. Sarah arrived with four other Filipino care assistants who were heading to the same company, all flying together from Manila, which she felt was 'a really big help.' This enabled them to bond and 'became strong' as well as to feel like 'one family' as she put it. This was reinforced through some of them living with this settled family. She found it tough living with children, however, the youngest reminding her of her own. She said, 'Whenever I saw her I feel sad. I miss my children more.' In this house they cooked food together although she said that because their hours were different they ate separately, and when they 'had the free time we just talk or get a rest.' Sarah spent a lot of time at home because she couldn't afford to go out since she remitted nearly 80 per cent of her income. As an oldest child she always had more responsibilities even in the Philippines, a sponsor role which was reinforced in England:

> It is because I have a big responsibility in the Philippines. My father is sick you know, and they have all this medicines and my mother as well and my brothers and my sister also, they all are depending on me. I mean they always asking me about all these things and everything. When I live in the Philippines with all these responsibilities and I still have to do it, even though I'm here.

When her oldest daughter asked for more things from Sarah she explained, 'That it's not as easy as that. I also told them that I am here because I really need to work so that we can save for the future.' Sarah felt like she was a role model for her children in demonstrating a work ethic:

> They have to understand that when they need certain things they have to also work for it. I don't want them to just sort of give things that easy. I want to give them, but I am afraid that they find things easy, you know.

She planned to sponsor them to England as a way to bring the whole family together under one roof that was not possible in the Philippines: 'It might give us a chance to be all together if he will join me here and later the kids can join us, only if we have a good job so that we can support the children.' But the position her husband obtained when he did arrive was in a nearby nursing home as a care assistant earning even less than Sarah. Sarah advised him about caring too:

> I asked him to make a note of all the cases and give him a brief summary and so he has an idea and conditions of clients what to do. I know they have a care plan but he needs to understand the cases. He has no idea.

Sarah felt the place that she lived in was in a 'quiet' area, which she felt was 'beautiful' and safer than where her children lived in the Philippines: 'because we are near the main road and I don't find it safe for the children. We don't have a wide ground to play for the children.'

On her breaks in this town she often pulled off to the side of the road and called or texted her eldest daughter while eating her lunch or at other times:

> If I get no chance to call the children, I send text. I ask my daughter to text to get to school. I want to make sure she is safe. They even say good night and morning through text. We are eight hours behind. When I wake up I can see the texts and get peace of mind. That is the least I can do for them. It's worth it.

Aside from working, sponsoring her family became a big project. Making herself into a legitimate sponsor was critical. Not only working long hours to save for expenses but she also obtained a house for rent, and visited schools in her town, learning that she needed to prepare her children to take exams. She said, 'I really have to also ask about everything about this. I want to really set up everything for them.' She also organized bank statements, bought another used car, and, finally, sponsored her husband. Her major worry was whether the Philippines embassy was going to grant the children sponsorship due to recently losing staff through layoffs. The children were excited to be sponsored and Sarah said they, 'keep on asking if they have their rooms now. What do they look like and when I am going to get them.' She didn't want them to be disappointed in case the sponsorship failed so she didn't give them dates until she had the documents in hand: 'I'm not assuring them yet. Let them get their visa because I don't want to disappoint them.'

She also prepared her children for using British English although they used American English at school. Sometimes Sarah wrote texts or emails in English like 'mum' and switched to Taglish. She encouraged her middle daughter who was not yet in school to speak English with her on the phone: 'My second daughter she's trying when I talk to her in English. She will tell me, mum I can't understand you what is that mean. So I try to tell her to say this, so she's trying...she's trying things to say in English and sometimes she just asks me how can she say it and things like that.' Sarah felt her oldest was more prepared because her school: 'really teach them, wants them to speak English well...I heard them, they are really good speaking.' The children also gave Sarah feedback on her English, which made Sarah feel good.

Still, Sarah claimed she was 'nervous and afraid' about bringing her children, particularly the oldest to England and hoped that she could 'guide her in a proper way.' Sarah remarked, 'It's really different you know...12-year old here is very different from what a 12-year old girl is there. She's still a baby you know. I see these 12-year olds here with all this makeup.' Once the paperwork was granted, she flew back to get them with her husband. Once the children were settled in England, Sarah experienced some problems. Firstly, she was disappointed in their schooling, which she described as 'backwards' and she said 'the children find it easy.' Overall Sarah remarked that the adjustment was 'really hard' but she now had 'peace of mind' because they were 'all together.' She said the teachers gave good feedback in reports, and she knew the children were doing well academically. Maintaining the family was tough, as in the Philippines they had more help. So she found it difficult balancing the cleaning, cooking, and ironing, and needs of her children on the back of her demanding care schedule but she felt they were coping. Her husband began to share more domestic duties in particular making meals ahead of time for them. She said her family had to be quiet though because they were renting one of the bedrooms to a newcomer Filipina.

Conclusion

These migrant care assistants felt tensions between the informal care that they gave to their families and their paid care to clients. It was often the case that their clients' needs came first and caused anxieties for the participants in staying in touch with family when they were constantly pulled away by their jobs. However, it was not a simple formula. Phone calls and visits were rescheduled and texts were somehow afforded monetarily and across time and space. The transnational communication alleviated some of these tensions but did not entirely erase them, becoming 'a kind of punctuated sociality that heighten[ed] emotional strain as well as alleviate[ed] it' (Vertovec, 2004, p. 223).

As pioneer migrants, these women were settling in to a new niche and new communities, while they worked hard—softening the feathers, so to speak—for their family who followed (Kofman, 1999). They were 'on the thresholds of belonging, between migration and settlement' (Fortier, 2000, p. 49) and were part of a historical flow of women, Irish, Italian, and Caribbean who moved to England in mid-century, with deep family ties, and lived between and in both worlds. I have viewed this movement of networks by pioneer migrant women as critical points of reference in history. These migrants manoeuvred these networks in dynamic and highly structured ways.

7
Conclusion: Counting Migrant Women's Education and Expertise

Introduction

This chapter turns the focus back on the participants and the ways gender, nationality and chance trumped their higher education and charted their 'race to the bottom' of the global economy as care assistants. With more women than ever before earning higher education degrees, it would seem that there would be more labour market opportunities for them. Yet their education may not yield enough power even with migration. In this chapter I explore this puzzle of self, nation, and higher education with labour market returns for migrant women.

First, I summarize the themes for each chapter with lessons that build theoretical understanding about gendered knowledge on labour migration. Then I discuss higher education as an affordance in women migrants' trajectories with the ways it reproduces gendered niches. In this section, I explore why it is more likely that highly educated women will migrate from particular countries due to lack of opportunities and labour market demands. With this, there will be attention to the relations between the labour market and higher education returns for women. Feminist interpretations of Pierre Bourdieu's theory on academic capital will further assist in theorizing these issues especially the failure to codify skills and portable qualifications and the resultant brain waste. On a more promising note, I will next discuss capabilities theory with regard to development and migration. This perspective challenges individualistic and economic-based models of migration. Typically migration models focus on decision-making processes, actors, networks, and structural factors in the pre-migration stage. Rarely, however, do they focus on both pre- and post-migration stages of adjustment especially on women and their perspectives on their progress (Ryan, Sales, Tilki, and Siara, 2008).

Finally, I propose a set of policies, practices, theory-building, and research directions, which are not meant to resolve the problems discussed in the book but which build on the findings and, as proposals, attempt to deal with current and future issues surrounding the feminization of skilled migration in the care industry and the advancement of women.

Lessons for engendering knowledge on women's labour migration

This book is a case study of migration, professional women, and care. Starting with Chapter 1, the focus was on engendering transnationalism through connecting the feminization of labour migration to a global care 'industry.' This chapter looked specifically at the role of this industry in prompting professional women to migrate. Taking high-stakes risks, the participants were selectively incorporated in the labour market due to a number of factors. The participants suffered from multiple discriminatory forces in the pre- and post-migration stages that worked against their career development and livelihoods. While migrant care assistants are included as important actors in market relations they are excluded socially in the top levels of the political economy of care (Bakker and Silvey, 2008). Although they were dislocated, they also discovered new ways of being transnationals (Grillo, 2007).

Chapter 2 builds on the gendered immigrant social spaces that were established in Chapter 1 to reflect the struggles of participants within three social locations, as: migrant care assistants, women, and former professionals. This cultural grouping (of diverse women put together through their worklives) was produced to challenge dominant models of socio-economic integration that see women as homogenous. This political identification also provided opportunities to reflect on different modes of gendered services in unequal labour markets and tell the participants' stories 'in a way that matters' (Behar, 1996, p. 166). Many of these participants' portraits, after all, defied popular stereotypes that the popular media cultivated about them as victims or suspects.

Chapter 3 focused on sectorial restructuring. While new migrant workers were in demand by England's upgraded care sector, the traditional workers were cast off in a new era of care market modernization (Boris and Parrenas, 2010). These new workers embodied the privatization and work ethic under a welfare reform that prized 'user involvement' (Cowden and Singh, 2007, p. 5), which was a rationale for job enlargement, strict standards, managerial imperatives, and commodified care. The 'bottom-line' (value for money) policies were the 'Janus face of community care and a low-cost solution to social problems' (Levick, 1992 in Cowden and Singh, 2007, p. 11). Placed at the bottom of the care hierarchy, migrant workers reworked their identities and claims to worth by becoming 'intimate citizens' (Plummer, 2003) to these 'service-users;' despite their lack of political citizenship, former health care professionals in particular drew on their expertise by responding to clients' medical problems. They were also 'intimate workers' (Boris and Parrenas, 2010, p. 4).

Chapter 4 captured the social geographies of the participants rushing from home to home, which reflected the oppressive rural worlds they inhabited in the local care sector. I show that these processes were already in motion before they arrived on the scene. Their stories illuminated their sense of belonging and being displaced at the same time. In belonging they actively marked out borders of a new place of settlement that produced them as 'different' which became a means for identity construction and performance (Fortier, 2000). They became marginalized and had to count on themselves to remember their former professional lives, which no longer counted (Pratt, 2004). They created solidarity outside of cities, typically places where migrant women would come together (Sassen, 2002).

Chapter 5 showed the impact of the participants' 'intimate labours' on their labour market trajectories (Boris and Parrenas, 2010). To draw on a timeworn metaphor they were 'canaries in the coal mine' for the new welfare reform in England. To this end they faced the emotional, physical, and social hazards of degrading and dangerous work in the global care industry (Pai, 2004), and they offered a warning about the nature of the global gendered division of labour on women's lives and career aspirations. These migrant women abided by the rules of the game and tried to conform at considerable expense and self-sacrifice. In order to play they became even more self-disciplined and self-monitoring even as they became more invisible and bonded to employers. The deeper their investments were in the industry, the longer their fates hung in limbo. From the beginning, their gendered decisions became a form of auto-discrimination consisting of a large set of self-selective disadvantages that like dominoes cascaded downwards.

Chapter 6 portrayed the participants as pioneers staging their migration for those who followed and they settled into England as transnationals with intact family systems for which they were responsible. These relations created tensions, sometimes maintaining and at other times altering conventional gender roles. The skilled migration chains they started were established in a world of weak and dense ties (Granovetter, 1983), which crossed borders virtually through technologies that 'reasserted time's place in care' (Tronto, 2003, p. 24). This informal care was organized differently than the time-and-space compressed labour they performed on their jobs, where time *was* money. Examples from this chapter illustrated the roles of non-migrants who were part of the participants' migration journeys.

Has higher education increased social mobility for skilled women migrants?

Highly skilled migration has increased dramatically since the 1990s (Lowell, Findlay, and Stewart, 2004). As hunger for 'knowledge workers' spread, demands increased for the services of this population (e.g. medical care) under global economic conditions of inequality. The highly skilled category is mostly reserved for businesspeople although it is commonly understood as, 'persons with a tertiary education' who are taken in as a temporary brain stock to fill skills shortages (Iredale, 2001; Koser and Salt, 1997; Lowell, 2008, p. 52). Because they are seen as carrying academic capital, they are also assumed to have economic resources and therefore less likely to be in low-end occupational niches. The assumption is that these migrants' brain power, middle-class status, and networks shield them from the low-wage market in the destination country and thus encourages social progress (Brown and Lauder, 2006), with their education reflecting their human capital worth (earnings, quality and stability of employment and greater upward mobility as well as language attainment).

Yet an analysis in London found that while migrant participants were well-educated, they also were a 'new underclass' because of their low-end employment status, demonstrating that a strong work ethic and high skill levels give these migrant workers few advantages in the global marketplace (Goodchild, 2007). Therefore the 'skills-mismatch' rationale wasn't operative so much as a lack of suitable jobs for these migrants. Immigration policies in OECD countries in attempting to attract 'the best and the brightest' cream a narrow band of the highly educated creating an oversupply of workers that cannot obtain quality positions. Skilled migrant women in particular are affected by this phenomenon.

It was clear that the highly skilled female participants in this study experienced a significant loss of their human capital in the post-migration stage. In the pre-migration stage, however, obtaining a university education appeared to significantly leverage their cultural capital in their families and communities—they moved to cities and some migrated to prestigious positions in the Middle East, as Chapter 5 showed. They didn't earn much, however, in the venturing out stage and their human capital was low. This led them to migrate to seek out greater labour market advantages. But as soon as they entered England's immigration system their credentials were not recognized and they became 'unskilled,' which dictated that they work as care assistants. Their visas put them in a weak labour market position and gave them little negotiating power, which encouraged their exploitation by employers. Viewed as unskilled, they were expected to do the dirty 'body' work, discussed in Chapter 4. The (now defunct) Learning and Skills Council (2006, p. 21) stipulated that 'aspiring migrants' like these participants should be:

> In low-skilled or unskilled roles while they improve their English or gain a relevant qualification to allow them to practise their profession [...] Aspiring migrants are happy to make easy money doing unskilled work and view it in the context of being an opening to greater opportunities.

This definition neglects the aforementioned structural barriers and begs the question as to whether these migrants are 'happy' to engage in low-grade work with mere promises of 'greater opportunities.' Participants' aspirations diminished when they discovered the meagre opportunities. As one said, 'I'm not living my dreams any more. I see the reality here.'

Women's participation in higher education incentivized their migration

Higher education and gender are 'deeply implicated' in globalization inequalities (Rizvi, 2007, p. 232) and universities are now critical to the migration industry. These universities adopt an entrepreneurial ethos, which push up costs as well as expectations (Nedeva, 2008). Raising standards for educational access creates an 'opportunity trap' forcing people to spend more on it with few guarantees, leading to an oversupply of qualified graduates with high hopes. This then leads to a surplus of graduates on the migration market. The 'internationalization of higher education' has been a major factor in the migration of students as well as workers (Iredale, 2001, p. 7). This scenario is the shadow-side of what is commonly known as the, 'knowledge-based economy,' which focuses on human capital (assets embodied in humans in the form of skills) for economic development, high technology jobs, goods, and services for global competition—a rationale that was cemented in the 2000 European Parliament Lisbon Policy (Commission of the European Communities, 2005). A 'Europe of Knowledge' (Bologna declaration) would be built to strengthen individual European countries through the mobility of knowledge-workers and students. Yet this labour market was also separated into those who were viewed as 'skilled' (associated science, financial, and IT fields, dominated by men) and those who weren't (mostly women who were in lower paid socially reproductive professions like nursing and teaching). Although health care was included in the OECD definition of the 'knowledge-based' economy it was always marginalized (Kofman, forthcoming). For many women (e.g. in health care), the knowledge economy has been highly contested because of its gender disadvantages (Walby, 2007b). For example, markets and states exert indirect control through setting qualification standards and defining 'technical' and expertise in particular ways (Koser and Salt, 1997, p. 287) that handicap women. Gendered pay gaps have been the end result, leading to an oversupply of highly educated women who often 'need to have comparatively higher levels of education to compete in the global auction' (Stromquist and Monkman, 2000, p. 10). One study found that this gap meant women have to obtain a doctorate in order to earn as much as a man with a Bachelor's degree (Carnvale, Rose, and Cheah, 2011, p. 7). But even education levels aren't effective at setting wages when, for example, male dropouts earn more than female graduates (Lafer, 2004, p. 112).

Almost all regions of the world have shown increases in tertiary education for women with female enrolments outnumbering men since the 1970s. When women access higher education they 'tend to exceed men in grades, evaluations and degree completion' (UNESCO, 2010, p. 71). Yet there are vast differences across the developing world and women from countries that have less female participation tend to study less feminized degree areas (like the Polish participants) (Jacobs, 1996; UNESCO, 2010). *Enrolments,* however, have been the focus for women's participation in higher education rather than their subject specializations in relation to labour market returns (Carnoy, 2005). This is important to examine because the subjects women take are in more marginalized and feminized areas like the humanities, teaching, and nursing with under-representation in the more lucrative and higher status computer sciences and engineering as well as the physical sciences fields (UNESCO, 1998). The outcomes for women's higher education often disadvantage them (Jacobs, 1996).

Nursing schools: A case of returns on investments in higher education

Universities in emerging countries are viewed as central actors in nurse migration, with the purpose of exporting nurse graduates—a common promotional slogan is 'your cap is your passport' (Kingma, 2006, p. 23). Mirelle Kingma refers to this system as an 'education export industry' (p. 90) and claims, 'no nurse can move either internally or externally if she does not have the proper education' (p. 81). Part of nursing education worldover entails interning at hospitals in a process known as 'bonding,' which allows them to run at very limited costs (p. 86). Expensive private nursing schools, in the Philippines for example, are on the rise and most are private and owned by doctors (p. 84). Many developing countries' governments are more reluctant to fund these schools especially if students leave and never return. This void forces many women to pay for their own education, making nursing, 'one of the expensive careers for girls to take [...] since they spend so much for their education, naturally their tendency after graduation is to go abroad.' (p. 85). There has been, after all, a demand for overseas graduates. In the UK, for example, in the mid 2000s, it was cheaper for hospitals to receive and adapt a migrant nurse from a developing country than to train one in their own (p. 192).

Many migrant nurses bear the costs of having to retrain as nurses. This is because adaptation and conversion systems for these nurses are quagmires. In the USA, for example, many foreign-educated nurses are left to 'sink or swim' due to the hoops they are expected to jump through (Xu, 2008). Post-arrival certification (adaptation) programmes have been characterized as 'hit or miss,' and there is a high failure rate for qualifying and licensing exams. While some states have waived the pre-exam to attract more migrant nurses to an expanding sector, most professional associations have opposed waivers that lift caps for migrating nurses. These contradictory forces have reduced the percentage of foreign-educated nurses in the USA to around 5 per cent, the lowest in industrialized countries (Haour-Knipe and Davies, 2008; Xu, 2008). In Canada nurses are given temporary licences but the time restriction is short and the national licensing exam takes so much time and effort to upgrade their credentials to the point that some 'nurses never re-establish their professional careers' (Baumann and Blythe, 2008). What makes Canada different, however, is that these nurses can count prior learning as part of the Canadian assessment system.

For those in non-nursing fields, systems do exist across Europe to convert foreign qualifications and promote higher education like The UNESCO Lisbon Recognition Convention, which, in theory, enables the transfer of qualifications from one country to another without losing their value. However, this system is only for Europeans and really focuses on academic student mobility. The same goes for the National Academic Recognition Information Centre (NARIC), the European Qualifications Framework system, and EUROPASS for lifelong learning that operate as credit systems to assess prior learning, skills and competencies so that governmental agencies can match systems of learning. For those who are not citizens of the EEA, however, professional bodies determine their trajectories as evident with the nurses, and discussed in Chapter 5. Furthermore, these associations often set high bars for non-EEA migrants.

Some efforts to focus specifically on professional mobility of migrants and refugees from outside the EEA have been made but the focus is often on basic skills, like language, or advice, information, and guidance (Gray, Sterland, and Aldridge, 2007, p. 20). The interventions focus on English language acquisition as the single most important factor in integrating into the employment market. An exceptional project (Houghton and Morrice, 2008) focuses on perspectives of migrants themselves and systemic issues in their education and employment journeys.

Gender selectivity and tracking skilled women into the migration stream

Migrating individuals are not a random sampling of a country's population but a highly selective group (Borjas, 1987). The well educated migrate because they *positively* self-select. They are viewed as having the wherewithal including the resources, stamina, entrepreneurialism, and ambition to adjust well to both the migration process and the destination country; those who are 'most efficient in the labour market are also more efficient in the migration and adjustment process' (Chiswick, 2000, p. 65). Additionally border controls, like England's points-based system, which looks for the 'right package of skills' (Raghuram, 2004, p. 309), privilege college-educated migrants.

Gender selectivity, however, is a different matter. It is the tendency for women from particular countries with a tertiary education to migrate more than men (Docquier, Marfouk, Salomone, and Sekkat, 2008).

In almost all cases, a higher education degree *increases* the likelihood of a woman migrating (Kanaiaupuni, 2000), a phenomenon bolstered by migration cottage industries like recruiters who target these skilled women. Although the pioneers, as Chapter 6 showed, didn't benefit from networked information, the participants viewed themselves as being positively self-selected in terms of their higher education (especially nurses). They expected that the receiving country's labour market would eventually see their true abilities and they would rise through the ranks when their competencies were recognized (Chiswick, 2000, p. 67; DuMont and Monso, 2007). They saw their employment dips being recovered quickly (Rabe, 2011).

From the policy-makers' perspectives, however, these 'aspiring migrants' were seen as lacking the requisite skills to acquire professional positions, that is, negative selection. Negative selection suggests that those with the least skills migrate (Feliciano, 2008). Indeed, the participants were less positively selected for the labour market in their sending countries and they had few opportunities after graduating from their professional schools. In a sense, they 'would have to go further in order to reduce the risk of discrimination' (Docquier et al., 2008, p. 23). But labour market deprivation in the sending country is not the only reason for migrating as Chapter 5 showed.

The failure to convert academic capital

Cultural capital in its institutionalized form, and as discussed in Chapter 3, is the codification of skills and qualifications from educational institutions. Cultural capital combines with family socialization and transmission as well as prestige (symbolic capital) to form what Bourdieu (1986, p. 51) has referred to as 'academic capital,' which can be converted into economic capital (financial resources). For these participants, academic capital was an important factor in their life trajectories. However, their hidden asset (e.g. higher education degrees) was rendered invisible in England through an immigration system that made them an 'out' group which did not determine the rules of the competition (Waters, 2009). In this case they lacked social capital—especially links to gatekeepers to help them convert their institutionalized cultural capital. This erasure was due to being from 'third world' countries and the participants' inability to confer social status by getting their qualifications recognized (Waters, 2009); their credentials weren't valued across time and place. This was also a major reason that many participants couldn't pass the upgraded IELTS exam, because of its in-built exclusive discourse. Moreover, their workplaces did not utilize their expertise. Although, as

Chapter 5 demonstrated, some participants aspired to change their situations by attempting to gain the academic capital needed to become professionals again, through upskilling in university-based adaptation programmes, most participants were unable to accrue academic capital in England. Only vocational and ESOL courses were available to them and their marginalized situations were reproduced in this second-class system; these women were being schooled in short-term vocational courses for the knowledge-based society ('for those that do *not* know') not the university-based, 'knowledge-based economy' ('of those that *do* know') (Brine, 2008, p. 347). Many of these women had a university education and academic capital but it did not confer the symbolic capital that could have created an edge for them in the receiving country.

Using a Bourdieuian analysis, the participants' reframing of their aspirations was a type of cultural reproduction of their status as they adjusted to a type of structure that organizes practices and dispositions. The participants played by the rules of this unequal game in their new social spaces in England. Their gender also infiltrated and influenced their pursuit of feminized occupations (Adkins, 2004; Moi, 1991, p. 1035). After they migrated they accommodated to their situations sometimes endorsing the gender contract and being proud of doing care as women, but also transforming care practices (discussed as a type of 'care capital' in Chapter 3). Also the migration regimes and professional regulations did not legitimize their belonging and so they formed a type of 'ethnic capital' (Erel, 2010, pp. 643–644) through their bridging and bonding to one another as Chapter 6 showed, validating their former identities. Again, these activities did not yield greater opportunities as the participants were cut off from 'professional diasporic networks' that could have helped them advance their careers (Rizvi, 2007, p. 227). They also saw themselves as ideal migrants reworking notions of motherhood, schooling, and family and using the discourse of greater human and cultural capital for their children, if not for themselves, by pushing them in their education (McLaren and Dyck, 2004). These women knew that their children (either in or outside of England) would need more academic capital in order to succeed in a highly stratified globalized labour market.

Brain waste and race to the bottom

These women, by most accounts, would be considered 'losers' in this system. As Chapter 5 showed, they migrated to make the cost and opportunities lent to them by a higher education degree pay off. However, they ran into detours when they became stuck in the care stepping-stones upon migrating to England, unable to exploit their expertise. This is not uncommon as migrant women change industries less than men (Boman, 2011). In short, their deskilling became brain waste in Britain. Brain waste is defined as the loss, or underutilization of human capital resources in a destination country, where the migrant workers' skills, qualifications, and professional experiences are not made use of in the labour market. As Chapter 3 showed the dispensing of medical tips and pointers by the former health care professionals was clandestine and the clients benefited from it, but there was no systematic knowledge-transfer of these care assistants' experiences to inform policies and services for older people. This is an example of brain waste. Brain waste involves 'a triple loss': to the destination country, the country of origin (lower remittances), and migrant workers (deskilling) (Chammartin, 2008, p. iv; Portes, 2009). While the migrant women's tax base bolstered England's economy (and they rarely used public services), their expertise was lost through the machinery of the care industry (e.g. the care plan) (Braverman, 1998). Meanwhile England benefited from the capital accumulation of their skills at the lowest levels and for a low cost. This generation of migrants was being used by England's labour market in a way that could be called 'accumulation through dispossession' (Harvey, 2005, p. 178) because wealth was being created (and secured) at their expense and they could be disposed of at any point because immigration policies made their labour position precarious.

The participants expected, however, to move up rather than down in English society. Imana, for example, was drawn to England to escape inequalities in India. She said, 'In India there is a caste system—here everyone is equal. I saw that on the telly program...a lot of people go to women and they have opportunities abroad.' Imana's trajectory is part of the legacies of Indians before her who migrated to England and were viewed as replacing the British (who emigrated to the USA) in a racist discourse called 'brains against browns' (Vinokur, 2006, p. 7). Imana represents the greatest proportion (of the highly skilled) who are now educated in non-OECD countries. But her story is not an unvarnished success story because she was a nurse where her mobility was based on a non-tradable service for which she paid the costs (Raghuram, 2009; Vinokur, 2006). This is the neoliberal solution of transferring all of the risks to self-sustaining individuals in a 'winner-takes-all' market (Brown and Lauder, 2006, p. 29). Imana's story is reflective of these downward pressures that led to her devaluation whereby new forms of social cachet are used for gaining advantages for some while reducing the bargaining power of others. This is a case of 'knowledge worked' rather than 'knowledge work' wherein capital-rich countries 'offshore' the skills they need and depend on individuals to support the costs of migrating, demonstrating that high-skill, high-wage magnet economies are only for the very few (Brown and Lauder, 2006, p. 42).

Deregulation and cost-cutting of public services to produce high rates of growth within advanced economies usually means lowering wages and has also created a 'race to the bottom' of the labour market for poor non-migrant women with whom migrant women are put into competition[1]; as Chapter 3 showed this situation pressured English nationals to put up with jobs that were restructured and intensified. Their work had been *downgraded* under neoliberal conditions that privatized social services by shifting them to the market, a move that 'tied women's hands' because of the lack of protections and opportunities (Collins and Mayer, 2010; Fraser, 2003). Individuals, considered to be market actors, engage in a 'solitary wage bargain' built on a male-model of work with no state support for care, ignoring the fact that women are often responsible for family care as well. This situation has been called a 'giant sinkhole pulling in to it the rest of the working class because it drives down wages and makes workers compete for low-paying jobs undermining any attempts to gain a solid foothold (Collins and Mayer, 2010, p. 153). This leads to asset stripping and downward mobility. Yet migrants have been blamed for this phenomenon.

Women's capabilities and development: Towards gender equity

Seeing these migrant women simply as 'losers,' however, loses the complexity of their situations. Most participants did not initially want to migrate but saw migration as the only way to achieve a greater livelihood (Sassen, 2006). The women's 'capacity to aspire' (Appadurai, 2004, p. 59), then, as Chapter 5 showed, was to become professionals and build a decent life in a new country for themselves and their families. As pioneer migrants they were equipped with high aspirations but also the resources and formal education to pay for the high costs of international migration. With their family responsibilities, they took considerable risks and had more to lose from a failed trip, not less (Lindstrom and Ramirez, 2010).[2] These pioneer participants also set in motion a chain of migration; the participants helped family and friends to adopt a migration path and reduced the shock for the followers that was absent for the pioneers due to their lack of networks in the pre-migration stage (Lindstrom and Ramirez, 2010).

Their own process looked clumsy, especially losing financial capital because of starting their journeys in debt but not being able to compensate for it once they settled because of receiving low wages. Although the participants expected some degree of uncertainty and disruption many did not anticipate what they found in England. This brings up questions about women's migration streams: Why as David Lindstrom and Adriana Ramirez (2010, p. 71) ask, 'does women's migration take off in some communities and not in others?' What they do *not* ask, however, is how gender and skills are a mediating variable in migration (Kofman, forthcoming). These women were mapping a new landscape with new circuits and new burdens placed upon them (Sassen, 2000, 2008). While they didn't blame themselves for their decision to migrate nor the routes they took, the participants often rebuked themselves for being *stuck* as care assistants; for example, one participant felt 'ashamed I am not a nurse.' It was not uncommon for participants to exclaim that the reason they had not become professionals like they initially planned was because they were 'lazy'—think of Jamuna in Chapter 5, and Lisette in Chapter 4 who stated: 'sometimes I feel lazy not reading,' after a ten-hour shift. This self-blaming was pervasive. Even an informant for the study did not understand why the participants migrated on student or care assistant work visas and questioned their commitment to their professions.

All of these participants were aiming to increase their individual capabilities to reach for a higher quality of life and they did so through migrating (Nussbaum, 2011). The capabilities approach aims at mobilizing for gender equity and the distribution of rights, services, opportunities, and protections on a global level (Unterhalter, 2007). This is particularly relevant for migrants in need of a rights approach to their livelihoods as they cross borders. Yet they are viewed almost solely as *economic* assets or burdens. It is important, therefore, to emphasize all dimensions of their human capabilities—'what people are actually able to do and to be' (Nussbaum, 2003, p. 1). Martha Nussbaum has focused on capabilities such as having bodily health and integrity, emotions, practical reasoning, affiliation, and control over one's environment. Although these have been critiqued as reductive and universalistic (see, Unterhalter, 2003), this approach is effective for calling attention to the participants' aspirations and the obstacles they faced to achieving them. Nussbaum argues that typical contractual/liberal views assume that immigration would cease to exist if states were self-sufficient and politically stable, ignoring that 'one of the greatest causes of immigration, economic inequality—is a global issue' (Nussbaum, 2004, p. 7). High inequalities produce vast amounts of low-paying jobs like care assistant work that become magnets. Women's decisions to migrate are influenced by these factors, which are gendered (Mahler and Pessar, 2006).

Nussbaum views education as 'the key to all human capabilities' (2004, p. 17) because this resource is the most unevenly distributed throughout the world, and it can support women migrants' social and cultural citizenship (e.g. access to services and knowledge about rights). Education, from literacy training to higher education, reflects an enlargement of freedoms to act (Nussbaum, 2006). Yet education in and of itself is not necessarily empowering. Although participants in this study had higher education, they weren't 'educating for world citizenship' (except for those who joined unions) (Friedman, 2000, p. 586) which left many of them feeling that they could not cope with the inequalities they faced upon migrating. Their professional education was for accessing the professions, not necessarily for building their own capabilities as workers in the labour market. They seemed to have a need for a feminist popular education, which goes beyond instrumental knowledge to focus on knowing about and demanding labour and immigration rights (Nadeau, 1996; Stromquist, 2006). Over and over again, participants declared that they did not know about their rights or how to assert and enforce them.

Amartya Sen's analysis of capabilities (1993, p. 35) goes further. It contains four concepts that advantage women migrants and their progress: *well-being achievement* (i.e. being able to *fully* participate in educational programmes), *agency achievement* (i.e. being able to choose a programme that matches a goal), *well-being freedom* (i.e. making choices about educational activities) and *agency freedom* (i.e. having the support to follow through with educational activities). Although all of these elements are important for migrant women, perhaps the first and last ones are the most critical because they highlight the process and outcomes of their capability to participate in higher education (well-being achievement) and the support that is needed to stay engaged through policies and programmatic structures (agency freedom). Yet in practice it can be problematic. Although the United Nations Development Program's (UNDP) Human Development Index assesses quality of life through socio-economic and political indicators on a country-to-country basis for health, education, literacy, and income including having a long life, and is based on Nussbaum and Sen's work, the index has conceptual problems (Klasen, 2006). For example, it doesn't encompass informal care and hours of work at home when women participate in the market economy; even when unpaid care work is referred to, it is vague in many aspects and narrow (Folbre, 2006). A gendered approach to education was needed.

Gender and Development (GAD) and gender mainstreaming

The United Nations (UN) Fourth World Conference on Women in Beijing and the Beijing Declaration of 1995 focused on assessing the progress of women. The Conference adopted key platforms of action for all areas of women's well-being, including rights and protections. The UN then launched a 'gender mainstreaming' campaign (UN, 2002). The goal was to achieve equal parity (economic and social) with men through compensatory goals and projects with the idea that 'development, if not engendered, is endangered' (UNDP, 1995, in Moser and Moser, 2005, p. 14). Introduced in 1997, gender mainstreaming was 'an organizational strategy to bring a gender perspective to all aspects of an institution's policy and activities through building gender capacity and accountability' (Reeves and Baden, 2000, p. 2). But as Sylvia Walby (2005) suggests, there are different operational definitions of gender mainstreaming in both theory and practice, which are highly contested (e.g. terms like 'mainstream' as well as 'gender equality'). Aside from its conceptual looseness, there are also inherent policy contradictions, organizational gaps, and implementation flaws in its potential as a 'radical political reform' (Clisby, 2005, p. 23; Moser and Moser, 2005). Yet as a practical tool, gender mainstreaming is attractive for it allows for gender-based budgeting and assessments to examine concrete outcomes for women's progress in the labour market (Walby, 2005).

Gender mainstreaming focuses on ending systemic gender discrimination and creating more opportunities for women to enter the workplace and other institutions. Most importantly, the idea is driven by a gender analysis of all public spheres (Heward, 1999; Reeves and Baden, 2000). It also aims at transforming gender roles and relations. The concept improves the first model, called Women in Development (WID), where women were viewed merely as a tool in poverty reduction strategies and gender relations were not challenged; programming under this model was usually directed *at* women but was not actually *for* them. Although WID was the first to challenge the view that women were passive recipients of welfare policies, GAD took this focus to the next level of involving gender in macro-economic and social planning policies; for example, closing the gender gap in education through attention to enrolments (Heward, 1999).

Aside from mention of remittances and brain drain, however, international migration is largely absent in the GAD literature. For example, a five-year review, 'Women 2000' by the International Organization for Migration (IOM) found that migrant women's needs were unrecognized (Paiva, 2000). The gender mainstreaming literature usually focuses on the poorest of the poor, which in this case, excludes participants in this study, thus becoming a missed opportunity to focus on deskilling of migrant women.

Embedding theory and research into practice and policies

A transnational feminist praxis

Although the term 'empowerment' is widely bandied about in development initiatives (e.g. the Millennium Development Goals) for developing achievements on a country-by-country basis, this study focuses on skilled migrant women and the structural disadvantages in their trajectories as well as their agency; their loss of status in the host country occurred through policies that gave them little bargaining power in the labour and higher education market. But they also found ingenious ways to deal with these oppressive forces and this study focused on increasing the support that they needed on a number of levels in the post-migration stage to ultimately help them gain 'power from within' (raising consciousness) and 'power to' (capacity building) as well as 'power with' (social mobilization) for their rights (Oxaal and Baden, 1997). A feminist transnational praxis aims to empower these migrant women in this way (Nagar and Swarr, 2010).

The advocacy part of the research was integrated throughout the study where participants, for example, in Strand 2, were asked about their needs for support to fulfil their goals. As well as career satisfaction from becoming professionals, many participants wanted a sense of belonging and to express their rights in other aspects of their daily life; one woman commented that England was an individualistic society with 'no public life.' Their labour rights were also important and this was a major theme early on in the study. Therefore, Strand 3 became part of a larger policy initiative to cover labour protections for migrant care assistants through advocacy approaches. A workshop for migrant care assistants that addressed educational and professional issues (to be described) was followed by another workshop focused exclusively on gender and labour rights. Activist care researchers, union organizers, sympathetic employers and workers, as well as national and international public service organizers participated. Those in the care field (social workers, nurses, midwives, and care assistants) discussed their experiences with one another to build professional networks and support.[3]

The study also attempted to engender knowledge about transnational migration and development to focus on global levels of women's displacement, disempowerment, stigmatization, and marginalization (Indra, 1999, p. 3). Nancy Naples (2003) discusses the importance of understanding marginalized women's standpoints within a globalized labour market, as well as their strategies for navigating policy limitations through an 'everyday world' approach. This orientation focuses on the tensions and contradictions that women migrants experience as they attempt to gain agency on a daily basis. So does Geraldine Pratt (2004, p. 93) who works 'at the borders of liberalism' by focusing on policy discourses that neglect women migrants, including their self-organizing tactics. Both researchers call attention to the ways marginalized women are 'othered' in policies and rendered invisible in globalization discourses but still create networks and solutions to common problems. These networks are activated for a broad political agenda, not one issue alone, and are considered alternatives to mainstream development in that they are non-hierarchical in structure and organization. They include education as part of larger empowerment objectives.

The women participants, as shown in Chapter 6, took part in the daily life in two or more nations and while their networks may have preserved social reproduction they also embodied new forms of equity (Fouron and Shiller, 2001). Most of the participants, for example, felt uncomfortable joining established organizations but liked ethnic-based associations and forming their own groups instead. Community-based 'open-to-migrant' institutions, like churches, were also used and the more 'open' they were, the better. Still, several women joined labour unions and their stories reflected more empowered voices, even while they were in the midst of struggling for status and self-respect. One of these union members said:

> I became a member of the union and they support me and if the fight is right, the truth will shine... I am confident in my skills. I have learned to speak what is right. You have to take this courage or be harassed.

With a stronger voice, she was on the path to not only asserting her labour rights, but also rearticulating her communities and challenging notions of nationhood and citizenry as part of 'transnationalizing the public sphere' (Fraser, 2007, p. 8). After all, the issues the participants were dealing with were not just migration-related, work-related, or educational, but stemmed from a variety of complex situations. Yet the new ethos of responsibility focused on individual economic accountability, expecting each migrant woman to 'manage her own human capital to maximal effect' (Fraser, 2003, p. 168).

A focus on practice: Popular education and migrant women

Strand 3 consisted of formulating and implementing a workshop oriented around a feminist transnational praxis that focused on global health care, deskilling, and advocacy knowledge for migrant women This deskilling workshop focused on Filipino care assistants (the largest sample in the study) and their capabilities, using Sen's ideas of agency, well-being, and achievement and feminist popular education models that attempt to rebuild civil society with non-governmental organizations (NGOs) (Walters and Manicom, 1996). The workshop aimed for three levels of empowerment—personal, social, and political. Personal referred to assertiveness and confidence; social entailed knowledge of access to higher education and other civil/state organizations; and political referred to knowledge of legal and labour-based rights. A participatory approach including reflecting and acting (praxis) was used with the idea that through action, marginalized people can acquire a critical awareness of their conditions, and, with their allies, struggle for empowerment. The workshop adapted curriculum from the globalization-from-below movement, which challenges unsafe working conditions and encourages full participation of migrant women in policy-making through learning about labour rights and community leadership. This approach sees connections between what occurs on the local level, with that of the global economy; Women's Education in the Global Economy (WEDGE) (Louie and Burnham, 2000) curriculum embodies this orientation and was adapted for the workshop. Folding the feminization of migration into popular education calls attention to a multi-dimensional and gendered notion of social equity.

The deskilling workshop took place at the Praxis community centre in London, and gathered 13 participants to discuss issues surrounding the global deskilling of migrant care assistants and to facilitate means for their career advancement, and to acquire knowledge about labour and immigration rights and the need for empowerment. The workshop aimed to raise awareness and create a supportive atmosphere to help participants continue with their plans for professional development and to organize with one another and link to advocacy organizations. It was sponsored by a community organization, Kanlungan, a consortium of Filipino advocacy groups based in Britain and it brought in the Philippines Nurses Association as a networking point. Worksheets also integrated union-based materials for migrant leadership. The day was filled with activities including videotaping participants' stories of struggle, large group discussions, information worksheets, and study circles. The themes which emerged from the workshop surrounded the participants' concerns: problems with work/student permits, poverty, unemployment in the Philippines, feeling entrapped in the workplace, lack of appreciation of skills (by the British government), discrimination and lack of knowledge and enforcement of employment and immigration rights. The open discussions enabled the participants to realize that not being able to reach their professional aspirations in England was not a personal flaw but that the existing system heavily impacted their status. The workshop appeared to boost their personal and social empowerment as they networked and felt more comfortable about discussing their problems with professionals in organizations to which they could connect.

The participants' concerns confirmed the need for greater political empowerment to overcome the institutional obstacles and systemic conditions that blocked their mobility. Although the video that came out of the workshop was promoted by several advocacy-based organisations and on websites, political empowerment was a process that had only begun in this workshop. In order to become visible, and find a collective voice, migrant care assistants would need to mobilize so as not to be caught, 'just stagnant in one place' as one participant expressed it.

Policies for recognizing qualifications and rewarding work

Recognition and redistribution need not compete and displace the other but can work in tandem (Fraser, 1996; Yuval-Davis, 2011). Nancy Fraser cites remedies for recognition such as representational change—moving migrant women from a place of invisibility, of being the 'absent centre' of public life as 'low-priced well-educated labour' (Momsen, 1999, pp. 7, 10), to that of being viewed as care experts. But recognizing qualifications does not necessarily guarantee that professionals will have a licence to practice (Liapi and Vouyioukas, 2009, p. 29). Rewarding professional work or redistribution usually signifies economic restructuring and policies that honour migrant women's qualifications to the extent that they can easily transfer them to England's professions at the same time that it ensures that all public service work is valued.

Feminist critical policy analysis (Marshall, 1999) re-centres women, gender, and power relations in institutions, which operate as gender-neutral and subsequently neglect their issues; examples are the discourses on migration that reinforce migrant women as 'other.' These policies are relevant for professional migrant women in particular who have lost their symbolic and human capital in England. But these barriers also exist in other countries too, for example, in the Middle East and in the places where they were born and trained. As Chapter 5 showed, family and schooling tracked many women into feminized professions while others faced discrimination as minorities (either by not being chosen for positions or being forced out of their jobs). They faced multiple economic, political, cultural, and social barriers. It was not a conspiracy so much as an interaction of different discriminatory practices operating simultaneously that marginalized them.

Expecting women migrants alone to solve these systemic inequalities is laughable, and so a number of policy strategies need to be developed to educate those in low and high places about the feminization of labour migration and the reasons that professional women end up in low-paying care work. Policies that recognize and reward should be informed by migrant women and highlight their voices and concerns in the adoption, implementation, and institutionalization phases. Dialogues already happen through conferences, websites, and reports spearheaded by organizations like Public Services International (PSI), UNIFEM, UNWOMEN, Gender and Migration Virtual Community, IOM Gender Division, and European Network of Migrant Women as well as other internationally based organizations. But these are not woven together for coherent policy development or to tackle migrant women's invisibility in the global economy and the sexual division of labour. A redistribution of public resources is clearly needed to support transnational programmes and organizations to develop comprehensive and long-term gender-sensitive policies for these migrant women. The following policy and research proposals arose from the study and are intended to confront multiple levels of discrimination that professional migrant women face.[4]

Fair immigration and recruitment policy issues

First, why so many highly educated women are migrating for care assistant jobs in such large numbers needs to be addressed. Few studies have researched these women's education levels or highlighted them. Quantifying how many care assistants there are in this situation would be important in highlighting deskilling and brain waste in OECD countries, like England. Defining 'highly skilled migrants' with a gender-based perspective is also important and challenges why some service sector positions like nursing are not labelled as such (Kofman, forthcoming). Immigration policies force these migrants into visa routes from which it is hard to escape and turn a blind eye to 'overseas' recruiters (some with sister companies and trainers in England/Europe). Recruitment companies need to be monitored, especially in the trafficking of student visas so that women are not pushed to desperate measures. Currently, these migrants are being set up as temporary guest workers with an implicit promise but no possibility of aspiring to better positions in society or of gaining citizenship (Bach, 2007; Castles, 2006). There are risk assessment packages, like those from PSI, and international codes of practices, as with the English organization, Skills for Care but none of these are enforced. A collaborative effort to formulate and enforce recruitment policies would involve internationally based unions, ethnic and professional associations, university advocate groups, and NGOs, as well as feminist organizations, in spreading information *across* borders to counter exploitative and discriminatory employment and immigration recruitment practices and the ways that borders, themselves, act as discriminatory mechanisms.

Even-handed workplace treatment

The second issue is migrant women's workplace treatment. Care work is a marginalized field. As Nancy Folbre (2006, p. 11) comments, 'economists sometimes refer to the service sector and pay attention to specific industries such as health but few acknowledge there is something called the care sector.' This problem is reflective of the downsizing of welfare systems, one where care assistant work has been rebranded as professional although lacking status. Policies should consider to what extent individual states and labour market institutions regulate employment of migrants (Lowell, Findlay and Stewart, 2004). As the participants' stories demonstrated, they were legal residents, their jobs were short-term and unstable and they were often overworked and had little support to help them advance. Also they couldn't easily exit these jobs. Government regulations need to be more finely tuned and strictly enforced so that migrants' workplace rights are protected; for example, Oxfam has advocated for the Gangmasters Licensing Authority in England to cover these care assistants (Poinasamy, 2009). Attention to reducing labour market segmentation for women in low-paying industries, with migrant women in particular stuck in the 2 C's (cleaning and caring) (see also, Anderson, 2000) or what Pierette Hondangnu-Sotelo (2007, p. 3) refers to as the 'New World Domestic Order,' is important for increasing their capabilities. Some studies (Rubin, Rendall, Rabinovich, Tsang, Oranje-Nassau, and Janta, 2008, p. 122) have shown that England

Conclusion: *Migrant Women's Education and Expertise* 215

is a liberal model with market-oriented solutions to care work with low-paid migrant women filling these jobs. Non-EU migrants in particular are on visas that lock them in to these types of jobs that make it difficult to switch or move up. The poor pay makes it hard to accrue resources and advance, because without helpful sources, the main focus is on survival. Unionization across the EU, particularly for migrants, can assist this effort as well as better enforcement of conditions and hours through a multi-agency collaboration involving government workplace regulation. A campaign to organize care workers across generations and on a larger scale is needed (Flanders, 2012). This improvement of the public sector would be considered a 'high-road' strategy (Folbre, 2005, pp. 19–20) that entails higher costs but also higher quality conditions for workers. Research that examines 'high-road' care services would be valuable.

Accepting qualifications

Third, there should be international agreements for converting participants' credentials into professional qualifications in a straightforward and practical manner. Currently no world wide multilateral agreements exist for such conversions across many sectors and fields. The participants' comments indicated that adaptation of their former qualifications was a prolonged and bureaucratic process that made them give up hope of ever becoming professionals again (see Liapi and Vouyioukas, 2009). The systems need to involve non-EU migrants so they can easily convert their qualifications or be on workable professional advancement routes without having to completely retrain. Adaptation courses could be more widely available and be for different professions as well as involving bridging programmes and prior learning assessments. Also, gatekeeping tests such as the International English Language Test System (IELTS) need to be better researched and monitored for their viability as to whether they are indeed necessary at all. Many feminized professions are tied to national professional licensing bodies that block migrant women's opportunities. Genuine opportunities should be available to them, especially with so many shortages of nurses and teachers (Kingma, 2006; Miller, 2008).

Improving women's opportunities in emerging countries

Fourth, improving the status and opportunities of professional women in developing countries is as important as it is in capital-rich countries in the pursuit of equal pay, rights, and opportunities. The participants' cases showed that they invested in a higher education in their countries of origin. They migrated in part because they could not locate appropriate work or professional development in their own countries or were paid far less than they should have been. As the Cuban and Filipina participants demonstrated, the feminization of skilled emigration from developing countries is widespread and diverse with differing educational, political, and economic systems (Cuba for example has a policy of free quality education throughout the lifespan and a highly professionalized workforce but faces an economic blockade by the USA). More research needs to focus on the ways wages, employment, professional development, networks, and socio-economic and political conditions interact with gender to drive professional migratory flows (Chappell and Glennie, 2010). The participants took jobs in England for which they were overqualified with the implicit promise that these would convert into better outcomes. Neither the jobs nor the opportunities transpired, as they had hoped, and they were faced with dilemmas about having to be 'just a carer' as one participant despaired or returning. Can changes be made under globalization processes that often undermine skilled women's capabilities—like the care industry that captures their labour? Improving conditions and rights of professional women needs to occur at international levels.

An international integrated approach

Lastly, an international, integrated approach is needed to secure 'bright futures' as a participant said (of achieving goals) for migrant women and their families. This would involve systematic efforts to improve women's progress in a global labour market that clearly disadvantages them, as this study, and much research, has demonstrated. As the women's stories showed, their reception in England was unfavourable in terms of being handicapped by their positioning in the care industry with their downward social trajectories. Institutional obstacles blocked their mobility in an industry and country that incorporated them as workers but did not enable them to advance. The ILO, for example, cites international human rights laws for its principles and rights to work as well as combating discrimination in the workplace. There is, however, little attention to any kind of gender empowerment and skilled women's labour market value. Research and policies are needed to understand the feminization of skilled labour migration at the cusp of the 21st century. One possible place to start for policy development is the 'UN Women' (formerly UNIFEM), which was established by the UN General Assembly in 2010. According to its aims, UN Women 'will significantly boost UN efforts to promote gender equality, expand opportunity, and tackle discrimination around the globe.'⁵ Through feminist policies and research UN Women, working with organizations like the IOM and ILO, as well as grassroots and feminist groups, can target interventions preventing migrant women's downward trajectories by focusing on the aforementioned barriers, like the immigration borders that entrap them as 'migrants.' While this entity is symbolically important, without substantial global policy tools and resources, the mission of equality may be missed.

Conclusion

In this chapter I focused on the ways that the feminization of skilled labour migration benefits the development of nation-states and with this, perhaps, some individuals, but does little for enhancing most migrant women's capabilities. I showed the ways that education was the backbone of migration policies aiming to bolster a skilled populace in global competition. I asked whether higher education leveraged women's socio-economic mobility. Higher education, for the most part, was not shown in this study to benefit migrant women's labour market outcomes. This was because immigration policies 'import labor not people' (Castles, 2006, p. 742) with national-based protectionism preventing translation of credentials and access to professional jobs citing migrant women's lack of experience in the country not to mention racism and sexism. This is paradoxical since many OECD nations like England are considered to be migrant countries (Miller, 2008, p. 15). A new vision of 'economic citizenship' (Collins and Mayer, 2010, pp. 13–15) would see higher rates of return for migrant women's higher education that lift them from the 'service pools' in which they are stuck in destination countries (Lutz, 2011, pp. 187–188).

The gender tracking process—of feminized subject specialties into gender-segmented labour markets—exerts pressure on women migrants' opportunities, especially exporting countries of health care professionals with their 'supply-side bottlenecks.' This complex triangle makes it difficult to tease apart the entrepreneurial university from the labour market and society from individual migrant women's goals. I have shown in this book that these were all 'mutually conditioning relations' (Brah, 1996; Cangiano, Shutes, Spencer, and Leeson, 2009, p. 89) that included migrant women's aspirations, trajectories, and practices within institutional discourses of labour, migration, and care. These relations also contributed to these women's high levels of deskilling and reduced their livelihoods.

Notes

1 Professional Women Migrants Becoming Care Assistants

1. This project includes a nine-month pilot study that was conducted in 2007.
2. This definition refers to 'personal *home* care workers' for elder care but adequately captures caregivers' labour in institutional sites.
3. There are exceptions to this rule (see, Raghuram, 2012). A fictional account by Deborah Moggach, *These Foolish Things* (Vintage/Random House, 2004), focuses on English elders moving to India for care.
4. This definition of 'pioneer' has been adapted from Portes and Rumbaut (2006, pp. 38–40) but is different in its focus on women. See Chapter 6 for a fuller explanation.
5. Five Indian participants came in 2005 and 2006 on student nursing visas despite the fact that their actual jobs were as care assistants.
6. An analysis of age, marital status, and number of children was conducted for 50 participants due to lacking this data for ten in Strand 3 of the study.

2 A Homework Methodology for Researching Migrant Women's Lives

1. Conditions in England's universities are far from ideal. But there is no doubt that working conditions, salaries, and treatment are considerably better than the care industry.
2. The research was based in England, although at times extended to other countries such as Poland and the Philippines (through informants). I also visited Poland for a month and took Polish language lessons there and in England for a year and a half.
3. The participants in Strands 1 and 2 were selected through employers who volunteered to participate and invited participants firstly through convenience sampling and secondly to gather diverse nationalities. Participants also invited one another to participate through a snowball approach. In Strand 3, participants were invited through advocacy-based organizations.
4. See, for example, Marina Lewycka's, *Two Caravans* (Penguin, 2008) and Rose Tremain's, *The Road Home* (Vintage, 2008), both of which feature narratives of migrant workers in nursing homes. Additionally the film, 'Caregiver,' starring Sharon Cuneta (2008, Star Cinema) takes the perspective of migrant workers in these homes.
5. Participants in the workshop had the option to be videotaped and photographed, with most of them granting written permission.

3 Care Industry Needs Skilled Migrant Labour

1. Upgrading here refers to changing standards. It is different from 'upskilling,' which refers to the role of higher education and professional development in raising workers' human capital potential, and is discussed in Chapter 7.
2. Here, the participant refers to a faecal 'accident' but also indicates that it might not have happened if she were to have visited the client sooner. The care plan, however, allowed clients a limited amount of toileting calls.
3. Lopez (2007) adopts the concept of 'mock routinization' from Alvin Gouldner's 1954 work on 'mock bureaucracy.'

4 A Place of Settlement and Upheaval

1. These 20 participants were selected from Strands 1 and 2 of the study, which entailed the most in-depth data.
2. Data on overseas workers is limited since the National Minimum Data set for this population was only started in January 2010 and holds overseas worker information on only a small amount of all worker records received.
3. Here, 5.5 per cent refers to non-UK *nationalities* of care assistants. The data also shows another figure of 14 per cent for those care assistants classified as 'born abroad.' This higher percentage suggests that those who are born abroad may have become citizens although this is uncertain. Nationality appears to be a more accurate measure.
4. Rotas have confidential details of clients, including names, addresses, times, and notes that cannot be shown. The critical aspect of a rota, here, is the amount of clients and the time and distance between homes.

5 The Disappointing Journey to Being 'Just a Carer'

1. This section was adapted from a forthcoming report written for the International Organization for Migration (IOM).
2. Maybud and Wiskow also discuss the International Labour Organization convention 157 for the harmonization and recognition of nursing qualifications (p. 226).
3. During the study period, these care assistants obtained work as nurses. It is highly possible that others found nursing posts but this was not known because of the study parameters.

6 Caring in Transnational Networks

1. Most of this sample (72%) was interviewed four times with the rest having three interviews per person.
2. Although 'pioneer' is not a perfect term, it is useful for highlighting the risks these migrant women took. For a good discussion, see Goulbourne et al. (2010, pp. 6–7).
3. These social support systems *did* change and these were incorporated into the mapping process during the study period.

7 Conclusion: Counting Migrant Women's Education and Expertise

1. 'Race to the Bottom' refers to a dismantling of regulations that increase economic global competition. Here it is being used to discuss the persistence of the low-wage labour market for women and which speaks to globalization fuelling poor labour standards for which they are affected (see Collins and Mayer, 2010).
2. Typically the profile of pioneer migrants tends to be younger and male (see Lindstrom and Ramirez, 2010).
3. The workshop information can be found at: http://www.genderandeducation.com/conferences-and-events/past_events/report-on-the-conference-care-work-in-focus-the-changing-nature-of-care-work-in-sectors/
4. This section was adapted from a forthcoming report for the IOM, called, *Crushed Hopes: Underemployment and Deskilling in Skilled Migrant Women*.
5. See website of UN Women for more information: http://www.unwomen.org/2010/07/statement-by-the-un-secretary-general-on-the-creation-of-un-women/

References

Ackers, L. (2004), 'Citizenship, Migration and the Valuation of Care in the European Union,' *Journal of Ethnic and Migration Studies*, 30 (2), 373–396.
Adams, T.L. (2010), 'Gender and Feminization in Health Care Professions,' *Sociology Compass*, 4 (7), 454–465.
Adkins, L. (2004), 'Introduction: Feminism, Bourdieu and After,' in L. Adkins and B. Skeggs (eds.), *Feminism After Bourdieu* (Oxford: Blackwell), 3–18.
Anderson, B. (2000), *Doing the Dirty Work: The Global Politics of Domestic Labour* (London: Zed Books).
Anderson, B. and Blinder, S. (2011), *Who Counts As A Migrant? Definitions and Their Consequences* (Oxford: COMPAS).
Antonucci, T.C. (1986), 'Social Support Networks: A Hierarchical Mapping Technique,' *Generations*, 10, 10–12.
Antonucci, T.C. (1990), 'Social Supports and Social Relationships,' in R.H. Binstock and L.K. George (eds.), *The Handbook of Aging and the Social Sciences* (San Diego, CA: Academic Press, Inc.), 205–226.
Antonucci, T.C. and Jackson, J.S. (1990), 'The Role of Reciprocity in Social Support,' in B.R. Sarason, I.G. Sarason, and G.R. Pierce (eds.), *Social Support: An Interactional View* (New York: John Wiley & Sons), 173–198.
Anttonen, A. and Zechner, M. (2011), 'Theorizing Care and Care Work,' in B. Pfau-Effinger and T. Rostegaard (eds.), *Care Between Work and Welfare in European Societies* (Basingstoke: Palgrave Macmillan), 15–34.
Apesoa-Varano, E.C. (2007), 'Educated Caring: The Emergence of Professional Identity Among Nurses,' *Qualitative Sociology*, 30, 249–274.
Appadurai, A. (2004), 'The Capacity to Aspire: Culture and the Terms of Recognition,' in V. Rao and M. Walton (eds.), *Culture and Public Action* (Stanford University Press), 59–84.
Aronson, J. and Neysmith, S.M. (1996), ' "You're Not Just in There to Do the Work": Depersonalizing Policies and the Exploitation of Home Care Workers' Labor,' *Gender and Society*, 10 (1), 59–77.
Bach, S. (2003), *International Migration of Health Workers: Labour and Social Issues* (Geneva: ILO), http://www.medact.org/content/health/documents/brain_drain/Bach%20Health%20worker%20Migration%20WP%20209.pdf, accessed 28 March 2012.
Bach, S. (2007), 'Going Global? The Regulation of Nurse Migration in the UK,' *British Journal of Industrial Relations*, 45 (2), 383–403.
Bach, S., Kessler, I., and Heron, P. (2012), 'Nursing a Grievance? The Role of Healthcare Assistants in a Modernized National Health Service,' *Gender, Work and Organisation* 19 (2), 205–224.
Bacigalupe, G. and Lambe, S. (2009), 'Virtualizing Intimacy: Information Communication Technologies and Transnational Families in Therapy,' *Family Process*, 50 (1), 12–26.

Bakker, I. and Silvey, R. (2008), 'Introduction,' in I. Bakker and R. Silvey (eds.), *Beyond States and Markets: The Challenge of Social Reproduction* (London: Routledge).

Baldassar, L. (2007a), 'Transnational Families and the Provision of Moral and Emotional Support: The Relationship Between Truth and Distance,' *Identities: Global Studies In Culture and Power*, 14, 385–409.

Baldassar, L. (2007b), 'Transnational Families and Aged Care: The Mobility of Care and the Migrancy of Ageing,' *Journal of Ethnic and Migration Studies*, 33 (2), 275–297.

Baldassar, L. (2008), 'Missing Kin and Longing To Be Together: Emotions and the Construction of Co-presence in Transnational Relationships,' Journal of Intercultural Studies, 29 (3), 247–266.

Balloch, S., Banks, L., and Hill, M. (2004), 'Securing Quality in the Mixed Economy of Care: Difficulties in Regulating Training,' *Social Policy & Society*, 3 (4), 365–373.

Barrera, M. (1986), 'Distinctions Between Social Support Concepts, Measures and Models,' *American Journal of Community Psychology*, 14 (4), 413–445.

Batnitzky, A. and McDowell, L. (2011), 'Migration, Nursing, Institutional Discrimination and Emotional/Affective Labour: Ethnicity and Labour Stratification in the UK National Health Service,' *Social & Cultural Geography*, 12 (2), 181–201.

Bauder, H. (2001), 'Culture in the Labor Market: Segmentation Theory and Perspectives of Place,' *Progress in Human Geography*, 25 (1), 37–52.

Baumann, A. and Blythe, J. (2008), 'Globalization of Higher Education in Nursing,' *The Online Journal of Issues in Nursing*, 13 (2), http://Nursingworld.Org/Mainmenucategories/Anamarketplace/Anaperiodicals/OJIN/Tableofcontents/Vol132008/No2May08/Globalizationofhighereducation.html, accessed 10 April 2012.

Behar, R. (1995), 'Introduction: Out of Exile,' in R. Behar and D. Gordon (eds.), *Women Writing Culture* (Berkeley: University of California Press), 1–29.

Behar, R. (1996), *The Vulnerable Observer: Anthropology That Breaks Your Heart*. (Boston: Beacon).

Bell, C., Nash, J., and Thomas, L. (2010), 'Social Care in England – A Brief History,' in C. Bell and P. Clarke (eds.), *Caring and Working In Ageing Societies* (Leeds: Skills for Care), 50–61.

Bennison, B. (2007), 'Heritage, Creativity and Innovation: Capturing the Past or Losing the Future?' Paper given at the Regions As Reservoirs of Innovation conference, Lancaster University, 26 April 2007.

Blake, W., Erdman, D.V., Bloom, H., and Golding, W. (1997), *The Complete Poetry & Prose of William Blake* (New York: Anchor).

Blunt, A. (2007), 'Cultural Geographies of Migration: Mobility, Transnationality and Diaspora,' *Progress in Human Geography*, 31 (5), 684–694.

Bolton, S. (2009), 'The Lady Vanishes: Women's Work and Affective Labour,' *International Journal Work, Organisation and Emotion*, 3 (1), 72–80.

Bolton, S. and Boyd, C. (2003), 'Trolley Dolly or Skilled Emotion Manager? Moving on from Hochschild's Managed Heart Work,' *Employment and Society*, 17 (2), 289–308.

Boman, A. (2011), 'Does Migration Pay? Earnings Effects of Geographic Mobility Following Job Displacement,' *Journal of Population Economics*, 24, 1369–1384.

Boris, E. and Parrenas, R.S. (2010), 'Introduction,' in E. Boris and R.S. Parrenas (eds.), *Intimate Labors: Cultures, Technologies, and The Politics of Care* (Stanford: Stanford University Press), 1–12.

Borjas, G.J. (1987), 'Self-Selection and Earnings of Immigrants,' *American Economic Review*, 77 (4), 531–553.

Bourdieu, P. (1986), 'The Forms of Capital,' in J. Richardson (ed.), *Handbook of Theory Research for the Sociology of Education* (New York: Greenwood Press), 241–258.

Boyd, M. (1984), 'At a Disadvantage: The Occupational Attainments of Foreign Born Women in Canada,' *International Migration Review*, 18 (4), 1091–1119.

Boyd, M. (2006), 'The Gender Dimensions of International Migration Commission on the Status of Women, 50th Session,' New York, 27 February – 10 March 2006, http://www.un.org/womenwatch/daw/csw/csw50/statements/CSW%20HLP%20Monica%20Boyd.pdf, accessed 14 April 2012.

Boyle, P. (2002), 'Population Geography: Transnational Women on the Move,' *Progress in Human Geography*, 26 (4), 531–543.

Brah, A. (1996), *Cartographies of Diaspora* (London: Routledge).

Braverman, H. (1998), *Labor and Monopoly Capital: The Degradation of Work in the Twentieth Century* (New York: Monthly Review Press).

Bremner, M. (2008), 'Maryport, West Cumbria, & East European Migrant Workers. Report for the Cumbria Equality & Diversity Partnership and Carlisle Diocese: Carlisle' (Maryport: Margaret Bremner).

Brine, J. (2008), 'The Boundaries of Competency Within Lisbon and Bologna: The Short-Cycle/Foundation Learner,' *European Educational Research*, 7 (3), 344–357.

Brown, A. and Kirpal, S. (2004), ' "Old Nurses with New Qualifications Are Best:" Managers' Attitudes towards the Recruitment of Health-Care Professionals in Estonia, France, Germany, Spain and The United Kingdom,' in C. Warhurst, E. Keep, and I. Grugulis (eds.), *The Skills That Matter* (New York: Palgrave Macmillan), 225–241.

Brown, J. and Talbot, I. (2006), 'Making a New Home in the Diaspora: Opportunities and Dilemmas in the British South Asian Experience,' *Contemporary South Asia*, 15 (2), 125–131.

Brown, P. and Lauder, H. (2006), 'Globalisation, Knowledge and the Myth of the Magnet Economy,' *Globalisation, Societies and Education*, 4 (1), 25–57.

Brush, B.L. and Vasupuram, R. (2006), 'Nurses, Nannies and Caring Work: Importation, Visibility, and Marketability,' *Nursing Inquiry*, 13 (3), 181–185.

Bryceson, D. and Vuorela, U. (2002), 'Transnational Families in the Twenty-First Century,' in D. Bryceson and U. Vuorela (eds.), *The Transnational Family New European Frontiers and Global Networks* (New York: Berg), 3–30.

Buch, E.D. and Staller, K.M. (2007), 'The Feminist Practice of Ethnography,' in S. Hesse-Biber and P.L. Leavy (eds.), *Feminist Research Practice* (London: Sage), 187–221.

Burawoy, M. (1998), 'The Extended Case Method,' *Sociological Theory*, 16 (1), 5–33.

Burawoy, M. (2005), '2004 American Sociological Association Presidential Address: For Public Sociology,' *The British Journal of Sociology*, 56 (2), 259–294.

Burawoy, M. (2008),'The Public Turn from Labor Process to Labor Movement,' *Work and Occupations*, 35 (4), 371–387.

Burawoy, M., Blum, J.A., George, S., Gille, Z., Thayer, M., Gowan, T., Haney, L., Klawiter, M., Lopez, S.H., and Riaian, S. (2000), *Global Ethnography* (Berkeley: University of California Press).

Buscher, M. and Urry, J. (2009), 'Mobile Methods and the Empirical,' *European Journal of Social Theory*, 12 (1), 99–116.

Campbell, K.E., Marsden, P.V., and Hurlbert, J.S. (1986), 'Social Resources and Socioeconomic Status,' *Social Networks*, 8, 97–117.

Cancian, F. and Oliker, S. (2003), *Caring and Gender* (New York: Rowman & Littlefield Pub. Co.).

Cangiano, A., Shutes, I., Spencer, S., and Leeson, G. (2009), *Migrant Care Workers in Ageing Societies* (Oxford: COMPAS).

Care Sector Alliance Cumbria (2008), 'Meeting the Need; Recruitment and Retention Strategy 2008–2013,' http://www.Cumbria.Gov.Uk/Elibrary/Content/Internet/327/5041/5044/39833111028.Pdf, accessed 4 April 2012.

Carey, M. (2007), 'White-Collar Proletariat? Braverman, the Deskilling/Upskilling of Social Work and the Paradoxical Life of the Agency Care Manager,' *Journal of Social Work*, 7 (1), 93–114.

Carnoy, M. (2005), 'Globalization, Educational Trends and the Open Society,' paper given at the OSI Education Conference, 'A Critical Look At New Perspectives and Demands,' http://www.international.ac.uk/resources/Open%20society%20Institute.pdf, accessed 12 October 2012.

Carnvale, A.P. Rose, S.J., and Cheah, B. (2011), *The College Payoff: Education, Occupations, Lifetime Earnings* (Washington, DC: Georgetown University Center on Education and the Workforce).

Castles, S. (2006), 'Guestworkers in Europe? A Resurrection,' *International Migration Review*, 40 (4), 741–766.

Castles, S. and Miller, M.J. (2009), *The Age of Migration: International Population Movements in the Modern World* (Basingstoke: Palgrave Macmillan).

Chammartin, G.M. (2008), 'Migration, Gender Equality and Development,' International Conference on Gender, Migration, Ration and Development: Seizing Opportunities, Upholding Rights, Manila, Philippines/September 25–26, 2008, http://www.icgmd.info/docs/paper_ilo.pdf, accessed 15 April 2012.

Chappell, L. and Glennie, A. (2010), 'Show Me the Money (and Opportunity): Why Skilled People Leave Home — and Why They Sometimes Return,' *Migration Information Source*, http://www.migrationinformation.org/Feature/display.cfm?id=779, accessed 17 April 2012.

Chappell, L. LatTorre, M. Rutter, J., and Shah, J. (2009), *Migration and Rural Economies: Assessing and Addressing Risks* (London: IPPR).

Charmaz, K. (2011), 'Grounded Theory Methods in Social Justice Research,' in N. Denzin and Y.S. Lincoln (eds.), *The Sage Handbook of Qualitative Research* (Thousand Oaks, CA: Sage), 359–380.

Chiswick, B.R. (2000), 'Are Immigrants Favorably Self-Selected?' in C.B. Bretell and J.F. Hollifield (eds.), *Migration Theory* (New York: Routledge), 61–76.

Clarke, C. and Sandlin, J. (2006), 'Wrestling with Reflexivity in Feminist Research: A Review of Qualitative Studies of Poor Women,' paper given at the American Educational Research Association, April, 2006.

Clisby, S. (2005), 'Gender Mainstreaming or Just More Main-Streaming? Experiences of Popular Participation in Bolivia,' *Gender and Development*, 13 (2), 23–35.

Cloke, P. (1999), 'Rurality and Racialised Others: Out of Place in the Countryside?' in N. Chakraborti and J. Garland (eds.), *Rural Racism* (Devon: Willan), 17–35.

Cohen, R. (2008), *Global Diasporas: An Introduction* (London: Routledge).

Collins, J. and Mayer, V. (2010), *Both Hands Tied: Welfare Reform and the Race to the Bottom in the Low-Wage Labor Market* (Chicago: University of Chicago Press).

Collins, P.H. (1991), *Black Feminist Thought: Knowledge, Consciousness, and the Politics of Empowerment* (New York: Routledge).

Commission of the European Communities (2005), 'Working Together for Growth and Jobs a New Start for the Lisbon Strategy' (Brussels: Commission of the European Communities).

Cook-Gumperz, J. and Hanna, K. (1997), 'Nurses' Work, Women's Work: Some Recent Issues of Professional Literacy and Practice,' in G. Hull (ed.), *Changing Work, Changing Workers* (New York: State University of New York Press), 316–334.

Cowden, S. and Singh, G. (2007), 'The 'User': Friend, Foe or Fetish?: A Critical Exploration of User Involvement in Social and Health Care,' *Critical Social Policy*, 27 (1), 5–23.

Cox, R. (2006), *The Servant Problem: Paid Domestic Work In A Global Economy* (London, I.B. Tauris).

Coyle, A. (2005), 'Changing Times: Flexibilization and the Re-Organization of Work in Feminized Labour Markets,' *Sociological Review*, 53, 73–88.

Crenshaw, K. (2011), 'Demarginalising the Intersection of Race and Sex: A Black Feminist Critique of Anti-Discrimination Doctrine, Feminist Theory and Anti-Racist Politics,' in H. Lutz, T.H. Vivar, and L. Supik (eds.), *Framing Intersectionality Debates on A Multi-Faceted Concept In Gender Studies* (Surrey: Ashgate), 25–42.

Crozier, G. (2010), 'Care Workers in the Global Market: Appraising Applications of Feminist Ethics of Care,' *International Journal of Feminist Approaches To Bioethics*, 3 (1), 113–137.

Cumbria County Council (2005), 'Local Matters: A Framework for Community Engagement 2005,' http://councilportal.cumbria.gov.uk/Data/Cabinet/20050405/Agenda/(item%209)%20Appendix%202%20to%20Community%20Engagement%20Strategy%20Document.pdf, accessed 4 April 2012.

Cumbria County Council (2010), 'Cumbria's Equality Story: The Changing Map of Cumbria July 2010,' http://Councilportal.Cumbria.Gov.Uk/Data/Scrutiny%20Management%20Board/20100716/Agenda/(Item%2010)%20Cumbrias%20Equality%20Story.Pdf, accessed 17 April 2012.

Datta, K., McIlwaine, C., Evans, Y., Herbert, J., May, J., and Wills, J. (2006), *Work, Care and Life Among Low-Paid Migrant Workers in London: Towards a Migrant Ethic of Care* (London: Queen Mary, University of London), http://www.geog.qmul.ac.uk/globalcities/reports/docs/workingpaper6.pdf, accessed 23 September 2012.

Datta, K., Mcilwaine, C., Evans, Y., Herbert J., May, H., and Wills, J. (2010), 'A Migrant Ethic of Care? Negotiating Care and Caring Among Migrant Workers in London's Low-Pay Economy,' *Feminist Review*, 94, 93–116.

Dent, M. (2006), 'Disciplining the Medical Profession? Implications of Patient Choice for Medical Dominance,' *Health Sociology Review*, 15, 458–468.

Department of Health (2000) 'Domiciliary Care National Minimum Standards,' http://www.dh.gov.uk/prod_consum_dh/groups/dh_digitalassets/@dh/@en/documents/digitalasset/dh_4083671.pdf, accessed 11 April 2012.

Department of Health (2008), 'Transforming Social Care,' http://www.cpa.org.uk/cpa/Transforming%20social%20care%20DH.pdf, accessed 24 September 2012.

Diamond, T. (1995), *Making Gray Gold: Narratives of Nursing Home Care* (Chicago: University of Chicago Press).

Director of Public Health (2009), 'The Annual Report of the Director of Public Health – Health In Cumbria 2009: Allerdale. Carlisle, Copeland. Eden, Furness, South Lakeland,' http://www.Cumbria.Nhs.Uk/Yourhealth/Publichealthinformation/Annualreport2009.Pdf, accessed 12 April 2012.

Docquier, F. Marfouk, A. Salomone, S., and Sekkat, K. (2008), *Are Skilled Women More Migratory Than Skilled Men?* (Louvain: Université Catholique De Louvain), http://sites.uclouvain.be/econ/DP/IRES/2009021.pdf, accessed 22 April 2012.

Dodson, L. and Zincavage, R. (2007), ' "It's Like A Family": Caring Labor, Exploitation, and Race in Nursing Homes,' *Gender & Society*, 21 (6), 905–928.

Doyle, L. (2009), *"I Hate Being Idle:" Wasted Skills and Enforced Dependence Among Zimbabwean Asylum Seekers in the UK* (London: Refugee Council).

Doyle, M. and Timonen, V. (2009), 'Breaking the Mould: New Trajectories in the Domiciliary Care of Older People in Ireland,' *International Journal of Social Welfare*, 17, 324–332.

Ducey, A. (2010), 'Technologies of Caring Labor: From object to Affect,' in E. Boris and R.S. Parrenas, *Intimate Labors: Cultures, Technologies and the Politics of Care* (Stanford: Stanford University Press), 18–32.

Duffy, M. (2007), 'Doing the Dirty Work: Gender, Race, and Reproductive Labor in Historical Perspective,' *Gender and Society*, 21, 313–336.

Duffy, M. (2011), *Making Care Count: A Century of Gender, Race, and Paid Care Work* (New Brunswick, NJ: Rutgers University Press).

Dumont, J. and Monso, O. (2007), 'Matching Educational Background and Employment: A Challenge for Immigrants in Host Countries,' in *International Migration Outlook* (Geneva: OECD), http://www.oecd.org/migration/internationalmigrationpoliciesanddata/41561786.pdf, accessed 4 October 2012.

Dyck, I. and Dossa, P. (2006), 'Place, Health and Home: Gender and Migration in the Constitution of Healthy Space,' *Health & Place*, 13, 691–701.

Eborall, C. (2010), 'Workforce Research at Skills for Care,' (Leeds: Skills for Care).

Eborall, C. Fenton, W., and Woodrow, S. (2010), *The State of the Adult Social Care Workforce in England, 2010* (Leeds: Skills for Care).

Eborall, C. and Garmeson, K. (2001), *Desk Research on Recruitment and Retention in Social Care and Social Work* (London: Christine Eborall).

Eckenwiler, L.A. (2010), 'Care Worker Migration and Global Health Equity: Thinking Ecologically,' in R. Shah (ed.), *The International Migration of Health Workers* (Basingstoke: Palgrave Macmillan), 25–43.

Ellery, S. (2006), 'Labour Pains,' *Guardian Unlimited*, 23 August 2006.

Elliot, A. and Urry, J. (2010), *Mobile Lives* (London: Routledge).

England, K. and Dyck, I. (2011), 'Managing the Body Work of Home Care,' *Sociology of Health & Illness*, 33 (2), 206–219.

England, K. Eakin, J. Gastaldo, D., and McKeever, P. (2007), 'Neoliberalizing Home Care: Managed Competition and Restructuring Home Care in Ontario,' in K. England and K. Ward, *Neoliberalization: States, Networks, Peoples* (Malden, MA: Blackwell), 169–194.

Erel, U. (2010), 'Migrating Cultural Capital: Bourdieu in Migration Studies,' *Sociology*, 44, 642–660.

Escriva, A. (2005) 'Aged Global Care Chains: A Southern-European Contribution to the Field,' International Conference on Migration and Domestic Work in Global Perspective Wassenaar, 26–29 May 2005, http://envejecimiento.sociales.unam.mx/articulos/conference.pdf, accessed 28 March 2012.

Feliciano, C. (2008), 'Gendered Selectivity: U.S. Mexican Immigrants and Mexican Nonmigrants, 1960–2000,' *Latin American Research Review*, 43 (1), 139–160.

Ferguson, H. (2009), 'Driven to Care: The Car, Automobility and Social Work,' *Mobilities*, 4 (2), 275–293.

Fitzgerald, D. (2006), 'Towards a Theoretical Ethnography of Migration,' *Qualitative Sociology*, 29 (1), 1–24.

Fivush, R. (2010), 'Speaking Silence: The Social Construction of Silence in Autobiographical and Cultural Narratives,' *Memory*, 18 (2), 88–98.

Flanders, N. (2012), 'Can "Caring Across Generations" Change the World?' *The Nation*. http://www.thenation.com/article/167354/can-caring-across-generations-change-world, accessed 31 July 2012.

Folbre, N. (2001), *The Invisible Heart: Economics and Family Values* (New York: New Press).

Folbre, N. (2005), 'Demanding Quality: Worker/Consumer Coalitions and "High Road" Strategies in the Care Sector,' paper given at, On Caring Labor, University of Washington, Seattle, WA 21, May, 2005.

Folbre, N. (2006), 'Measuring Care: Gender, Empowerment, and the Care Economy,' *Journal of Human Development*, 7 (2), 183–199.

Fonow, M.M. and Cook, J.A. (1991), 'Back to the Future,' in M.M. Fonow and J.A. Cook (eds.), *Beyond Methodology: Feminist Scholarship As Lived Research* (Bloomington: Indiana University Press), 1–15.

Fortier, A. (2000), *Migrant Belongings: Memory, Space, Identity* (Oxford: Berg)

Fouron, G. and Shiller, N. (2001), 'All in the Family, Gender, Transnational Migration and the Nation-State,' *Identities*, 7 (4), 539–582.

Fraser, N. (1996), 'Social Justice in the Age of Identity Politics: Redistribution, Recognition, and Participation,' paper given at Stanford University 30 April–2 May 1996, http://www.tannerlectures.utah.edu/lectures/documents/Fraser98.pdf, accessed 17 April 2012.

Fraser, N. (2003),'From Discipline to Flexibilisation? Rereading Foucault in the Shadow of Globalization,' *Constellations*, 10 (2), 160–171.

Fraser, N. (2007), 'Transnationalizing the Public Sphere,' *Theory, Culture, Society*, 24 (4), 7–30.

Fresnoza-Flot, A. (2009), 'Migration Status and Transnational Mothering: The Case of Filipino Migrants in France', *Global Networks*, 9 (2), 252–270.

Friedman, M. (2000), 'Educating for World Citizenship,' *Ethics*, 110 (3), 586–601.

Froggatt, K., Davies, S., and Meyer, J. (2009), 'Research Development in Care Homes,' in K. Frogatt, S. Davies, and J. Meyer (eds.), *Understanding Care Homes: A Research and Development Perspective* (London: Jessica Kingsley Pub), 9–22.

Fudge, J. (2010), 'Global Care Chains: Transnational Migrant Care Workers,' http://www.ialsnet.org/meetings/labour/papers/FudgeCanada.pdf, accessed 28 March 2012.

Gee, J.P. and Hayes, E.R. (2011), *Language and Learning in the Digital Age* (New York: Routledge).

Gee, J.P., Hull, G., and Lankshear, C. (1996), *The New Work Order: Behind the Language of the New Capitalism* (Sydney: Westview Press).

George, S. (2005), *When Women Come First: Gender and Class In Transnational Migration* (Berkeley: University of California Press).

Gergen, K.J. (2002), *Cell Phone Technology and the Challenge of Absent Presence* (Swarthmore, PA: Swarthmore College) http://www.swarthmore.edu/Documents/faculty/gergen/Cell_Phone_Technology.pdf, accessed 14 April 2012.

Glenn, E.N. (2010), *Forced to Care: Coercion and Caregiving in America* (Cambridge: Harvard University Press).

Gilligan, C. (1982), *In A Different Voice* (Cambridge, MA: Harvard University Press).

Goodchild, S. (2007), 'Migrant Workers—The New Underclass' [ESRC website is no longer active].

Gordolon, L. and Lalani, M. (2009), *Care and Immigration: Migrant Care Workers In Private Households* (London: Kalayaan).

Goulbourne, H., Reynolds, T., Solomos, J. and Zontini, E. (2010), *Transnational Families: Ethnicities, Identities and Social Capital* (London: Routledge).

Graham, E. Jordon, L. and Yeoh, B. (2010), 'Transnational Families, the Care Triangle and the Well-Being of "Left-Behind" Children in South-East Asia,' Paper given at, 'Changing Families in a Changing World,' Edinburgh, 16–18 June 2010 http://www.crfr.ac.uk/events/intconference10/presentations-wed/EGraham.pdf, accessed 14 April 2012.

Granovetter, M. (1983), 'The Strength of Weak Ties: A Network Theory Revisited,' *Sociological Theory*, 1, 201–233.

Gray, R., Sterland, L., and Aldridge, F. (2007), *Advising for Adaptation: A Guide To Personal Adviser Mediated, IAG, Careers, and Skills Adaptation Support for Migrants and Refugees* (Leicester: NIACE).

Grillo, R. (2007), 'Betwixt and Between: Trajectories and Projects of Transmigration,' *Journal of Ethnic and Migration Studies*, 33 (2), 199–217.

Grugulis, I. Warhurst, C., and Keep, E. (2004), 'Whats Happening to "Skill?" in C. Warhurst, I. Grugulis, and E. Keep (eds.), *The Skills That Matter* (London: Palgrave Macmillan), 1–18.

Hannam, K., Sheller, M., and Urry, J. (2006), 'Editorial: Mobilities, Immobilities, and Moorings,' *Mobilities*, 1, 1–22.

Haour-Knipe, M. and Davies, A. (2008), *Return Migration of Nurses* (Geneva: International Centre for Nurse Migration).

Harvey, D. (2005), *A Brief History of Neoliberalism* (Oxford: Oxford University Press).

Held, V. (2002), 'Care and Justice in the Global Context,' *Ratio Juris*, 17 (2), 141–155.

Heward, C. (1999), 'The New Discourses of Gender, Education, and Development,' in C. Heward and S. Bunwaree (eds.), *Gender, Education and Development Beyond Access To Empowerment* (London Zed Books), 1–14.

Hochschild, A. (1997), *The Time Bind: When Work Becomes Home and Home Becomes Work* (New York: Holt).

Hochschild, A. (2000), 'Global Care Chains and Emotional Surplus Value,' in W. Hutton and A. Giddens (eds.), *On the Edge: Living with Global Capitalism* (London: Jonathan Cape), 130–146.

Hochschild, A. (2002), 'Love and Gold,' in B. Ehrenreich and A.R. Hochschild (eds) *Global Woman: Nannies, Maids and Sex Workers in The New Economy* (New York: Henry Holt and Company), 15–30.
Hochschild, A. (2003a), *Commercialization of Intimate Life: Notes From Home and Work* (Berkeley: University of California Press).
Hochschild, A. (2003b), *The Managed Heart: The Commercialization of Human Feeling* (Berkeley: The University of California Press).
Hondagneu-Sotelo, P. (2000), 'Feminism and Migration,' *ANNALS of the American Academy of Political and Social Science*, 571, 107–120.
Hondagneu-Sotelo, P. (2007), *Domestica: Immigrant Workers Cleaning and Caring in the Shadows of Affluence* (Berkeley University of California Press).
Houghton, A. and Morrice, L. (2008), *Refugees, Asylum Seekers and Migrants: Steps on the Education and Employment Progression Journey* (Leicester: NIACE).
Huang, S., Yeoh, B. and Toyota, M. (2012), 'Caring for the Elderly: The Embodied Labour of Migrant Care Workers in Singapore,' *Global Networks*, 12 (2), 195–215.
Huisman, K. (2008), ' "Does This Mean You're Not Going to Come Visit Me Anymore?" An Inquiry into an Ethics of Reciprocity and Positionality in Feminist Ethnographic Research,' *Sociological Inquiry*, 78 (3), 372–396.
Husso, M. and Hirvonen, H. (2012), 'Gendered Agency and Emotions in the Field of Care Work,' *Gender, Work, and Organisation*, 19 (1), 29–51.
Hussein, S., Stevens, M., and Manthorpe, J. (2010), *International Social Care Workers In England: People, Motivations, Experiences, and Future Expectations* (London: King's College).
Hyland, T. (1994), 'Silk Purses and Sows' Ears: NVQs, GNVQs and Experiential Learning', *Cambridge Journal of Education*, 24 (2), 233–243.
Hyland, T. (1998), 'Exporting Failure: The Strange Case of NVQs and Overseas Markets,' *Educational Studies*, 24 (3), 369–381.
Indra, D. (1999), 'Not a Room af One's Own Engendering Forced Migration Knowledge and Practice,' in D. Indra (ed.), *Engendering Forced Migration Theory and Practice* (New York: Bergahn Press), 1–22.
International Labour Organisation (ILO) (2008), 'Draft ISCO-08 Group Definitions: Occupations in Health,' http://www.Ilo.Org/Public/English/Bureau/Stat/Isco/Docs/Health.Pdf, accessed 27 March 2012.
Iosifides, T. Lavrentiadou, M. Petracou, E., and Kontis, A. (2008), 'Forms of Social Capital and the Incorporation of Albanian Immigrants in Greece Ethnic and Migration Studies,' *Journal of Ethnic and Migration Studies*, 33 (8), 1343–1361.
Iredale, R. (2001), 'The Migration of Professionals: Theories and Typologies,' *International Migration*, 39 (5), 7–24.
Isaksen, L.W., Devi, S.U., and Hochschild, A.R. (2008), 'Global Care Crisis: A Problem of Capital, Care Chain, or Commons?' *American Behavioral Scientist*, 52 (3), 405–425.
Jackson, N. (1991), 'Skills Training in Transition: Implications for Women,' in J. Gaskell and A. McLaren (eds.), *Women and Education* (Calgary: Detselig), 351–370.
Jackson, N. (2001), 'Writing Up People at Work: Investigations of Workplace Literacy,' *Literacy & Numeracy Studies*, 10 (1 and 2), 5–21.

Jacobs, J.A. (1996), 'Gender Inequality and Higher Education,' *Annual Review of Sociology*, 22, 153–185.
Jubany, O. (2009), 'Skilled Female Labour Migration, Policy Brief 13,'http:// www.hwwi.org/uploads/tx_wilpubdb/PB_13_skilled_fem_l_m.pdf, accessed 14 October 2012.
Kanaiaupuni, S.M. (2000), 'Reframing the Migration Question: An Analysis of Men, Women, and Gender in Mexico,' *Social Forces*, 78 (4), 1311–1347.
Kelly, P. and Lusis, T. (2006), 'Migration and the Transnational Habitus: Evidence from Canada and the Philippines,' *Environment and Planning*, 38, 831–847.
Kendall, J., Matosevic, T., Forder, J., Knapp, M., Hardy, B., and Ware, P. (2003), 'The Motivations of Domiciliary Care Providers in England: New Concepts, New Findings,' *Journal of Social Policy*, 32 (4), 489–511.
Kim, T. (2009), 'Shifting Patterns of Transnational Academic Mobility: A Comparative and Historical Approach,' *Comparative Education*, 45 (3), 387–403.
Kingma, M. (2006), *Nurses on the Move: Migration and the Global Health Care Economy* (Ithaca, NY: ILR Press).
Klasen, S. (2006), 'UNDP's Gender-Related Measures: Some Conceptual Problems and Possible Solutions,' *Journal of Human Development*, 7 (2), 243–274.
Kleinman, S. (2007), *Feminist Fieldwork Analysis* (Los Angeles: Sage).
Kofman, E. (1999), 'Female Birds of Passage a Decade Later: Gender and Immigration in the European Union,' *International Migration Review*, 33 (2), 269–299.
Kofman, E. (forthcoming), 'Gender and Skilled Migration in Europe,' in *Cuadernos De Relaciones Laborales*.
Kofman, E., Phizacklea, A., Raghuram, P., and Sales, R. (2000), *Gender and International Migration In Europe: Employment, Welfare and Politics* (London: Routledge).
Kofman, E. and Raghuram, P. (2009), *The Implications of Migration for Gender and Care Regimes in the South* (Geneva: United Nations Research Institute for Social Development).
Koser, K. and Salt, J. (1997), 'The Geography of Highly Skilled International Migration,' *International Journal of Population Geography*, 3, 285–303.
Lafer, G. (2004), 'What Is Skill? Training for Discipline in the Low-Wage Labour Market,' in C. Warhurst, E. Keep, and I. Andgrugulis (eds.), *The Skills That Matter* (New York: Palgrave Macmillan), 109–127.
Lawrence-Lightfoot, S. (1997), 'A View of the Whole: Origins and Purposes,' In S. Lawrence-Lightfoot and J.H. Davis (eds.), *The Art and Science of Portraiture* (San Francisco: Jossey-Bass), 3–16.
Learning and Skills Council (2006), *Migrant Workers and the Labour Market* (Coventry: Learning and Skills Council).
Lee-Treweek, G. (1996), 'Emotion Work, Order and Emotional Power in Care Assistant Work,' in V. James, and J. Gabe (eds.), *Health and the Sociology of the Emotions* (Malden: Blackwell), 115–132.
Levitt, P. and Lamba-Nieves, D. (2011), 'Social Remittances Revisited,' *Journal of Ethnic and Migration Studies*, 37 (1), 1–22.
Levitt, P. and Schiller, N.G. (2007), 'Conceptualizing Simultaneity: A Transnational Social Field Perspective on Society,' in A. Portes and J. Dewind (eds.), *Rethinking Migration: New Theoretical and Empirical Perspectives* (New York: Berghahn Books), 181–218.

Lexander, K.V. (2011), 'Texting and African Language Literacy,' *New Media Society*, 13, 427–443.
Liapi, M. and Vouyioukas, A. (2009), 'Language Skills, Educational Qualifications and Professional Skills,' in M Kontis (ed.), *Integration of Female Immigrants In Labour Market and Society, Comparative Analysis* (Frankfurt Goethe University).
Lindstrom, D.P. and Ramirez, A.L. (2010), 'Pioneers and Followers: Migrant and Selectivity and the Development of U.S. Migration Streams in Latin America,' *The ANNALS of the American Academy of Political and Social Science*, 630, 53–77.
Llewelyn, S. (2007), 'A Neutral Feminist Observer? Observation-Based Research and the Politics of Feminist Knowledge Making,' *Gender & Development*, 15 (2), 299–310.
Lopez, S.H. (2006), 'Emotional Labor and Organized Emotional Care: Conceptualizing Nursing Home Care Work,' *Work and Occupations*, 33, 133–160.
Lopez, S.H. (2007), 'Efficiency and the Fix Revisited: Informal Relations and Mock Routinization in a Nonprofit Nursing Home,' *Qualitative Sociology*, 30, 225–247.
Louie, M., and Burnham, L. (2000), *Women's Education in the Global Economy (WEDGE) Workbook* (Berkeley, CA: Women of Color Resource Center).
Lowell, L. (2008), 'Highly Skilled Migration,' in G. Appave and R Cholewinski (eds.), *IOM World Migration 2008: Managing Labour Mobility in the Evolving Global Economy* (Geneva: IOM), 51–76.
Lowell, L., Findlay, A., and Stewart, E. (2004), *Brain Strain: Optimising Highly Skilled Migration From Developing Countries* (London: IPPR).
Lu, M. (2007), 'Rereading Adult Literacy Research Against the Grain of Fast Capitalism,' in B. Daniells and P. Moretenson (eds.), *Women and Literacy: Global and Local Inquiries for A New Century* (Metuchen, New Jersey: Lawrence Ehrlbaum), 297–319.
Lutz, H. (2011), *The New Maids: Transnational Women and the Care Economy* (London: Zed Books).
Macdonald, C.L. (2011), *Shadow Mothers: Nannies, Au Pairs, and the Micropolitics of Mothering* (Berkeley: University of California Press).
Madge, C. Raghuram, P. and Noxolo, P. (2009), 'Engaged Pedagogy and Responsibility: A Postcolonial Analysis of International Students,' *Geoforum*, 40, 34–45.
Madianou, M. and Miller, D. (2011), 'Crafting Love: Letters and Cassette Tapes in Transnational Filipino Family Communication' *South East Asian Research*, 19 (2), 249–272.
Madianou, M. and Miller, D. (2012), *Migration and New Media: Transnational Families and Polymedia* (London: Routledge).
Mahler, S.J. and Pessar, P.R. (2006), 'Gender Matters: Ethnographers Bring Gender from the Periphery toward the Core of Migration Studies,' *International Migration Review*, 40 (1), 27–63.
Marcus, G.E. (1998), *Ethnography Through Thick and Thin* (Princeton, N.J.: Princeton University Press).
Marginson, S. (2008), 'Have Global Academic Flows Created a Global Labour Market,' in D. Epstein, R. Boden, R. Deem, F. Rizvi, and S. Wright, *World Yearbook of Education 2008* (New York: Routledge), 305–317.

Marshall, C. (1999), 'Researching the Margins: Feminist Critical Policy Analysis,' *Educational Policy*, 13, 59–76.
Mason, L. (2009), 'Revised: Workforce Development Strategy for Adult Social Care,' http://www.Cumbria.Gov.Uk/Elibrary/Content/Internet/327/946/39583105143.Pdf, accessed 11 April 2012.
Massey, D. (2008), *New Faces In New Places: The Changing Geography of American Immigration* (New York: Russell Sage Foundation).
Maybud, S. and Wiskow, C. (2006), 'Care Trade: The International Brokering of Health Care Professionals,' in S. Kuptsch, *Merchants of Labor* (Geneva: ILO).
McCall, L. (2005), 'The Complexity of Intersectionality,' *Signs: Journal of Women in Culture and Society*, 30 (3), 1771–1800.
McCann, S., Ryan, A.A. and McKenna, H. (2005), 'The Challenges Associated with Providing Community Care for People with Complex Needs in Rural Areas: A Qualitative Investigation,' *Health Social Care Community*, 13 (5), 462–469.
McDowell, L. (2004), 'Work, Workfare, Work/Life Balance and an Ethic of Care,' *Progress In Human Geography*, 28 (2), 145–163.
McDowell, L. (2009), *Working Bodies: Interactive Service Employment and Workplace Identities* (Chicago: Wiley/Blackwell).
McGregor, J. (2008), ' "Joining the BBC (British Bottom Cleaners)": Zimbabwean Migrants and the UK Care Industry,' *Journal of Ethnic and Migration Studies*, 33 (5), 801–824.
McKay, D. (2003) 'Filipinas in Canada – De-Skilling as a Push towards Marriage,' in N. Piper and M. Roces (eds.), *Wife Or Worker? Asian Women and Migration* (Lanham: Rowman and Littlefield), 23–52.
McKay, D. (2005), 'Migration and the Sensuous Geographies of Re-Emplacement in the Philippines,' *Journal of Intercultural Studies*, 26 (1–2), 75–91.
McKay, D. (2007), 'Sending Dollars Shows Feeling' – Emotions and Economies in Filipino Migration,' *Mobilities*, 2 (2), 175–194.
McKenna, H.P., Hasson, S., and Kenney, S. (2004), 'Patient Safety and Quality of Care: The Role of the Health Care Assistant,' *Journal of Nursing Management*, 12, 452–459.
McLaren, A. and Dyck, I. (2004), 'Mothering, Human Capital, and the "Ideal Immigrant," *Women's Studies International Forum*, 27, 41–53.
McLimont, B. and Grove, K. (2004), *Who Cares Now? An Updated Profile of The Independent Sector Home Care Workforce In England* (Carshalton, UKHA).
Menjivar, C. (2000), *Fragmented Ties: Salvadoran Immigrant Networks in America* (Berkeley: University of California Press).
Miller, D. (2008), 'Downgrading and Discounting the Qualifications of Migrant Professionals in England: The Case of Overseas-Trained Teachers,' *Education, Knowledge & Economy*, 2 (1), 15–25.
Milligan, C. (2009), *There's No Place Like Home: Place and Care In An Ageing Society* (Surrey: Ashgate).
Milligan, C. and Wiles, J. (2010), 'Landscapes of Care,' *Progress in Human Geography*, 34 (6), 736–754.
Misra, J. Woodring, J. and Merz, S. (2006), 'The Globalization of Care Work: Neoliberal Economic Restructuring and Migration Policy,' *Globalizations*, 3 (3), 317–332.

Moi, T. (1991), 'Appropriating Bourdieu: Feminist Theory and Pierre Bourdieu's Sociology of Culture,' *New Literary History*, 22 (4), 1017–1049.
Momsen, J.H. (1999), *Gender, Migration, and Domestic Service* (London: Routlege).
Moser, C. and Moser, A. (2005), 'Gender Mainstreaming Since Beijing: A Review of Success and Limitations,' in *International Institutions Gender and Development*, 13 (2), 11–22.
Nadeau, D. (1996), 'Embodying Feminist Popular Education Under Global Restructuring,' in S. Walters and L. Manicom (eds.), *Gender In Popular Education: Methods for Empowerment* (London: Zed Books), 40–60.
Nagar, R. (2002), 'Footloose Researchers, "Traveling" Theories, and the Politics of Transnational Feminist Praxis,' *Gender, Place and Culture*, 9 (2), 179–186.
Nagar, R. and Swarr, A.L. (2010), 'Introduction: Theorizing Transnational Feminist Praxis,' in A.L. Swarr and R. Nagar (eds.), *Critical Transnational Feminist Praxis* (New York Suny Press), 1–22.
Nannestead, P., Svendsen, G.L, and Svendsen, G.T. (2008), 'Bridge Over Troubled Water? Migration and Social Capital,' *Journal of Ethnic and Migration Studies*, 34 (4), 607–631.
Naples, N. (2003), *Feminism and Method: Ethnography, Discourse Analysis, and Activist Research* (New York: Routledge).
Nash, J. (2008), 'Re-thinking Intersectionality,' *Feminist Review*, 89, 1–15.
National Health Service (2007), 'Putting People First a Shared Vision and Commitment to the Transformation of Adult Social Care,' http://www.dh.gov.uk/prod_consum_dh/groups/dh_digitalassets/@dh/@en/documents/digitalasset/dh_081119.pdf, accessed 4 April 2012.
Nedeva, M. (2008), 'New Tricks and Old Dogs? The "Third Mission" and the Re-Production of the University,' in D. Epstein, R. Boden, R. Deem, F. Rizvi, and S. Wright (eds.), *The World Yearbook of Education 2008: Geographies of Knowledge/Geometries of Power: Framing The Future of Higher Education* (New York: Routledge), 85–105.
NHS Information Centre (2009), *Community Care Statistics 2008 Home Care Services for Adults, England* (London: NHS Information Centre).
Nussbaum, M.C. (2001), *Upheavals of Thought: The Intelligence of Emotions* (New York: Cambridge University Press).
Nussbaum, M.C. (2003), 'Capabilities as Fundamental Entitlements: Sen and Social Justice Draft Paper. Paper given "On Sen's Work,"' The University of Bielefeld, Germany, June 2001, http://www2.lse.ac.uk/humanRights/articlesAndTranscripts/Constitutions_and_Capabilities.pdf, accessed 8 November 2012.
Nussbaum, M.C. (2004), 'Beyond the Social Contract: Capabilities and Global Justice,' *Oxford Development Studies*, 32 (1), 3–18.
Nussbaum, M.C. (2006), 'Education and Democratic Citizenship: Capabilities and Quality Education,' *Journal of Human Development*, 7 (3), 385–395.
Nussbaum, M.C. (2011), *Creating Capabilities: The Human Development Approach* (Cambridge: Harvard University Press).
Ogaya, C. (2004), 'Social Discourses on Filipino Women Migrants,' *Feminist Review*, 77, 180–182.
Orellana, M. (2001), 'The Work Kids Do: Mexican and Central American Immigrant Children's Contributions to Households, Schools and Community in California', *Harvard Educational Review*, 7 (3), 366–389.

Oxaal, Z. and Baden, S. (1997), *Gender and Empowerment: Definitions, Approaches and Implications for Policy* (Sussex: University of Sussex, Institute of Development Studies).
Pai, H. (2004), 'An Ethnography of Global Labour Migration,' *Feminist Review*, 77, 129–136.
Paiva, R.G. (2000), 'Women 2000: Gender Equality, Development and Peace for the Twenty-First Century,' New York, 9 June 2000, http://www.un.org/womenwatch/daw/followup/beijing+5stat/statments/omi9.htm, accessed 16 April 2012.
Parrenas, R.S. (2001), 'Mothering from a Distance: Emotions, Gender, and Intergenerational Relations in Filipino Transnational Families,' *Feminist Studies*, 27 (2), 361–390.
Parrenas, R.S. (2005), *Children of Global Migration: Transnational Families and Gendered Woes* (Stanford: Stanford University Press).
Parrenas, R.S. (2008), *The Force of Domesticity: Filipina Migrants and Globalization* (New York: NYU Press).
Patai, D. (1994), 'When Method Becomes Power (Response),' in A. Gitlin (ed.), *Power and Method: Political Activism and Educational Research* (New York: Routledge), 61–76.
Peixoto, J. (2009), 'New Migrations in Portugal: Labour Markets, Smuggling and Gender Segmentation,' *International Migration*, 47 (3), 185–210.
Phillips, N. (2009), 'Migration as Development Strategy? The New Political Economy of Disposession and Inequality in the Americas,' *Review of International Political Economy*, 16 (2), 231–259.
Pillow, W. (2003), 'Confession, Catharsis, or Cure? Rethinking the Uses of Reflexivity as Methodological Power in Qualitative Research,' *Qualitative Studies In Education*, 16, (2), 175–196.
Piper, N. (2005), *Gender and Migration* (Brussels: Global Commission of International Migration, IOM).
Plummer, K. (2003), *Intimate Citizenship: Private Decisions and Public Dialogues* (Seattle: University of Washington Press).
Poinasamy, K. (2009), *Who Cares? Oxfam Briefing Paper* (London: Oxfam).
Portes, A. (1998), 'Social Capital: Its Origins and Applications in Modern Sociology,' *Annual Review of Sociology*, 24, 1–24.
Portes, A. (2009), 'Migration and Development: Reconciling Opposite Views', *Ethnic and Racial Studies*, 32 (1), 5–22.
Portes, A., Luis E. Guarnizo, L.E., and Landolt, P. (1999), 'The Study of Transnationalism: Pitfalls and Promise of an Emergent Research Field,' *Ethnic and Racial Studies*, 22 (2), 217–237.
Portes, A. and Rumbaut, R.G. (2006), *Immigrant America: A Portrait* (Berkeley: University of California Press).
Pratt, N. (2004), *Working Feminisms* (Philadelphia: Temple University).
Prensky, M. (2001), 'Digital Natives, Digital Immigrants,' *on The Horizon* 9, 5, http://www.Marcprensky.Com/Writing/Prensky%20-%20digital%20natives,%20digital%20immigrants%20-%20part1.Pdf, accessed 14 April 2012.
Procter, J. (2003), *Dwelling Places: Post-War Black British Writing* (Manchester: Manchester University Press).
Pyle, J.L. (2006), 'Globalization, Transnational Migration, and Gendered Care Work: Introduction,' *Globalizations*, 3 (3), 283–295.

Rabe, B. (2011), 'Dual-Earner Migration: Earnings Gains, Employment and Self-Selection,' *Journal of Population Economics*, 24, 477–497.
Raghuram, P. (2004), 'The Difference that Skills Make: Gender, Family Migration Strategies and Regulated Labour Markets,' *Journal of Ethnic and Migration Studies*, 30 (2), 303–321.
Raghuram, P. (2007), 'Interrogating the Language of Integration: The Case of Internationally Recruited Nurses,' *Journal of Critical Nursing*, 16, 2246–2251.
Raghuram, P. (2009), 'Caring About "Brain Drain": Migration in a Postcolonial World,' *Geoforum*, 40, 25–33.
Raghuram, P. (2012), 'Global Care, Local Configurations – Challenges to Conceptualizations of Care,' *Global Networks*, 12 (2), 155–174.
Raghuram, P. and Kofman, E. (2004), 'Out of Asia: Skilling, Reskilling and Deskilling of Female Migrants,' *Women's Studies International Forum*, 27, 95–100.
Raghuram, R. Bornat, J., and Henry, L. (2011), 'The Co-Marking of Aged Bodies and Migrant Bodies: Migrant Workers' Contribution to Geriatric Medicine in the UK,' *Sociology of Health & Illness*, 33 (2), 321–335.
Rainbird, H. and Munro, A. (2003), 'Workplace Learning and the Employment Relationship in the Public Sector,' *Human Resource Management Journal*, 13 (2), 30–44.
Rainbird, H., Munro, A., and Senker, P. (2005), ' "Running Faster to Stay in the Same Place?" The Intended and Unintended Consequences of Government Policy on Workplace Learning in the UK,' in A. Cumming, N. Bascia, A. Datnow, K. Leithwood, and D. Livingstone (eds.), *International Handbook of Educational Policy* (Hingham, MA: Kluwer Academic Publisers), 885–901.
Reeves, H. and Baden, S. (2000), *Gender and Development: Concepts and Definitions* (Sussex: University of Sussex, Institute of Development Studies).
Riessman, C.K. (1993), *Narrative Analysis* (Newbury Park, CA: Sage).
Ritzer, G. (2008), *The McDonaldization of Society* (Los Angeles: Pine Forge Press).
Rizvi, F. (2007), 'Brain Drain and the Potential of Professional Diasporic Networks,' in L. Farrell and T. Fenwick (eds.), *Educating The Global Workforce: Knowledge, Knowledge Work, and Knowledge Workers* (Abingdon: Routledge), 227–238.
Roberts, C. (2010), 'Language, Migration and the Gatekeepers,' *Language Issues*, 2 (21), 4–18.
Roberts, C., Mort, M., and Milligan, M. (2012), 'Calling for Care: "Disembodied" Work, Teleoperators and Older People Living at Home,' *Sociology*, 46 (3), 490–506.
Rose, G. (1997), 'Situating Knowledges: Positionality, Reflexivities and Other Tactics,' *Progress in Human Geography*, 21 (3), 305–320.
Rostagaard, T. Chiatti, C., and Lamura, G. (2011), 'Tensions Related to Care Migration: The South-North Divide of Long-Term Care,' in B. Pfau-Effinger and T. Rostegaard (eds.), *Care Between Work and Welfare In European Societies* (Basingstoke: Palgrave Macmillan), 98–114.
Rubery, J. and Urwin, P. (2011), 'Bringing the Employer Back in: Why Social Care Needs a Standard Employment Relationship,' *Human Resource Management Journal*, 21 (2), 122–137.
Rubin, J., Rendall, M.S., Rabinovich, L., Tsang, F., Oranje-Nassau, C.O., and Janta, B. (2008), *Migrant Women in the European Labour Force* (Cambridge: Rand Europe).

Ruhs, M. and Anderson, B. (2010), 'Introduction,' in R. Ruhs and B. Anderson (eds.), *Who Needs Migrant Workers? Labour Shortages, Immigration, and Public Policy* (Oxford: Oxford University Press), 2–14.

Ryan, L., Sales, R., Tilki, M., and Siara, B. (2008), 'Family Strategies and Transnational Migration: Recent Polish Migrants in London,' *Journal of Ethnic and Migration Studies*, 35 (1), 61–77.

Rybas, N. (2012), Producing the Self at the Digital Interface,' in P.H. Cheong, J.N. Martin and L.P. MacFadyen (eds.), *New Media and Intercultural Communication: Identity, Community and Politics* (New York: Peter Lang Publishing), 93–108.

Salt, J. and Stein, J. (1997) 'Migration as a Business: The Case of Trafficking,' *International Migration*, 35 (4), 467–494.

Sassen, S. (1998), *Globalization and Its Discontents: Essays on the New Mobility of People and Money* (New York: New Press).

Sassen, S. (2000), 'Women's Burden: Counter-Geographies of Globalization and the Feminization of Survival,' *Journal of International Affairs*, 53 (2), 503–524.

Sassen, S. (2002), 'Global Cities and Survival Circuits,' in B. Ehrenreich and A. Hochschild (eds.), *Global Woman: Nannies, Maids and Sex Workers in the New Economy* (New York: Henry Holt & Co.), 254–274.

Sassen, S. (2006), 'The Numbers and the Passions are not New,' *Third Text*, 20 (6), 635–645.

Sassen, S. (2008), 'Two Stops in Today's New Global Geographies Shaping Novel Labor Supplies and Employment Regimes,' *American Behavioral Scientist*, 52, 457–496.

Scheeres, H.B. and Solomon, N.V. (2006), 'The Moving Subject: Shifting Work Across and Beyond Organisational Boundaries,' in S. Billett, T. Fenwick, and M. Somerville (eds.), *Work Subjectivity and Learning* (Dordrecht, The Netherlands: Springer), 87–104.

Schneider, J. (2005), *Donna Haraway: Live Theory* (New York: Continuum).

Scott, J.W. (1992), 'Experience,' in J. Butler and J.W. Scott (eds.), *Feminists Theorize the Political* (New York: Routledge), 22–40.

Secretary of State for Health (1998), 'Modernising Social Services: Promoting Independence, Improving Protection, Raising Standards' (London: The Stationery office).

Secretary of State for Health (2009), 'Shaping the Future of Care Together,' http://www.dh.gov.uk/prod_consum_dh/groups/dh_digitalassets/documents/digitalasset/dh_102732.pdf, accessed 4 April 2012.

Sen, A. (1993), 'Capability and Well-Being,' in M.C. Nussbaum and A. Sen (eds.), *The Quality of Life* (Oxford: Clarendon Press), 30–53.

Shamir, R. (2008), 'The Age of Responsibilization: On Market-Embedded Morality,' *Economy and Society*, 37 (1), 1–19.

Skeggs, B. (1997), *Formations of Class and Gender* (London: Sage).

Skills for Care (2007), 'Overseas Workers in the UK Social Care Sector, Draft Final Report,' http://www.Skillsforcare.org.Uk/research/research_reports/overseas_workers.aspx, accessed 28 March 2012.

Skills for Care (2011), 'NMDS-SC Briefing. Issue 14 Migrant Workers' (Leeds: Skills for Care), https://www.Nmds-Sc-Online.Org.Uk/Get.Aspx?Id= 648745, accessed 4 April 2012.

Skills for Care Northwest (2010), *National Minimum Data Set for Social Care North West Regional Report* (Leeds: Skills for Care Northwest).

Smith, D. (2005), *Institutional Ethnography* (New York: Rowman and Littlefield).
Smith, P. and MacKintosh, M. (2007), 'Profession, Market and Class: Nurse Migration and the Remaking of Division and Disadvantage,' *Journal of Clinical Nursing*, 16 (12), 2213–2220.
Solari, C. (2006), 'Professionals and Saints: How Immigrant Careworkers Negotiate Gender Identities at Work,' *Gender & Society*, 20 (3), 301–331.
Spencer, S., Martin, S., Bourgeault, I.L., and O'Shea, E. (2010), *The Role of Migrant Care Workers in Ageing Societies: Report on Research Findings in the U.K., Ireland, The U.S. and Canada* (Geneva: IOM).
Spivak, G.C. (1988), 'Subaltern Studies: Deconstructing Historiography,' in R. Guha (ed.), *Subaltern Studies IV: Writings on South Asian History and Society* (New Delhi: Oxford University Press), 3–34.
Stacey, J. (1988), 'Can There be a Feminist Ethnography,' *Women's Studies International Forum*, 11 (1), 21–27.
Strathern, M. (2000), 'The Tyranny of Transparency,' *British Educational Research Journal*, 26 (3), 309–321.
Strathern, M. (2006), 'Useful Knowledge,' paper given at the Centre for Science Studies at Lancaster University, 13 May 2006.
Strauss, A. and Corbin, J. (1990), *Basics of Qualitative Research: Grounded Theory Procedures and Techniques* (Newbury Park, CA: Sage).
Strauss, A. and Corbin, J. (1998), *Basics of Qualitative research: Techniques and Procedures for Developing Grounded Theory* (London: Sage).
Stromquist, N.P. (2006), 'Women's Rights to Adult Education As a Means towards Citizenship,' *International Journal of Educational Development*, 26, 140–152.
Stromquist, N.P. and Monkman, K. (2000), 'Defining Globalization and Assessing its Implications on Knowledge and Education,' in N.P. Stromquist and K. Monkman (eds.), *Globalization and Education: Integration and Contestation Across Cultures* (Lanham: Rowman & Littlefield Pub.), 3–26.
Sullivan, T. (1984), 'The Occupational Prestige of Women Immigrants: A Comparison of Cubans and Mexicans,' *International Migration Review*, 18 (4), 1045–1062.
Tanner, C. Benner, P., Chesla, C., and Gordon, D. (1996), 'The Phenomenology of Knowing the Patient,' in D. Gordon, S. Benner, and N. Noddings (eds.), *Caregiving: Readings In Knowledge, Practice, Ethics, and Politics* (Philadelphia: University of Pennsylvania Press), 203–220.
Taylor, I., Evans, K., and Fraser, P. (1996), *A Tale of Two Cities: A Study In Manchester and Sheffield* (London: Routledge).
Temple, B. (1999), 'Diaspora, Diaspora Space and Polish Women,' *Women's Studies International Forum*, 22 (1), 17–24.
Thane, P. (2009) 'History of Social Care in England. Memorandum to the House of Commons,' http://www.historyandpolicy.org/docs/thane_social_care.pdf, accessed 11 April 2012.
Thoits, P. (1982), 'Conceptual, Methodological and Theoretical Problems in Studying Social Support As a Buffer Against Life Stress,' *Journal of Health and Social Behavior*, 23, 145–159.
Thomas, M. and Lim, S. (2011), 'On Maids and Mobile Phones: ICT Use by Female Migrant Workers in Singapore and its Policy Implications,' in J. Katz (ed.) *Mobile Communication: Dimensions of Social Policy* (New Jersey: Transaction), 175–190.

Timonen, V. and Doyle, M. (2010), 'Migrant Care Workers' Relationships with Care Recipients, Colleagues and Employers,' *European Journal of Women's Studies*, 17, 25–41.
Tolia-Kelly, D. (2007), 'Fear in Paradise: The Affective Registers of the English Lake District Revisited,' *Senses and Society*, 2 (3), 329–352.
Tronto, J.C. (1992), 'Women and Caring: What Can Feminists Learn about Morality from Caring?,' in A.M. Jaggar and S.R. Bordo (eds.), *Gender/Body/Knowledge: Feminist Reconstructions of Being and Knowing* (New Brunswick: Rutgers University Press), 172–187.
Tronto, J.C. (2003), 'Time's Place,' *Feminist Theory*, 4 (2), 119–138.
Tronto, J.C. (2006), 'Vicious Circles of Privatized Caring', in M. Hamington and D. Miller (eds.), *Socializing Care: Feminist Ethics and Public Issues* (Lanham, MD: Rowman and Littlefield), 3–26.
Tronto, J.C. (2010), 'Creating Caring Institutions: Politics, Plurality, and Purpose,' *Ethics and Social Welfare*, 4 (2), 158–171.
Twigg, J. (2000), *Bathing: The Body and Community Care* (London Routledge).
Twigg, J., Wolkowitz, C., Cohen, R.L., and Nettleton, S. (2011), 'Conceptualising Body Work in Health and Social Care,' *Sociology of Health & Illness*, 33 (2), 171–188.
UN (2002), *Gender Mainstreaming: An Overview* (New York: United Nations Department of Economic and Social Affairs).
UNESCO (1998), 'Women in Higher Education: Issues and Perspectives,' *Conference at UNESCO*, Paris, 5–9, http://unesdoc.unesco.org/images/0011/001166/116618m.pdf, accessed 24 September 2012.
UNESCO (2010), *Global Education Digest: Comparing Education Statistics across the World* (Montreal, Quebec: UNESCO Institute for Statistics), http://www.uis.unesco.org/library/documents/ged_2010_en.pdf, accessed 14 April 2012.
Ungerson, C. (2004), 'Whose Empowerment and Independence? A Cross-National Perspective on "Cash for Care" Schemes,' *Ageing & Society*, 24, 189–212.
Unterhalter, E. (2003), 'Education, Capabilities and Social Justice,' paper commissioned for the EFA Global Monitoring Report 2003/4, *The Leap to Equality*. http://unesdoc.unesco.org/images/0014/001469/146971e.pdf, accessed 16 April 2012.
Unterhalter, E. (2007), 'Cosmopolitanism, Global Social Justice and Gender Equality in Education,' paper given at The HDCA Conference, July, In New York.
Urry, J. (2007), *Mobilities* (Cambridge: Polity).
van Hooren, F.J. (2012), 'Varieties of Migrant Care Work: Comparing Patterns of Migrant Labour in Social Care,' *Journal of European Social Policy*, 22 (2), 133–147.
Vertovec, S. (2004), 'Cheap Calls: The Social Glue of Migrant Transnationalism,' *Global Networks*, 4 (2), 219–224.
Vertovec, S. (2007), 'Migrant Transnationalism and Modes of Transformation,' in A. Portes and J. Dewind (eds.), *Rethinking Migration: New Theoretical and Empirical Perspectives* (New York: Berghahn Books), 181–218.
Vinokur, A. (2006), 'Brain Migration Revisited,' *Globalisation, Societies and Education*, 4 (1), 7–24.
Wacquant, L. (1997), 'For an Analytic of Racial Domination,' in D.E. Davis (ed.), *Political Power and Social Theory II* (Greenwich, CT: Jai Press), 221–234.

Waerness, K. (1996), 'The Rationality of Caring,' in D. Gordon, S. Benner, P., and N. Noddings (eds.), *Caregiving: Readings In Knowledge, Practice, Ethics, and Politics* (Philadelphia: University of Pennsylvania Press), 231–255.
Wainwright, R. (2009), *An Overview of the UK Domiciliary Care Sector* (Sutton: UKHA).
Walby, S. (2002), Gender and the Economy: Regulation Or Deregulation? Paper for the ESRC seminar 'Work, Life and the New Economy,' Lancaster University. http://www.lancs.ac.uk/fass/sociology/papers/walby-genderandthenew economy.pdf, accessed 11 April 2012.
Walby, S. (2005), *Measuring Women's Progress in a Global Era* (Oxford: UNESCO).
Walby, S. (2007a), 'Complexity Theory, Systems Theory, and Multiple Intersecting Social Inequalities,' *Philosophy of the Social Sciences*, 37 (4), 449–470.
Walby, S. (2007b), 'Introduction: Theorizing the Gendering of the New Economy: Comparative Approaches,' in S. Walby, H. Gottfried, K. Gottschall, and M. Osawa (eds.), *Gendering The Knowledge Economy: Comparative Perspectives* (Basingstoke: Palgrave Macmillan), 3–50.
Waldinger, R. Lim, N., and Cort, D. (2007), 'Bad Jobs, Good Jobs, No Jobs? The Employment Experience of the Mexican American Second Generation,' *Journal of Ethnic and Migration Studies*, 33 (1), 1–35.
Walters, S. and Manicom, L. (1996), 'Introduction,' in S. Walters and L. Manicom (eds.), *Gender in Popular Education* (London: Zed Books), 1–22.
Warhurst, C. (2008), 'The Knowledge Economy, Skills and Government Labour Market Intervention,' *Policy Studies*, 29 (1), 71–86.
Warhurst, C. and Nickson, D. (2007), 'Employee Experience of Aesthetic Labour in Retail and Hospitality Work,' *Employment and Society*, 21 (1), 103–120.
Warhurst, C. and Thompson, P. (2006), 'Mapping Knowledge In Work: Proxies Or Practices?' *Work, Employment and Society*, 20 (4), 787–800.
Wasserfall, R. (1993), 'Reflexivity, Feminism and Difference,' *Qualitative Sociology*, 16 (1), 23–41.
Waters, J.L. (2009), 'Transnational Geographies of Academic Distinction: The Role of Social Capital in the Recognition and Evaluation of "Overseas" Credentials,' *Globalisation, Societies and Education*, 7 (2), 113–129.
Wellman, B. and Wortley, S. (1990), 'Different Strokes from Different Folks: Community Ties and Social Support,' *American Journal of Sociology*, 96 (3), 558–588.
White, A., Laoire, C.N., Tyrell, N., and Carpena-Méndez, F. (2011), 'Children's Roles in Transnational Migration,' *Journal of Ethnic and Migration Studies*, 37 (8), 1159–1170.
Wibberley, G. (2011), 'The Invisibility and Complexity of Domiciliary Carers' Work, around, in and out of Their Labour Process,' Unpublished Ph.D Thesis, (Lancaster: Lancaster University).
Williams, F. (2010), 'Migration and Care: Themes, Concepts and Challenges,' *Social Policy & Society*, 9 (3), 385–396.
Wills, J. Datta, K. Evans, Y. Herbert, J. May, J., and McIlwaine, C. (2010), *Global Cities At Work: New Migrant Divisions of Labour* (New York: Pluto Press).
Winkelmann-Gleed, A. (2004), *Migrant Nurses* (Oxford: Radcliffe Medical Press).
Wolf, A. (2002). *Does Education Matter? Myths about Education and Economic Growth* (London: Penguin).

Wolkowitz, C. (2006), *Bodies at Work* (London: Sage).
Xu, Y. (2008), 'Communicative Competence of International Nurses and Patient Safety and Quality of Care,' *Home Health Care Management & Practice*, 20, 430–432.
Yeates, N. (2009), *Globalizing Care Economies and Migrant Workers: Explorations in Global Care Chains* (Basingstoke: Palgrave Macmillan).
Yeates, N. (2012), 'Global Care Chains: A State-of-the-Art Review and Future Directions in Care Transnationalization Research,' *Global Networks*, 12 (2), 135–154.
Yuval-Davis, N. (2011), 'Beyond the Recognition and Re-Distribution Dichotomy: Intersectionality and Stratification,' in H. Lutz, T.H. Vivar, and L. Supik (eds.), *Framing Intersectionality Debates on A Multi-Faceted Concept in Gender Studies* (Surrey: Ashgate), 155–170.

Index

abuse, abusive, bullying, 33, 54–5, 67, 97, 111, 114, 133–4, 162
academic capital, 194, 197, 202–3
accent(s), 17, 34, 68, 108, 117, 119
  see also England, British-born; English language, English to Speakers of Other Languages (ESOL)
accountability, regimes, 35, 47
adaptation, 58–61, 88, 128, 130, 141, 143–4, 146, 151, 154–5, 181, 200, 203, 215
  adapt, 17, 58, 61, 124, 128, 143, 155, 200
adopt, 157, 198, 205, 219
advance, advancement, 2, 4–5, 8, 10, 14, 18, 20, 23–4, 38, 58, 61, 65, 68, 70, 120, 128–9, 131, 136, 138, 140, 143, 145, 147–9, 151–2, 155, 157, 161, 169–70, 178–9, 181, 187, 195, 203, 205, 211, 214–16
advanced economies, 5, 8, 10, 38, 161, 170, 205
  see also OECD
advocacy, advocate, 3–4, 34–6, 38, 50, 79, 145, 148, 178, 209, 211–12, 214, 218
aesthetic labour, 51, 75–9
  see also Warhurst, Chris
Africa, African, 37, 62, 124, 171
African-American, 62, 124
ageing, 5, 8–9, 41, 99, 165, 179
agency (regulations), 133
Anderson, Bridget, 6–9, 16, 214
aspirations, 3–4, 16, 25, 33, 49, 103, 135, 145–8, 156–8, 181, 196, 198, 203, 205–6, 212, 217

Australia, 23, 128, 131, 148, 171
autonomy, 51, 62–3, 89–90, 127

bargaining power, 56, 150, 204, 209
  risks, gamble, 24, 204
barriers, 2, 14, 18, 64, 66, 97, 114, 124, 131, 134–5, 142, 145, 148–50, 157, 160, 168, 198, 213, 217
Behar, Ruth, 29–30, 195
belonging, 43, 127, 159, 173–5, 185, 193, 196, 203, 209
black, 47, 62–3, 75
bodywork, 85, 102
  see also care
bond, bonding, 80, 82, 110, 148, 156, 162–3, 176–8, 180–2, 185, 190, 196, 200, 203
border crossing, borders, 5, 14, 38, 42, 159, 181, 196–7, 206, 210, 214, 217
Boris, Eileen, 5, 62–3, 102, 195–6
boundaries, 30–1, 33, 36, 63–4, 89, 91, 95, 122, 126, 174
  see also care, caring
Bourdieu, Pierre, 80, 194, 202–3
brain waste, 194, 203–5, 213
Braverman, Harry, 150, 204
breadwinner, 3, 125, 127, 161, 164, 169–70, 183
bridging, 162, 178, 181–2, 203, 215
Burawoy, Michael, 41–2, 45
businesses, 52, 90, 93, 97

Canada, 16, 22–3, 52, 113, 128, 148, 182, 200–1
capabilities, 2, 32, 34, 194, 205–8, 211, 214, 216–17
  see also Nussbaum, Martha

241

242 Index

care
  care about, 33, 86, 145, 147, 171
  care industry, 1, 4, 7–8, 10–11, 15, 19, 41, 51–87, 219
  care work, 3, 62
  caring, 159–93
  caring for, 8, 14, 30, 34, 36, 55, 63, 98, 147, 159–60, 164–5, 167
  fast care, 53, 89
  care assistant
  carer, 6
  care worker, 3, 6, 10, 16, 36, 57, 81, 92, 215
  care capital, 11, 80–1, 87, 203
  care ethic, 31, 34–6
    ethic of caring, 36
    feminist care ethic, 35
    see also care, caring
  care plans, 14, 54, 60, 64, 69–70, 73, 76–9, 82–4, 89, 102–3, 106, 112, 191, 204, 219
cars, 18, 99–102, 106–7, 121, 175
  driving, 99–102
Caucasian, 19
children, 7, 10, 23, 40, 59, 78, 94–5, 112, 127, 130–2, 134, 146, 157–8, 160–4, 166–9, 170–7, 181–3, 186–93, 203
  education, 40, 95, 130
  pregnant, 133
choice, 8, 16, 52–3, 71, 75–6, 81–3, 90, 125, 136–7, 187, 207
  see also social care
church, 63, 95, 172–3, 210
citizen, citizenship, 15, 22, 35, 61, 94, 96, 121, 128, 140, 154, 196, 201, 207, 210, 214, 217, 219
Citizens Advice Bureau, 96
clients, 3, 8, 9, 14, 15, 17, 30, 43–4, 49, 51–5, 57, 59, 63–4, 69–72, 75–92, 96–106, 108, 110–11, 119–22, 124–5, 134, 142, 146–7, 162, 171–2, 174–5, 177, 180, 186, 191, 193, 196, 204, 219
co-ethnic, 173, 175, 178
Collins, Patricia, 32, 36, 205, 217
commercial care sector, 52
commodified care, 196
  see also care

communication, communicating, communicate, 18, 24, 52, 56, 68, 71–2, 75–7, 89, 97, 106, 162–4, 167, 170, 175, 177, 181–5, 188, 193
community, communities, 3, 11, 13–16, 25, 35, 40, 49, 61, 78, 87–8, 95–8, 100, 102, 113, 119, 125, 135, 162–4, 169, 173–4, 181, 186–93
competencies, 52, 66, 185, 201–2
  see also skilled migrants
competition, productivity, 8, 15, 53, 62, 199, 202, 205, 217, 220
  see also socioeconomic
constrain, 7–8, 59, 106
Corbin, Juliet, 45
costs, 15, 18, 22, 24, 41, 53, 98, 120, 127, 141, 142–3, 185, 198, 200, 204–5, 215
  see also remittances, remit; poor pay
Cox, Rosie, 8, 10
credential, 28, 130, 135, 143, 151, 156, 198, 200, 202, 215, 217
Cuba, Cuban, 21, 216
cultural capital, 52, 80, 87, 150, 198, 202–3
  see also Bourdieu, Pierre
Cumbria, Northwest England, 88, 93–9, 101, 115, 120–2

daughter(s), 28, 73, 78, 81, 111–12, 130–1, 133, 137, 161, 163–71, 179, 183–4, 188–92
dead end, 55, 135, 142–5
decision-making, 14, 24, 89, 163, 194
Delphi study, 48
deportation, 28, 160
deprofessionalization, 42
  see also deskilling; professionalization
deskilling, 4, 7, 14, 16, 41–2, 44–5, 50, 87, 144, 149–52, 157, 204, 209, 211, 213, 217
  see also Braverman, Harry
development (as with developing countries)
  developing countries, 200, 215–16
  low-income countries, 51, 150

diaspora, 37, 122, 159, 173–8
disadvantages, 63, 89, 150, 196, 199–200, 209, 216
disappointment, 2, 18, 27, 114–15, 121, 137, 145
discrimination, 5, 16–19, 95–6, 108, 138, 155, 196, 202, 208, 212–13, 216
displace(d), 196, 212
distance, 33, 77, 82, 97, 102, 108, 119, 159–60, 162, 165, 167, 170–1, 181–2, 185
divorce, 6, 23, 111, 133, 160, 165–7, 172
domestic workers, 6, 146
domiciliary care, home-based care, home help, 25, 64, 74, 81, 88–94, 96–106, 108–9, 186
dream, 2, 12, 24–5, 114–15, 120, 123, 134, 136, 139, 141, 143, 157, 166, 187, 198
  see also aspirations

elder care, 2, 5, 42, 88, 153, 218
empower, empowerment, 12, 32, 76, 207, 209–12, 216
engendering transnationalism, 5, 15, 195
England, British-born, 1, 8–10, 51, 92
English language
  English to Speakers of Other Languages (ESOL), 3, 12, 18, 33, 40, 46–8, 68, 122, 131, 143–4, 153, 185, 195, 203
  see also accent(s)
English, UK, 175
environmental scan, 48
Europeans, non-Europeans, A–8, 10, 22, 95, 125, 140, 144, 153–5, 165, 167, 171, 176, 199, 201, 213
  Romanian, Romania, 17, 21–2, 140, 152–3, 165–8, 170
  see also Poland, Polish
expectations, 16, 22, 24, 55–6, 91, 119, 126, 132, 134, 163, 179–80, 184, 198
expertise, 11, 14–15, 16, 30, 37, 61, 68, 80–1, 124, 144, 149, 181, 194–217
exploitation, exploit, 17, 22–3, 28, 32, 35, 50, 91, 155, 198, 204

extended case, 29, 41–2, 44
  see also Burawoy, Michael
extra care, 81–2

Feminist, 16, 29, 32, 34–6, 38, 42, 194, 207, 209–12, 214, 217
Feminist transnational praxis, 34, 209, 211
feminization of migration
  feminization of labour migration, 12–13, 19, 195, 213
  gender selectivity, 201
  skilled labour migration, 41, 216–17
Feminized, 12, 19, 29, 42, 86, 124, 126, 135–7, 156, 199, 203, 213, 215, 217
  see also feminization of migration; care; service economy
fieldwork, 49
flexible, 45, 65, 106, 114
Folbre, Nancy, 24, 208, 214–15
food, 43–4, 69, 84, 86, 94, 103, 120, 132, 142, 166, 169–70, 173–4, 176, 190
foreign, foreign-educated, 6, 28, 114, 120–1, 135, 200–1
fourth shift, The, 58–61
second shift, 58–9
shifts, shift, 58–61
third shift, 58–9, 182
  see also workplace; Hochschild, Arlie
Fraser, Nancy, 121, 205, 210–12

gender and development, 208–9
  see also United Nations
gendered
  contract, 7, 24, 124, 203
  drivers, 126–34
  employment, 3
  identities, 123–4, 126, 156
  ideologies, 16
  labour, 125
  motivations, 124–30
  occupations, 66
  practices, 16
  relations, 39, 208
  roles, 125, 163, 197, 208
  skills, 4, 66
  strategies, 124, 126, 134–48

gender mainstreaming, 208–9
gender roles, 125, 163, 197, 208
   see also gendered
gender selectivity, 201–2
   see also feminization of migration
global care chains, 4, 10–11, 42, 162
   see also Hochschild, Arlie
globalization, 4, 13, 16, 161, 198, 210–11, 216
God, religious, 63, 113, 125, 152, 155, 169
grey market, grey pound, 81, 95
   see also ageing
Grounded Theory, 44–7
   see also Strauss, Anselm; Corbin, Juliet
guardian, 85–6, 187

hazards, 95, 196
   see also workplace
health care, 4, 7, 14, 19, 25, 27, 48, 51, 58, 60, 62, 65, 74, 78–87, 123–6, 144, 169–70, 188, 196, 199, 204, 211, 217
health care professionals, 14, 25, 27, 48, 51, 58, 60, 65, 78–87, 123–4, 126, 170, 196, 204, 217
   midwives, 51, 114, 209
   nurses, 3, 10, 17, 20–1, 23, 49, 51, 62–4, 70, 78, 81, 85–6, 124–5, 129, 134, 136–7, 141, 145, 152–5, 170–1, 200–2, 209, 211, 215, 219
   occupational and physical therapists, 20, 51, 84, 133–4, 140, 144, 180–1
   see also nurses, nursing profession
hidden curriculum, 25, 31, 66–8
higher education, 5, 135, 148–51, 194, 197–203, 207, 209, 211, 215, 217
   tertiary education, 7, 28, 38, 197, 199, 201
   universities, 2, 198, 203
Hochschild, Arlie, 4, 10–12, 58–9, 77, 82, 136, 161–3
hoists, medical equipment, 103–4
home, 146, 169–73, 218

homework, 26–50, 67, 177, 190, 218
   see also methodology
Hondagnu-Sotelo, Pierette, 126, 163
hospital, 7, 21–2, 28, 40, 60–2, 65, 75, 81, 94–5, 97, 129, 131–2, 136, 138–9, 143–4, 153, 155, 164, 170, 186, 200
human capital, 80, 149–51, 197–9, 204, 211, 213, 219

ICTs, 181–5
   see also technology, technologies
ideal migrants, 40, 186, 203
identity, identities, 3–6, 18, 25, 32, 40, 43, 46, 64, 69, 80, 103, 109, 121, 123–7, 135, 139, 147, 155–6, 159, 181, 196, 203
immigration
   immigration legislation, 48, 150
   managed migration, 9
   migration model, 3, 127, 163, 194
   points-based system, 9, 22, 201
independent/independence, 8, 53, 76, 81–3, 87, 89–91, 105, 110, 120–1, 132–4, 139, 157–8
India, Kerala
   Keralite, 125, 141
inequality(ies), 9, 18–19, 35, 39, 41, 127, 197–8, 204, 206–7, 213
informant, 31–3, 36
   see also methodology
insider/outsider, 31–4
institutional settings, 91
   see also nursing home
intensification, 56, 92
intermediaries, 5
   brokers, 5, 135, 148, 179
   gatekeepers, 15, 18, 60, 178, 202
   mediators, 94, 163
   sponsors, 182–3
internalized, 55, 121, 125, 130, 145
International English Language Test System (IELTS), 18, 114, 128–30, 143, 154, 202, 215
internationalization, 198
International Labour Organization (ILO), 6, 216–17, 219

International Organization for
  Migration (IOM), 209, 213, 217,
  219
Internet, 115, 134, 155, 168–9, 183–5,
  190
intersectional, intersectionality,
  16–19, 31–2
intervention, 4, 30, 33, 35, 41, 67–8,
  71, 77, 79, 114, 118, 145, 168,
  201, 217
intimate labour, 5, 102, 196
  see also Boris, Eileen; Parrenas,
    Rhacel; bodywork
invisible, invisibility, 19, 30, 34, 47,
  63–4, 95, 121, 196, 202, 210,
  212–13
Irish, 63, 96–7, 193

job expansion, 56, 79

Kingma, Mirelle, 134–6, 143, 148, 153,
  155, 158, 170, 200, 215
knowledge-based, 35, 199, 203
  see also universities, higher
    education
Kofman, Eleanor, 5, 9, 13–14, 124,
  162–3, 178, 193, 199, 206,
  213

labour market (tests), 18, 148, 150
  in low-income countries, 51, 150
  segmented labour market, 217
Labov, William, 46
legislation, 19, 48, 53, 66, 90, 98, 150
liberal, 8, 42, 62, 169, 206, 215
  see also neoliberal
lifestyle, 84, 120, 130
Lightfoot, Sarah, 44, 46
link, 5, 10, 15, 23, 37, 41–2, 45, 56,
  68, 122, 124, 127, 147–8, 177–9,
  182, 202, 211
literacy, 33, 51–2, 65, 68, 74, 181, 185,
  207
  digital literacy, 181, 185
  see also paperwork
livelihood, 2, 10, 30, 41, 82, 124, 131,
  133, 156, 157, 160, 174, 195,
  205–6, 217

local, 42, 53, 55, 58–9, 65, 88, 90,
  92–4, 96, 110, 121–2, 125, 127,
  138, 140, 159–60, 162, 164, 171,
  174–8, 182, 185, 190, 196, 211
lost, 13, 34, 57, 130, 138, 149–52, 204,
  213

macro-level, 127, 179
male care assistants, 93, 109
management, 13, 23, 37, 54, 56–7, 69,
  71, 75, 77, 79, 85, 89–90, 102,
  113, 143, 147, 150, 167, 169
  see also workplace
manipulate, 116, 133, 179
mapping, map, 4, 7–11, 16, 25, 41,
  43–4, 48–9, 102, 179–81, 206, 219
  see also network, social networks,
    support networks; workplace
marginalized, marginalization, 15, 19,
  30, 37, 174, 185, 196, 199, 203,
  210–11, 213–14
  othering, othered, 210
market care, 8
married, 23, 94, 133, 139, 143, 165–6
marriage, 120, 133
McDonaldization, 54
media, mass media, 4, 49, 51, 119,
  159, 163, 173, 176–7, 182, 184–5,
  195
mediator, 94, 163
methodology, 26–50, 218
Middle east, 198, 213
  Gulf, The, 23, 165
migrant academic, 37
migration model, 3, 127, 163, 194
migratory flows, 1, 216
mobilities, mobility
  downwardly mobile, 4
  physical mobility, 109, 121
  professional mobility, 201
  social mobility, 109, 149, 197–205
mothers
  motherhood, 183, 203
  mothering, 58, 161, 163, 167, 187

Naples, Nancy, 30, 32, 210
NARIC, 144, 201

narratives, 3, 24, 29, 41, 44–6, 128, 143, 157
narrative analysis, 3, 29
  see also Labov, William
nationality, 16, 19–20, 25, 33, 81, 94, 173, 194
neighbor, neighbourhood, 101
neoliberal, 204–5
network
  personal networks, 163–4, 178, 180–1, 184
  social networks, 14, 96, 160–2
  support networks, 25, 160, 177–8
  see also transnational families
new place of settlement, 4, 19, 94–8, 196
norms, 126, 163, 178–9, 181
Nurse Midwifery Council (NMC), 114, 130, 143, 154
nurses, 3, 10, 17, 20–1, 23, 49, 51, 62–4, 70, 78, 81, 85–6, 124–5, 129, 134, 136–7, 141, 145, 152–5, 170–1, 200–2, 209, 211, 215
  nursing profession, 2, 155
  nursing school, 125, 137, 200
  nursing home, 1–2, 6, 19–21, 23, 32, 44, 55, 64, 71, 86, 123, 129–30, 142, 144, 153–5, 180, 191
nurturing fields, 124–5, 156
Nussbaum, Martha, 161, 206–7

obligation, 12, 24, 125, 130–1, 156, 162–3
occupation, 7–8, 51, 58, 62, 156
  occupational, 4, 13, 17, 20, 51, 61–4, 66, 84, 87, 123–4, 126–8, 136, 140, 142, 148, 156, 180–1, 197
OECD, 9, 28, 52, 150, 197, 199, 204, 213, 217
older persons, 2, 4–7, 9–10, 41, 51, 53, 80, 82, 87, 90–1, 96–7, 118, 122
opportunities (opportunity), 5, 7, 12–13, 24–5, 32–3, 53, 61, 76, 115, 127–32, 136–43, 148, 151–2, 157–8, 161, 163, 169, 179, 181, 187, 189, 194–5, 198, 202–6, 208–9, 215–17
outsourced, outsourcing, 7–8, 124

over-qualified/qualification, 2, 56–7, 150, 216
overseas workers, 55, 219
overworked, 60, 138, 143, 170, 186, 214
Oxfam, 17, 98, 214

panel study, 49
paperwork, 28, 48, 51–2, 55–6, 59–60, 69–75, 84, 100, 103, 140–1, 151, 154, 186, 193
  documentation, 16, 73–4, 88–9, 140
  see also immigration; workplace
Parrenas, Rhacel, 5–6, 62–3, 102, 161–3, 167, 183, 186, 189, 195–6
pathway, 13, 134, 136, 143–4, 148, 156
penalties
  ethnic/linguistic penalty, 16–18, 24
personalization, personalisation, personalized, person-centred care, 48, 51–61, 75–7, 87, 90–1, 96
personal services, 91–2, 99
  see also service economy
Philippines, Filipino(s), 10, 17, 20, 22, 34, 58, 80–1, 94, 113, 162, 173, 175–6, 180–1, 190, 211
phone, 27, 43, 50, 85, 100, 108, 110, 118, 142–3, 160, 163–4, 167–8, 170–3, 175, 181–5, 189–90, 192–3
pilot study, 43, 48, 218
Poland, Polish, 10, 17, 19, 31, 49, 114–17, 120, 125, 137, 139, 142, 145, 148, 165, 184, 218
political economy of care, 10–11, 195
poor pay, 10, 56, 142, 215
popular education, 207, 211–12
portraiture, 44–7
  portraits, 45, 49, 90, 105, 107, 109–20, 195
  see also Lightfoot, Sarah
post-migration, 179, 194–5, 209
post-welfare, 4, 9–10, 48
poverty, 13, 95–6, 161, 170, 208, 212
  see also poor pay
Pratt, Geraldine, 16, 156, 196, 210
pre-migration, 126, 169–71, 194, 198, 205
presence, 39, 42, 62, 95, 183–5

private companies, 57, 89
private schools, 130, 136, 166
privatization, 41–2, 93, 196
professional development, 52, 127–30, 142, 211, 216
professionalization, 53, 86–7
professionals, 1–25, 32–3, 41, 52, 54, 60, 62, 64, 69, 73, 77, 79–80, 82, 102, 114, 124, 126–30, 131–2, 134–5, 139, 142, 144, 146–8, 150–1, 153–5, 156–7, 160–1, 178–9, 182, 195, 200–3, 207, 209, 211–17, 218
public
  management, 53–4
  sphere, 208, 210
  value, 35

qualifications, 5, 7–8, 12, 53, 55–7, 64–6, 68, 80, 124, 126, 128, 135, 140, 142–4, 148–51, 153, 156, 179, 181, 194, 198–9, 201–2, 204, 212–13, 215
  National Vocational Qualifications, 55, 65
qualitative, 24, 40, 46, 79
  see also methodology

race to the bottom, 4, 157, 194, 203–5
race, racist, racism, 4, 9, 15–16, 19, 35–6, 43, 48, 62, 80–1, 102, 108, 112, 124, 138, 149, 204, 217
  see also gendered; Intersectional, intersectionality; white; black; Caucasian
Raghuram, Parvati, 5, 11, 13, 17, 36, 79, 124, 155, 162–3, 178, 201, 204
raising standards, 52–61, 198
  see also workplace
receiving countries, 13, 127, 135, 202–3
reciprocal, reciprocity, 24, 162, 179, 181
recruiter, 5, 12, 16–17, 22–4, 27–8, 42, 55, 58, 65, 94, 108, 113, 133, 140–2, 144, 154, 156–7, 202, 214
recruitment, agencies, 27, 50, 115, 133, 140, 157, 189

reflexivity, reflexive, reflective, 25, 30, 36–41, 46, 49, 53, 69, 204, 214
reframing, 4, 135, 145–8, 203
registration, 22, 53, 114, 130, 134
  register, 22, 55, 154
regulations, 8–9, 51, 53–4, 87, 97, 133–4, 140, 203, 205, 214–15
  see also migration model
relationships
  expectations, 119
  family, 145–6, 171
  research, 32
  transnational networks, 159–93
  at work, 33, 113, 183
  see also care, caring; reflexivity, reflexive, reflective; clients
remittances, remit, 11, 109, 131–2, 161, 163, 169, 179, 181–2, 204, 208
representation
  politics of representation, 36–41
  see also methodology
residential home, 7, 54, 72
reskilling, 151
resources, 10–12, 14, 36, 40, 52–3, 61, 80, 97, 104, 114, 134–6, 138, 145, 148, 156–7, 161, 164, 174, 176, 178–9, 181–2, 185, 197, 201–2, 204–5, 213, 215, 217
responsibilization, 52
retention, 4, 80, 93
rotas, 71, 89, 102, 219
  see also workplace
route(s), 6, 22, 27, 65, 67, 89, 91, 101–2, 135, 140–2, 160, 206, 214–15
rural, 44, 88–90, 92–9, 109, 122, 136, 176, 184, 196

sacrifice, 13, 134, 143, 180, 188, 196
saints, 4, 125–6, 146–7
Sassen, Saskia, 5, 9, 13, 122, 127, 170, 196, 205–6
Saudi Arabia, 109, 113, 164, 171
schedule, 58–60, 71, 73–4, 89, 100, 106–8, 114, 116, 142, 156, 164, 174–7, 184, 187, 190, 193
  see also rotas

selective, selectivity, 9, 13–14, 22, 45, 65, 140, 195–6, 201–2
Sen, Amartya, 207, 211
sending countries, 12, 15, 18, 150, 202
servant, slave, 8, 62, 109, 125, 142, 174–5
service economy, 7, 16, 96, 121–2
service-users, 53, 196
sexism, 169, 217
  see also gendered
sheltered home, 6–7, 72
short-term, 22, 28, 148, 157, 170, 203, 214
  temporary, 148
silence, 33, 69, 102, 111, 123, 133
  see also methodology
sister(s), 22, 110, 115, 125, 129, 136–7, 141, 160–1, 165–6, 168, 184–5, 189, 191, 214
skilled migrants, 4–5, 29, 37, 41, 48, 51–88, 150, 197, 209, 213, 219
  highly skilled, 37, 43, 197, 213
  migrants, 37, 41, 51–2, 61, 87, 150, 213
  migrant workers, 197, 204
  pioneers, 160, 196
Skype, 167, 184–5
social capital, 178, 202
social care, 2, 6–8, 51, 60–2, 64, 70–1, 85, 90–1, 95–6, 106, 115, 126, 179
  care industry, 1, 4, 7–11, 13, 15, 19, 24–5, 37, 41–2, 48, 51–87, 88, 93, 122, 125, 153, 156, 174, 195–6, 204, 216, 219
  care sector, 2, 17, 31, 41, 51, 53, 55–7, 60–2, 65, 70, 91, 93, 95, 106, 115, 126–7, 150, 179, 195–6, 214
social service, 95–7, 148, 172, 205
social workers, 53–4, 62–3, 84–5, 209
  social work, 20, 31, 33, 35, 53–4, 56, 58, 61–3, 71, 84–7, 115–16, 124–8, 138, 172, 209
socioeconomic, 38, 96, 99, 178, 195, 207, 216–17
specialism, 139
  specialist, 20, 55–6, 67–8, 138, 151

sponsor (family), 23, 125, 169, 183, 191–2
sponsorship, 160, 168–9, 192
staffing, 5, 7–11, 53, 66
  staff shortages, staff demands, 62, 96, 138
stepping stone(s), 24, 45, 64, 115, 126, 138, 140, 148, 152, 156, 203
strategic essentialism, 33
strategies, 2–4, 44, 49, 79, 88, 123–4, 126, 134–5, 145, 148–9, 151, 157, 159, 163, 208, 210, 213
stratification, 13, 17, 19, 35
Strauss, Anselm, 45
stress, 22, 35, 59–60, 111, 113–14
  stressor, 144
stuck, 33, 45, 57, 116, 120, 144–5, 148–9, 203, 206, 214, 217
study, studied, 1–4, 8–10, 12–13, 15–19, 22–3, 25, 27–9, 31–2, 34–7, 41, 43–5, 47–9, 51, 53–8, 60–8, 71–2, 79, 81–2, 86–7, 92–7, 108, 113, 122, 124–7, 129–31, 134–5, 137, 139, 142, 146–7, 149, 151, 153, 156, 161–2, 174, 177–9, 182–3, 185, 195, 198–9, 206–7, 209–13, 216–17
  see also higher education
subjectivity, subjectivities, 32, 39, 121
support
  educational, 179, 181
  emotional, 7, 136, 167, 171–3, 177, 179
  financial, 131
  instrumental, 178, 207
  support system, 35, 84, 164, 179–80
survive, 4, 40, 59, 88–9, 109, 112, 122, 161, 178, 181
  survivor circuits, 122

Tagalog, 101, 175, 176
Taglish, 175, 192
technology, technologies, 49, 98, 100, 128–9, 151, 159, 163, 181–2, 185, 197, 199
  computers, 163, 167–8, 182
  television, 40, 169, 177, 190
  texting, 182–3, 185

texts, 47, 69–70, 74, 163, 168, 182, 185, 192–3
  see also paperwork, documentation
therapeutic, 81, 84–5, 100
ties, 159, 160–5, 178–9, 193, 197
  see also bond, bonding
time (related to work), 24, 28, 33, 49, 54, 100–1, 106, 138
  hours, 100–1, 106, 138
trafficking, 214
training, 7, 17–18, 23, 27–8, 31–2, 42, 48–9, 51–8, 61–2, 64–8, 71, 76, 83, 85, 87–8, 97, 102, 113–15, 120, 128, 133–4, 136, 140, 142, 144, 150–1, 154, 160, 180, 207
  retrain, 143–4, 200, 215
  trainer, 28, 61, 66–7, 76–7, 214
  training centre, 133
transnational families, 159, 160–3, 167, 168, 171, 178, 180, 182
  see also network
transnational families, 159, 161–3, 180, 182–3, 189
transnational feminist praxis, 209–11
  see also feminization of migration
transnational, transnationalism, 5, 14–16, 41–2, 160–77, 181–93, 195
  see also relationships, transnational networks
Tronto, Joan, 34–6, 98, 100, 147, 197

UNESCO, 199–201
unions, 57, 91, 145, 207, 210, 214
United Nations, 207–8
universities, higher education, 2, 198, 203

unskilled, 12, 51, 150, 198
upgrade, upgrading, 51–2, 61, 79, 86–7, 115, 129, 152, 178, 195, 200, 202, 219
upskilling, 151–2, 203, 219
Urry, John, 42, 99, 121, 149, 181–2
USA, 9, 22–3, 34, 52, 62–3, 71, 114–15, 120, 124–5, 148, 171, 200, 204, 216

visa
  student visa, 1, 22, 27–8, 32, 65, 128, 133–4, 139, 141, 143, 146, 160, 214
  work visa, 28, 206
vocational courses, 28, 120, 203

waiting, 26, 103, 142, 155, 171–4
  wait, 54, 67, 85, 106, 118, 141, 153, 155
Warhurst, Chris, 76, 79, 151, 157
white, 38, 47, 62, 75
women's work, 5, 87, 124, 126, 214
working conditions, 28, 57, 64, 92, 139, 211
workplace, 3–5, 8, 15–18, 22, 25, 28, 31, 43, 48–50, 57–8, 64, 67–9, 87, 91, 95, 99, 120, 138, 148–9, 151, 153, 159, 167, 169, 180–1, 202, 208, 212, 214–16

Yeates, Nicola, 5, 9–11, 42, 61, 63–4, 138, 156–7

Zambia, 21, 43, 123, 131–2, 172–3

GPSR Compliance

The European Union's (EU) General Product Safety Regulation (GPSR) is a set of rules that requires consumer products to be safe and our obligations to ensure this.

If you have any concerns about our products, you can contact us on

ProductSafety@springernature.com

In case Publisher is established outside the EU, the EU authorized representative is:

Springer Nature Customer Service Center GmbH
Europaplatz 3
69115 Heidelberg, Germany

www.ingramcontent.com/pod-product-compliance
Lightning Source LLC
LaVergne TN
LVHW011007250326
834688LV00004B/116